Professional
Playwrights

Professional Playwrights

MASSINGER, FORD, SHIRLEY, & BROME

Ira Clark

THE UNIVERSITY PRESS OF KENTUCKY

Publication of this book was assisted by grants from the
University of Florida Division of Sponsored Research
and College of Liberal Arts and Sciences.

Scholarly publisher for the Commonwealth,
serving Bellarmine College, Berea College, Centre
College of Kentucky, Eastern Kentucky University,
The Filson Club, Georgetown College, Kentucky
Historical Society, Kentucky State University,
Morehead State University, Murray State University,
Northern Kentucky University, Transylvania University,
University of Kentucky, University of Louisville,
and Western Kentucky University.

Editorial and Sales Offices: Lexington, Kentucky 40508-4008

Library of Congress Cataloging-in-Publication Data

Clark, Ira.
   Professional playwrights : Massinger, Ford, Shirley, and Brome /
Ira Clark.
     p. cm.
   Includes bibliographical references (p.   ) and index.
   ISBN 0-8131-1787-9 :
   1. English drama—17th century—History and criticism.
2. Massinger, Philip, 1583-1640—Criticism and interpretation.
3. Ford, John, 1586-ca. 1640—Criticism and interpretation.
4. Shirley, James, 1596-1666—Criticism and interpretation.
5. Brome, Richard, d. 1652?—Criticism and interpretation.
I. Title.
PR671.C5 1992
822'.409—dc20   91-45853

Contents

For Joanna,
who knows why

Acknowledgments

I owe general thanks, perhaps too often silent, to scholarly interpreters of history and literature, who will appreciate my society of books. I owe particular thanks to social scientists, undoubtedly some unidentified, who may wonder at my apparently nonsocial, impractical applications of their disciplines to a society of texts. Both groups will understand my thanks to critics who took the time and effort to make this a better work than it would have been; they should not be held accomplices to its waywardness. Teresa Bruckner, Arthur Kinney, David Locke, Jeremy Maule, and Marie Nelson gave me useful information and helpful advice on various sections at various times; Michael Mooney helpfully read most parts of it in various states. Melvyn New, John Perlette, and an undetermined number of anonymous readers made valuable comments on the whole of what, at different times, I believed to be a submissible manuscript.

All these scholars will share my special thanks to the University Press of Kentucky, which took the risks commendable in scholarly presses of publishing a work with prospects somewhat short of booming sales. To these I add my thanks to the Division of Sponsored Research of the University of Florida for a summer grant during which I did considerable revision of the manuscript, and to the Division of Sponsored Research and the College of Liberal Arts and Sciences of the University of Florida for subsidies to help defray the publication costs. Finally, I thank future scholars. They will venture, I hope, to redress the inescapable abstraction of scholarly criticism which I have compounded into overgeneralization because of some current lacks. They should be able to improve our meager store of information about such basic matters as the texts, attributions, dates, and histories of the plays and playwrights of the Caroline era, raise our critical estimate of and interest in them, and increase the amount of our publication space devoted to them. Caroline drama deserves and will reward more detailed attention.

1

The Caroline Professionals

The Profession

Among the four professional playwrights who have dominated studies of English drama of the 1620s and 1630s, only James Shirley has not been dubbed the foremost decadent. Perhaps the label "decadent" derives partly from the fact that all four—Philip Massinger, John Ford, James Shirley, and Richard Brome—came to prominence at ages older than most of their predecessors and much older than the prodigy who proved their chief competitor, Sir William Davenant. The long time required for these playwrights to gain artistic maturity suggests the extraordinary complexity that drama had rapidly achieved: the trove of traditional dramatic techniques had accumulated to the extent that apprentices had to take a good while learning their craft. The conspicuous craft of these playwrights has too often been belittled as a facility for slick imitation: if discovery is deemed profound, then repetition, variation, and development must be shallow. Along with poor marks because of their polished craft, the four have also been disparaged for catering to an audience labeled dissolute. These playwrights are supposed to have purveyed sensational fantasies, escapes from an era that was falling into revolution. Moreover, the fantasies purportedly paint flattering portraits that hide the failings of presumably debased, sycophantic courtiers. Thus both the craft and the sociopolitics of Massinger, Ford, Shirley, and Brome have been condemned as decadent. In the submerged metaphor of the medlar, borrowed from the Elizabethans this schema exalts, the Caroline professional playwrights got rotten before they got ripe.

I propose a different estimate. I do not limit consideration to their artistry, abandoning them to Muriel C. Bradbrook's strictures against a so-called wornout imitation. Nor do I extend their beliefs to some inevitable support of absolutism, opening them to John F. Danby's charge of reactionary adolescence. I aim to correct the fusion of these views evident in T.S. Eliot's allegation that these playwrights lacked a commitment to aesthetics and morality.[1] To reverse such criticisms, I consider recent approval of the Caroline professional playwrights' artful variations of dramatic traditions that are related to social conventions and transactions maintaining and reforming the self, the family, and the community. My understanding is illuminated by recent social theories of psychosocial interactions, rituals, role playing, and recreation aligned with well-known dramatic traditions. And I place this consideration within the context of new views of the Caroline audience as one torn between prolonging the past and promoting the future. My perspective suggests that Massinger, Ford, Shirley, and Brome self-consciously offered sociopolitically as well as aesthetically sophisticated representations of their society to a privileged audience more complexly troubled than has generally been recognized.

By way of introduction, in this chapter I distinguish these Caroline professional playwrights from other important playwrights in the period. Then I situate my procedure among important historical studies of English Renaissance drama. Next, with help mainly from social historians, I sketch my construal of the era's political and social concerns. And to conclude the introduction I outline my study and characterize the sociopolitical and aesthetic attitudes of Massinger, Ford, Shirley, and Brome.

The Caroline professional playwrights came to their vocation during the reign of James I: Massinger by the middle of the seventeenth century's second decade, Ford a little later, Shirley shortly before James's death in 1625, and Brome about that same time. They were surrounded by a host of other dramatists who also deserve our attention. Thomas Heywood and Thomas Dekker, who remained active early in the era, appear with Massinger, Shirley, and Brome on the list of "regular" or "attached professionals" that Gerald Eades Bentley compiled for *The Profession of Dramatist in Shakespeare's Time, 1590-1642*.[2] But Heywood and Dekker began writing plays in the 1590s and achieved their characteristic habits near the turn of the century; they did the bulk of their work before 1625 and turned more to masques and civic pageants for their earnings during this era, which they did not survive. Therefore they do not seem distinctively Caroline. Similar reasons disqualify Ben Jonson, who was trying to make a comeback during this period and who, along with Ford and the others, appears on Bentley's longer list of playwrights paid to produce most of the plays staged between 1590 and 1642.[3]

Ford's output of about one play per year when active, rather than the two Bentley required for his "regular professionals," is still large enough to distinguish him from the rest of his contemporaries except for Sir William Davenant. Davenant, though absent from Bentley's list, matched Ford's annual production. But apparently neither Ford nor Davenant earned his living by the stage in the same sense that Massinger, Shirley, and Brome did. Neither was likely to have commanded their pay since neither had an agreement such as Massinger had with the King's Men at Blackfriars and the Globe; Shirley with Queen Henrietta's Men at the Phoenix or Cockpit on Drury Lane, John Ogilby's theater in Ireland, and the King's Men; or Brome with the proprietors of Salisbury Court.[4] Telling evidence of this is that neither Ford nor Davenant exhibits the others' avoidance of print, an avoidance that indicates a need to keep their plays on the boards.[5] Davenant, moreover, turned mainly to masques and topics fashionable at court after 1634, when *The Wits* and, likely, *Love and Honour* won greater applause from the court than from the crowd.[6]

Even though Ford did not write primarily for one company, his plays, like those of Massinger, Shirley, Brome, and Davenant, appeared primarily at private theaters in front of privileged audiences.[7] This fact leads to two related observations that set Ford—with Massinger, Shirley, and Brome—apart from Davenant. Initially, though, this grouping seems odd, since Ford was descended from an established gentry family and had the closest blood connections to the privileged audience all five wrote for. As the son of a vintner, Davenant's origins seem closer to those of Massinger, who sought patronage from the noble family his father served; to Shirley, who aspired to court gentility from a middling background; and to Brome, who rose from obscurity. But Ford and the others, unlike Davenant, began their careers by working for a long time with dramatists who wrote plays for a living. Massinger and Ford wrote collaborations with established playwrights: Massinger worked with at least Field, Dekker, and especially Fletcher, before he inherited Shakespeare's and Fletcher's post. Ford wrote with at least Dekker, Rowley, and Webster. Brome served as Jonson's "man." And Shirley avowed his recognizably autodidactic imitation of the masters of the English stage. On the contrary, Davenant, who declared himself to be at least the spiritual son of Shakespeare and who was influenced by Jonson and Fletcher, served a very brief apprenticeship, if it was one, in the household of a statesman and patron, the sonneteer, memorialist of Sir Philip Sidney, and closet dramatist Fulke Greville, Lord Brooke.[8]

It is not so much the commemorations of the other playwrights as it is the allusions, imitations, and variations in their plays that proclaim the dedication of the Caroline professionals to the traditions of their craft. This sets them apart from Davenant. One readily apparent indication is their reliance on metadramatic techniques such as plays within plays, dumb shows, disguisings, and stagings popular among theater people. Davenant, however, made prominent use of metadramatic techniques only in *The Just Italian* (1629) and in *The Distresses*, his last Caroline play if this title is just another name for *The Spanish Lovers* (1639).

The second point that distinguishes Massinger, Ford, Shirley, and Brome from Davenant is that their chief associates apparently remained among theater professionals, members of the inns of court, or gentry, whereas Davenant's associates increasingly came from the ranks of courtiers close to royal circles. Before he entered Greville's household Davenant served as a page to Frances, the first Duchess of Richmond and a prominent figure in the Stuart court; and after Greville's death his chief patrons were Queen Henrietta Maria, Henry Jermyn, one of her favorites, and especially Endymion Porter, the king's confidant. Apart from Porter, Davenant's closest friends were probably Edmund Waller, surely William Habington and Thomas Carew, and particularly Sir John Suckling. Nor did Davenant enter into the links of association, except with Ford, that the four Caroline professional playwrights forged with each other.[9] The four often looked to the same patrons. Ford dedicated nondramatic works to the Pembroke family, Massinger's primary patrons. Both Ford and Brome dedicated plays to Shirley's notable patron, William Cavendish, successively the Earl, Marquess, and Duke of Newcastle.[10] Shirley not only offered Newcastle a dedication and an ode, he also, according to rumor, helped Newcastle write *The Variety*, a play Brome commended. More significantly, the four looked to each other. Massinger wrote a commendatory poem for Shirley's *The Grateful Servant*. Ford did the same for Massinger's *The Roman Actor* and *The Great Duke of Florence*, Shirley's *The Wedding*, and Brome's *The Northern Lass*. Shirley provided commendations for Massinger's *The Renegado*, Ford's *Love's Sacrifice*, and Brome's *A Jovial Crew*. The four also seem to have occasionally adapted each other's successful techniques, characters, and situations.

In effect, Davenant joined a group of amateur courtly and court-aspiring gentlemen, usually called "cavaliers" or "courtiers," who as dramatists posed a genuine economic and a perceived aesthetic threat to the professional playwrights.[11] In *Criticism and Compliment* Kevin Sharpe has rightly shown that Davenant and the courtiers were capable of criticizing the court, and has argued that critics should raise our estimate of Davenant.[12] But Davenant's critique of the courtiers and the court, like that of the others, issues from an insider, not an outsider. So, for example, his criticisms of court corruption honor the camp, not the country. And he habitually insults both the country and the city, an attitude the four rarely present.

Most important, the Caroline professional playwrights specifically set themselves apart from the courtiers. This is especially true of the younger competitors—Shirley, who lost the laureateship to Davenant, and Brome, who satirized them sharply. But it is also true of Massinger, who engaged in an angry poetic exchange with Carew over dramatic poetry. And it is true even of Ford, who had friends among the courtiers; a commender of his *The Fancies* specifically acclaims him for being professional. In a sometimes envious, occasionally invidious rivalry with the courtiers, Massinger, Ford, Shirley, and Brome marked distinguishing traits. Brome offered perhaps their fullest case in the epilogue to his *The Court Beggar* (1639-40), a satire that features a caustic attack on Davenant's close friend, the notorious courtier Sir John Suckling. The epilogue's conclusion, after various ladies, courtly gentry, and citizens of the city have begged for applause in couplets, is delivered in prose by a plain-dealing countryman. Swaynwit declares that there is no need for the actors to beg applause for a professional playwright:

> [W]hy should we? has not he money for his doings? and the best price too? because we would ha' the best: . . . If it were for one of the great and curious Poets that give these Playes as the Prologue said, and money too, to have 'em acted; For them, indeed, we are bound to ply for an applause. Because they look for nothing else. . . . But take heed [of criticizing them severely, that] you displease not the Ladies tho' who are their partiall judges, being brib'd by flattering verses to commend their Playes . . . and by their powerfull voyces to be cry'd up wits o' Court, the right worshipfull Poets boast to have made those enterludes, when for ought you know they bought 'em of Universitie Scholars. . . . But this small Poet vents none but his own, and his by whose care and directions this Stage is govern'd, who has for many yeares both in his fathers dayes, and since directed Poets to write and Players to speak.

The first major characteristic that distinguishes the professional playwrights from courtier playwrights is that, far from paying others to write, perform, and praise "his" work, the professional earns his livelihood by his craft. And this means writing enough good plays to get wages directly from stage companies and ultimately from theater audiences, not from patrons who reward the literary with the other service of their retainers. As the prologue warns, because courtly playwrights purchase fame *"you sometimes pay deare for't, since they write / Lesse for your pleasure than their own delight."* The second major distinction is proffered through the compliment to Beeston, a veteran impresario who demanded standards of craft implicitly violated by courtier playwrights. As the prologue puts this difference, the poet condemns their *"new strayne"* and maintains the traditional quality of plays *"writ / By our great Masters of the Stage and Wit."* Brome reiterates the Caroline professionals' claims in opposition to the courtiers: professionals produce plenty of plays worthy of pay because they have studied drama's heritage and practice its proven techniques. The sum of Massinger's, Ford's, Shirley's, and Brome's differences from the courtiers amounts to their writing more plays and plays of higher quality for pay out of the proceeds of acting companies.

A Perspective on the Professionals

All four Caroline professional playwrights reward formal approaches of the sort Lois Potter promises in her preface to *The* Revels *History of Drama in English, 1613-1660*: her critics respond to literary "refinement" and "skill." Massinger has been well served aesthetically by such studies as *The Pattern of Tragicomedy in Beaumont and Fletcher* by Eugene M. Waith, Ford by formal and thematic analyses of recurring image clusters by

Donald K. Anderson, Jr.[13] But Brome has been better served historically than his peers. Instead of dismissing him for alleged escapism, his seminal critic, Ralph J. Kaufmann, portrays him as a reporter of the fashionable personages, places, and manners of his time.[14] Appreciation of the others in their context has been tardy. In his dissertation at the University of Birmingham (1966) Douglas Sedge became one of the first scholars to consider how these playwrights presented social problems. The first sophisticated historical treatment of them came almost twenty years later, in Martin Butler's *Theatre and Crisis, 1632-1642*, which concentrates on the spectrum of political issues presented in popular as well as elite and courtly dramas and masques.[15] By taking the political reflections of the Caroline playwrights seriously he has recovered one perspective.

Considering Clifford Leech's important studies of Caroline plays to be representative, Butler finds two major problems with earlier scholars: first, they see Caroline society through the lens of the Revolution, anachronistically observing cavalier-Puritan civil strife before the conflict; and second, they see the era through whiggish, anti-royalist eyes.[16] To counter these failings Butler draws on revisionist historians who emphasize the mutual interests of the Carolines as these are revealed through analyses of the era's sociopolitical network of associations and patronage. He thereby comes closer to achieving the goals of traditional theorists of literary history, such as R.S. Crane, who want to place literature in a context broader than the evolution of techniques and genres.[17] Enlarging Butler's focus on political issues, such as absolutism and social mobility, so as to include more social concerns, mainly family and gender relations, I can take advantage both of the traditional analogy comparing the family and the state, which extends at least from Aristotle and includes Sir Robert Filmer's prominent *Patriarcha*, and of recent social historians who write about adolescents and women, specifically those who describe courtship and marriage.

A new scholarly consensus demands still more from historical studies than an accommodation of new data and a closer fit of hypothesis to data. When Butler accuses Leech of presenting an anachronistic view he suggests two goals. He usefully proposes that we try to understand another era on something like its own terms. But he also implicitly charges us with an impossible task: regarding and judging an earlier era without anachronism, as if we could forget the past or ourselves. So the new historicists who currently dominate criticism of English Renaissance literature seem motivated by dual goals: to regard historical figures as particular psychosocial constructs and not individual representatives of universals, and to recognize historians as creatures of their own cultures. Both figures and historians are viewed as products of conflicting beliefs, values, needs, and desires.

New historicists seem to hold in common the image of a Renaissance marked by the discontinuities that characterize transition. To them Renaissance society displays extraordinary fissures in what its members held to be the facts, truths, and values that people assume in order to cope with the world they perceive. But new historicists treat the culture of the English Renaissance diversely because they come from different backgrounds and have different needs and because they employ methods from an array of literary, philosophical, and social disciplines. One prominent set of these critics, working more with continental Marxist and philosophical historians and focusing more on ideological ruptures, have taken the label students of "cultural materialism." The other, taking comfort in the "thick descriptions" advocated by symbolic anthropologists and focusing more on sutures, appear as students of "the poetics of culture."[18] Like all of these critics I focus on sociopolitical rifts, but on rifts that were presented as significant by the Caroline professional playwrights. So instead of opening with some striking historical illustration (an incident, account, or fantasy from society's margins) whose representativeness might seem tenuous or whose choice might seem unusually arbitrary, I begin with generalizations that meet two criteria: they are derived from detailed interpretations of a variety of sociopolitical data gathered by recent historians; and they illuminate social and political problems that play prominent roles in Caroline plays.

This reconstitution of the era further concentrates on traditionally literary works, the Caroline professional playwrights' somewhat consistent representation of certain ideas, situations, character types, styles, and so on. And it relies on other contemporary texts for exemplification. Finally it depends for an interpretive framework on social sciences much more than on philosophy or economic politics, and more on social historians, sociologists, and social psychologists than on anthropologists or psychologists. Thus I am closer to a third, less prominent set of critics who contribute to a new history. My study emulates Frank Whigham's analysis in "Sexual and Social Mobility in *The Duchess of Malfi,*" and it extends to more playwrights, genres, and social studies Lawrence Danson's thesis in "Jonsonian Comedy and the Discovery of the Social Self."[19]

From the seminal theories of University of Chicago sociologist George Herbert Mead to the ingenious experiments staged by social psychologists, social scientists have borrowed metadrama's world-stage trope, extended its implications, and tested the consequent hypotheses.[20] Their fundamental postulate issuing from the metaphor is that personality is constructed by the interactions between an individual and society when someone acts out parts in a variety of situations among diverse people in particular times and places. Put another way, our roles create our selves as we create our roles in specific social conditions. Peter L. Berger and

Thomas Luckmann outline the general proposition in *The Social Construction of Reality:* humans believe in realities they create in a dialectic between themselves and society; identity emerges from the interaction of an individual and a society; the internalization of social reality, the creation of a self through roles habituated for dealing with others in given situations, continuously constitutes and maintains both identities and social reality.[21]

To exemplify the theory, Danson draws on the horrifying experiment staged by social psychologist Stanley Milgram, which demonstrated that Americans have a powerful propensity to obey scientists' orders to administer severe shock to supposed test subjects. And he cites the compelling experiment during which Philip G. Zimbardo found that subjects who were self-consciously playing randomly assigned roles of prisoner and guard so thoroughly became those roles that he and his associates had to shut down their experiment before it was half over.[22] Danson thus sets an argument for a sociological view of the drama and stereotypical characters of Ben Jonson, which have been denigrated from the psychological view satisfying to Shakespeareans. I liberalize Danson's determinism by emphasizing the renewed interest among social scientists in both the consequences of unanticipated, uncontrollable interventions and the potential of agents playing roles in such ways that constraints serve as enablings, rules as resources.[23] Moreover, I extend Danson's thesis to later playwrights who were influenced more by Jonson and Fletcher than by Shakespeare; so I oppose critics who assume a psychological perspective, place the highest value on "essential" selves, and condemn as shallow the characters presented by Caroline playwrights. Placing great value on "social" selves, the adoptions, adaptations, and interactions of types, I claim that these dramatists explored the potential for character creation within a variety of situations and roles sanctioned by their society.

This amounts to using social scientists' reinterpretations of the world-stage trope to read plays by the Caroline professionals. By my estimate, they did more than put characters in settings and situations and then imagine the personal consequences, as many critics assume writers do. They restaged scenes much as social psychologists do; they focused attention on social and sociopolitical circumstances and consequences much more than on psychological ones. Alternatively, the plays wrought by the Caroline professionals seem to yield uncommonly useful insights into that era when examined as if the playwrights set in motion imaginative social experiments.[24] Thus, Massinger in *The Picture* makes characters consider their mutually reflective and interactive roles. Ford in *The Broken Heart* makes them undergo ritual refinement into ideal roles. Shirley in *Hyde Park* makes them choose among fashionable roles. And Brome in *The Antipodes* makes them experiment with inverted roles.

Several prominent characteristics common to the plays indicate that the playwrights were aware of focusing attention on the ongoing creation of people through roles that interact with the ongoing definition of society. These playwrights repeatedly presented academies of behavior where inept gulls, who aspire to circles of privilege close to court, seek training from venal tutors in how to dress, behave, and talk, that is, how to pose appropriately. Shirley's earliest extant play, *The School of Compliment*, features such an institution; so does Brome's *The New Academy, or The New Exchange*. Massinger frequently ridicules proposals to establish academies of courtly behavior, and Brome often shows city slickers selling social instruction to climbing country bumpkins. Ford, however, demonstrates in *The Fancies Chaste and Noble* that an academy can offer advantages. Another trait suggesting that the Caroline professionals focused on the interaction of roles and society is that they repeatedly presented social events. Massinger's contributions in collaborative plays are frequently identified by scenes that feature arguments in judicial or quasi-legal hearings. These often feature, as in *The Parliament of Love*, social and personal as well as political problems. Ford has been characterized as the dramatist of public ceremonies: feasts, coronations, and weddings that celebrate alliances among families and states. Shirley is usually less formal, setting his plays at *The Ball* or, as in *Hyde Park*, at the opening of the spring racing season. And Brome is notable for settings that feature popular locales, as do *The Weeding of the Covent Garden* and *The Sparagus Garden*.

A final preliminary characteristic suggesting that the Caroline professionals focused on the interdependent creation of selves and society is that they habitually featured role playing. Ford's *Perkin Warbeck* provides the obvious example; a fraudulent pretender creates a role so authentically regal that he appears to convince himself of his royalty as much as he persuades other characters and modern critics of it. Conversely, the self-confirming regality of Massinger's exiled pilgrim, Antiochus the Great, "King of Lower Asia," in *Believe As You List*, reflects genuine authentication through role playing. From a different vantage Massinger's Paris in *The Roman Actor* offers a prominent example of questioning the relationship of roles to identity. Shirley's title paragons, from *The Grateful Servant* to *The Royal Master* and including *The Example*, and his title machiavels, from *The Traitor* to *The Politician* and *The Cardinal*, perpetually consider their means, their settings, their goals, and their co-actors; in essence they calculate the potential their roles hold for meeting situations, winning their ends, and affecting their audiences. Brome's most famous plays, *The Antipodes* and *A Jovial Crew*, follow from one of his earliest, *The City Wit*, in that characters explore pretended roles as they try to turn themselves and their situations to advantage.

Such preliminary illustrations show that the Caroline professional playwrights focused on the mutual creation of selves and society. Yet the mere evidence of their presentation of types in social settings is vacuous, since it lacks framing estimates of what they depicted their political, social, family, and gender relations to be like and of what issues they described as vital.

A Sociopolitical Context

The associates, the patrons, and the audiences the Caroline professional playwrights addressed were elite. In *The Privileged Playgoers of Shakespeare's London, 1576-1642* Ann Jennalie Cook has written that "Thanks to wealth or birth, to education or achievement, privileged Englishmen followed a life considerably different from the rest of their countrymen."[25] This does not mean that all of that audience was courtly. The two other leading scholars of the Caroline audience, Martin Butler and Andrew Gurr, agree with Cook that the professional drama companies should not be identified with the cavaliers and the royal court since the first label perpetuates an anachronism and since both labels oversimplify and hide diversity. The fact, then, that the sustaining patrons of the private theatrical companies—with which all these playwrights were associated—were elite does not entail that all were elite in the same way. Cook describes how "the group called the privileged, though limited in size, was not at all limited in degree, for it ranged from the threadbare scholar or the prospering landholder, newly risen from the yeomanry, all the way up to nobility and royalty itself."[26] Privileged Carolines held a wide range of sociopolitical preferences. As they confined their differences on a single spectrum of identification with each other as members of the elite, so they differed over a set of common concerns they wanted to resolve amiably inside a rather closed society of those who counted.

The privileged Carolines addressed by their professional playwrights had been educated to hold in common a set of expectations and aesthetic values. Most were brought up in grammar schools. Many continued in one of the universities; others attended the inns of court; and some did both. The curricula of all of these training grounds were based on rhetoric, the study and practice of persuasion in declamations and disputations. Moreover, each institution often presented dramatic productions: revivals, adaptations, original works for special occasions, and the like. The privileged Carolines who provided the primary support of the professional playwrights understood drama: they could appreciate expert displays of their rhetorical professions, they had backgrounds in drama, and many of them had theatrical experience. Such privileged playgoers participated most influentially in making and carrying out the nation's political and social policies; and they were among those most directly affected by the policies. This sociopolitical and dramatic context, despite what some critics have averred, proved propitious for Caroline drama. It, in turn, proves all the more interesting as another index of the last era before the English Revolution.

The Carolines could not, in all likelihood, have recognized a political use of the term *revolution*. If they did, it is even less likely that they could have conceived of themselves as revolutionaries. In retrospect, however, labeling them revolutionary seems appropriate in two seemingly contradictory yet truly complementary senses. In their view they often promoted a return to a state they presumed had existed earlier; sociopolitically they wanted to revert. From our view they often promoted extraordinary change in politics, society, religion, and culture. Whenever they differed on an issue, usually both sides called themselves traditional and presented themselves as the heirs to an idealized Elizabethan era, the transmitters of folk culture, or the revivalists of an ancient heritage of truth and goodness.[27] For example, although factions emphasized either one or the other word in the *lex rex* debates, the overture to a division on ultimate sovereignty, all pledged allegiance to the traditional, conciliatory, general, and hence problem-charged phrase *king-in-Parliament*. This agreement on tradition indicates the fundamental community of the privileged. They all repeatedly invoked accommodation and unity as what they valued most while at the same time as individuals and cliques they vied for advantage. In the twentieth century a neo-Whiggish historian, Margaret Atwood Judson, as well as a revisionary one, Conrad Russell, agree: the primary objective of the rare sessions of Parliament was to provide a forum that could contain disputes within the tradition of consensus.[28] And Esther S. Cope's study of the local politics that prevailed during most of the period, *Politics without Parliaments, 1629-1640*, traces the continuous efforts of the privileged to maintain harmony despite the increase in problems, grievances, and conflicts.[29]

While members of the privileged assumed the principle and goal of a unified, ordered commonweal, they became increasingly disturbed by political and social rifts that threatened to become oppositions. Because of the increasing array of disputes, from settling on final sovereignty in the nation to setting seating precedents in parish churches, the privileged members of this stratified society were concerned, even alarmed, at perceiving ever greater instability.[30] Moreover, as they deliberated about how to maintain order while they were struggling to define a host of issues, they became increasingly alert to the economic, political, and social rewards of relative dominance within any consensus. And they became more uncertain, more troubled because of their dilemma of needing to choose between personal advantages and social cohesion.[31] The era's predicaments have generated so much argument among later historians, who need categories, that most of the oppositions proposed for under-standing the progression into the Revolution have been disqualified. Royalist-parliamentary, arminian-puritan, ins-outs, feudal-bourgeois, aristocracy-gentry, court-country have been shown to consist of shifting memberships, to be based on inconsistent, often anachronistic criteria or on indistinct, overlapping, incomplete, unrepresentative memberships. Indeed, the only tentative agreement among historians resembles Law-rence Stone's and J.H. Hexter's extension to the elite as a whole of Harrington's familiar judgment in specific that the "dissolution of this Government caused the War": the disintegrating unity of the privileged members of society caused however much Revolution there was.[32]

If the concerns recurring in the Caroline professionals' plays provide a useful indication, several sociopolitical, social, and family issues seemed crucial to an audience fearful of disintegration. Common sociopolitical issues focus on the dilemma of keeping faith with values associated with court or with country; on the problem of the relative power of the king and parliament; and on whether to determine rank by lineage, patronage, public service, or wealth. Common social and family issues focus on the prerogatives of fathers versus the rights of children and adolescents, on inheritance patterns, and on the prerogatives of husbands and men versus the rights of wives and women. The domains of politics and the family provide mutual reinforcement because the privileged adhered, albeit with diverging interpretations, to patriarchal order in the state and in the household.

Allegiance to the court or the country signalled an inclination toward certain values more than a position or an alliance. In Lawrence Stone's modification of Perez Zagorin's persuasive but questionable thesis, coun-try was placed generally against the corruptions of the court and the city and stood for the ancient moral superiority of forthright honesty, thrift, stoical Christian simplicity, and health; in particular English country ways were presumed to include old-fashioned hospitality, tight-knit paternal-ism, local control, and county regionalism within the commonwealth.[33] The term evokes a heritage of humanistic education in classical and Christian morality. Hesiod's *Works and Days,* Horace's odes, and Virgil's *Georgics* extoll agrarian life. And the Bible and Augustine's *The City of God* exalt the opposition of faithful herdsmen to decadent artisans, cities, and courts. The evocation of country proved so potent in literature's pastoral retreats and green-world romances that the Elizabethan and early Stuart courts appropriated its force by playing shepherds and shepherdesses in self-presentations; perhaps the roles became central to some courtiers' self-conceptions.[34] The vogue was prominent enough that Davenant, who usually pitted the camp against the court and occasionally against the country and the city as well, laughingly depicted the ruler Theander donning a courtly shepherd's garb and gab in *The Platonic Lovers* (1636). The country, then, provided a favored mode for proclaiming absolute royal prerogatives as well as for advocating parliamentary balance. Thus, among the Caroline professional playwrights country was invoked as readily for the royalism of Shirley's *The Triumph of Peace* as for the more typical anti-court attitude of Brome's *The Queen and Concubine.*

The era's encompassing political question asked who, in the formula king-in-Parliament, was to wield ultimate sovereignty. Charles's position, as James's, was that the king, as God's representative on earth, held all prerogatives; his own will made law. Royal rights included deciding who is qualified to sit in Parliament, how it is to be ruled, what it discusses, how to punish MPs who broach *arcana imperii,* whether or not to impose special royal collections and maintain prerogative courts, and so on. James frequently rephrased his 1609 declaration before the House of Commons: "Kings are not only God's lieutenants on earth and sit upon God's throne, but even by God Himself they are called gods."[35] In 1626 Charles let members of the House of Commons know that their very existence as a body depended on his will: "Parliaments are altogether in my power for their calling, sitting, and dissolution; therefore, as I find the fruits of them good or evil, they are to continue, or not to be." And he began his 1629 explanation of why he dissolved the latest Parliament by reiterating his central principle: "princes are not bound to give account of their actions, but to God alone."[36]

Adherents to the position that Parliament could constrain the king's rights were less definitive.[37] But a position can be traced through a celebrated series of constitutional incidents, including the Bates Case of 1606, the impeachment of royal ministers in 1621 and accusation of them in 1626, the Five Knights' Case in 1627, the Petition of Right in 1628, and the Ship Money Case of 1638. These seem to sustain the spirit of the *Form of the Apology and Satisfaction,* which a committee of the House of Commons penned in 1604 but never forwarded to James. The document refutes the counsel of the king's advisers, who wanted to curtail Parliament's traditional powers; so it enumerates them. The central parliamentary prerogative is that the membership elected to the House of Commons constitutes, with the monarch and the House of Lords, the highest court of the realm and that therefore the House of Commons retains jurisdiction over itself and its members. As the legislative representative of the people of the commonwealth, it speaks for the nation. Moreover, it is the only legal body with full taxing and central legislative powers. In brief, Parliament can curb the king's will.[38] This position garnered support from Sir Edward Coke and other common-law spokesmen who cited precedents. Revolutionary in both senses, Coke's contingent argued for pro-Parliament interpretations of the Magna Carta and for restrictions on royal rule issuing from the so-called ancient constitution of *jus non scriptum*. This unwritten, immemorial code was presumed to embody an Anglo-Saxon tradition of freedom in accord with common law and in opposition to such monarchical innovations as prerogative courts and special administrative fines and assessments.[39] Cope has shown that during the Caroline era local leaders carried on by some such code while they awaited parliamentary curbs on monarchy.

The stage did not ignore the issue of whether ultimate sovereignty rested with the monarch, with Parliament, or in their conjunction. A famous passage from Beaumont and Fletcher's *Philaster* (1608-10) recalls drama from the past and sets a recurring scene for the future; at the same time it creates a problem for interpreters. A king, desperate over the disappearance of his daughter, makes almighty commands to one of his councillors, the Lord Dion:

> I doe command you all, as you are subjects,
> To shew her me: what, am I not your King?
> If I, then am I not to be obeyed?
> *Dion.* Yes, if you command things possible, and honest.
> *King.* Things possible and honest? Heare me, thou,—
> Thou traitor,—that dar'st confine thy King to things
> Possible and honest. . . . tis the King
> Will have it so! whose breath can still the Winds,
> Uncloud the Sunne, charme down the swelling Sea,
> And stop the flouds of heaven: speake, can it not?
> *Dion.* No.
> *King.*   No? . . . . Alas, what are we Kings?
> Why doe you gods place us above the rest,
> To be serv'd, flatter'd, and ador'd, till we
> Beleeve we hold within our hands your thunder?
> And when we come to try the power we have,
> There's not a leafe shakes at our threatenings. [IV.iv.26-51][40]

John F. Danby has led a number of critics in arguing that this passage at least accedes to James's claims of absolute rule.[41] But Douglas Sedge counters that the king's initial orders (even in excessive grief) are patently absurd and that his subsequent guilt over presumption emphasizes the arrogance and the failure of claims for the absolute sovereignty of a monarch.[42] Later scholars, most recently Albert H. Tricomi, recognize that early Stuart dramatists sometimes guardedly, sometimes obviously, depicted opposition to absolutism.[43] Often Caroline dramatists assume royal absolutism. Davenant rarely admits the question, but when he does, the challenger, such as Oramond in *The Fair Favourite* (1638), quickly resigns himself to the monarch's divine prerogatives (II.i/223).[44] Shirley's position for royal absolutism is invariable, as in *The Coronation*, and Ford's is consistent, as in *Perkin Warbeck*. But Massinger can imply a strong critique of absolutism, as in *The Roman Actor* or *The Emperor of the East*, and so can Brome, as in *The Queen and Concubine*. More likely than criticizing, Caroline plays—for instance, Massinger's *The Great Duke of Florence* or perhaps Ford's *Love's Sacrifice*—seem ambiguous about the resolution of ultimate sovereignty. Perhaps some of the presenters were ambivalent.[45]

The sociopolitical conflicts most often represented on the Caroline stage were how to define gentility, what constituted an adequate basis for social mobility, and what amount of it was acceptable. Not that anyone questioned hierarchy. People were placed and they acclaimed the system that placed them. Richard Hooker's memorable sentence from *Of the Laws of Ecclesiastical Polity* aligns all the universe and all society in an order as precise and integrally layered as his magnificent period. Shakespeare's celebrated speech on the necessity of degree, from *Troilus and Cressida*, provides another reminder of the reverence evoked by hierarchy; the fact that Ulysses, a machiavel, employs the principle to make this affecting exhortation attests to its enduring power. Keith Wrightson opens his account of *English Society, 1580-1680* with the observation that commentators during the era invariably began by delineating distinctions among social ranks.[46] And Lawrence Stone is one among many historians who note that the very leaders of the Revolution clung to established hierarchies.[47]

The foremost audience of Caroline drama was drawn from the small contingent of the population (perhaps 5 to 7.5 percent) who were in the top ranks.[48] They fit Sir Thomas Smith's brief characterization: "In these days he is a gentleman who is commonly taken and reputed. And whosoever studieth in the universities, who professeth the liberall sciences and to be short who can live idly and without manuall labour and will beare the port charge and countenance of a gentleman, he shall be called master."[49] Perhaps disgruntled that anyone could appear to be genteel, Smith emphasizes the essential requisite for any pretense to privilege—leisure, escape from the long days of manual labor required of all others by the Elizabethan Statute of Artificers, 1563. Other marks of privilege included the right to possess coats of arms, to bear arms (particularly swords), to wear silks and velvets and satins, and to be exempt from such commoners' punishments as being put in the stocks or whipped. Such outward signs were so important that the Tudor establishment wrote and Charles extended sumptuary legislation aimed at governing display so as to reinforce the recognition of status: certain fabrics and styles of clothing, materials and types of jewelry, kinds and amounts of foods were restricted to specific ranks.[50]

Besides signifying social stratification, sumptuary legislation provides one sign of a deep concern over social mobility. Attempts to limit perquisites and govern opportunities indicate both that social mobility was deemed critical and that significant distinctions were perceived as dismayingly imitable. At least by the time of Sir Thomas Wilson's "The State of England (1600)" social changes were rousing comment. This lawyer was troubled by mobility, both upward and downward, between the social strata: commonalty, *nobilitas minor,* and *nobilitas major.* Some yeomen decay into gentlemen's servants while others gain so much wealth that "my yonge masters the sonnes of such, not contented with their states of their fathers to be counted yeoman and called John or Robert (such an one), but must skipp into his velvett breches and silken dublett and, getting to be admitted into some Inn of Court or Chancery, must ever after thinke skorne to be called other then gentlemen"; later they fall faster than they rose. Some of the *nobilitas minor* are made knights with "competent quantity of revenue" from their ancestors; others rot. Among the *nobilitas major* "I find great alteracions almost every yeare, so mutable are worldly thinges and worldly mens affaires . . . . some daily decay, some encrease accordinge to the corse of the world." [51] In a passing observation in his *Description of England* William Harrison includes merchants among those who are socially mobile: they "often change estate with gentlemen, as gentlemen do with them, by a mutual conversion of the one into the other." [52] The remarkable extent of mobility has caught the attention of historians, particularly since Stone's demonstration of it in *The Crisis of the Aristocracy.* [53] The obvious illustrations, then and now, are the competition to purchase lands, the inflation of honors bestowed by James and Charles, and the scramble to hire genealogists to discover and legitimize family lineages, coats of arms, and ranks. [54]

Social mobility plays a frequent, prominent role in the period's plays. [55] A cynical observation about interchanges between merchants and gentry is made by Old Barnacle in Shirley's *The Gamester:*

> we that had
> Our breeding from a Trade, cits as you call us,
> Though we hate gentlemen our selves, yet are
> Ambitious, to make all our children gentlemen,
> In three generations they returne agen,
> We for our children purchase Land, they brave it
> I'th Countrie, begets children, and they sell,
> Grow poore, and send their sonnes up to be Prentises:
> There is a whirle in fate, the Courtiers make
> Us cuckolds; marke, we wriggle into their
> Estates, poverty makes their children Citizens;
> Our sonnes cuckold them, a circular justice,
> The World turnes round.   [I.i/201][56]

Old Barnacle's social theory implies a set of important criteria for status among the privileged. The rapid three-generation turnover in his hypothesis indicates a social disqualification of short-term landholders and suggests that a family's legitimation comes from a long-term tenure on its estate. But the primary consideration of his social theory is obviously the wealth that could buy leisure and the luxuries of social ostentation—sumptuous clothing, jewelry, food, gambling, crowds of retainers, special means of transportation, monumental building—that marked off ever higher social rungs.

Old Barnacle observes that there could be no question about whether or not mobility was acceptable. Mobility was presupposed. But two consequent questions remained at issue: how much mobility was good and, especially, what criteria ought to be applied in selecting who would ascend and descend. These issues were extensively discussed in contemporary accounts, including those by the teacher Richard Mulcaster and the writer Thomas Churchyard as well as Sir Thomas Wilson and William Harrison. The major criteria for Old Barnacle were commonplace but inverted. Preeminent was the inheritance of valuable ancestral lands (the more generations the more prestige). Close behind was wealth, often commercial wealth. Other criteria included intellectual gifts and university or legal training, membership in the professions (especially the clergy and the military), and administrative service for royal, noble, and county patrons. The key to social status was ultimately wealth, less because of its power to purchase honor (the financially strapped early Stuarts required these fees) than because of the necessity for maintenance. Precisely the lack of family resources, as Old Barnacle explains, generates the cycle. Nevertheless, elite society placed different social values on various modes of accumulation. While managerial posts were not acceptable, directorships could be. And directors who belonged to privileged circles plied their skills to earn untainted wealth from the development of demesne farming, minerals, and smelting, from speculation on urban real estate, privateering, and colonizing, and from Old Barnacle's marital alliances.[57] In brief, enormous opportunities for success and risks of failure required continual redistribution of political and social clout to match economic power. Thus social mobility occurred within the hierarchical patronage system; but that mobility was based on conflicting criteria.

Considerable evidence shows that commentators had qualms over the ease of mobility and the relative value of criteria, particularly over what honor was owed to the accumulation of wealth.[58] As sumptuary legislation indicates, most of those whose families had maintained their privileged status for some while held against mobility and demanded rigorous screening for lineage. But others favored considerable mobility on a number of grounds, primarily wealth or achievement. Ever more frequently, honors devolved on commercial, administrative, or other contributions to the commonwealth. One oft-quoted testament comes from Henry Oxinden, a gentleman from Kent who decided

> not to value anie man by having anie inward respect or conceite of him before another, beecause he excells in degrees of honour, but according to the concomitant ornaments, as vertue, riches, wisdom, power etc. etc.
>
> If I see a man of what low degree or quality soever that is vertuous, rich, wise or powerful, him will I preferre beefore the greatest Lord in the king-dome that comes short of him in these.[59]

Drama of the era presents proponents of recognizing status for achievement, that is status earned by merit, as well as proponents of recognizing status by ascription, that is status granted for birth or show. In *Everyman out of his Humor* (1599) Carlo Buffone represents an ascriptive stance in his satiric account of "Mushroom gentlemen" who spend "what-soever it costs" to "shoot up in a night to place and worship" by purchas-ing ostentatious outfits and foods, gambling, buying acquaintances, and issuing challenges: "First (to be an accomplisht gentleman, that is, a gentleman of the time) you must giue o'er house-keeping in the countrey, and liue altogether in the city amongst gallants; where, at your first apparance, 'twere good you turn'd foure or fiue hundred acres of your best land into two or three trunks of apparel (you may doe it without going to a coniurer. and be sure you mixe your self still, with such as flourish in the spring of fashion" (I.i.37-44).[60] On the other hand, Bosola's invective from *The Duchess of Malfi* (1612-14) represents the disillusion of many who aspired to status on the basis of their achievements and who felt barred from the rewards that went with gentility. Embittered by failure, they discredited supposed prizes for achievement:

> Who wold relie upon these miserable dependances, in expectation to be advanc'd to-morrow? what creature ever fed worse, then hoping *Tantalus?* nor ever di[e]d any man more fearefully, then he that hop'd for a pardon: There are rewards for hawkes, and dogges, when they have done us service; but for a Souldier, that hazards his Limbes in a battaile, nothing but a kind of Geometry, is his last Supportation. . . . [to] swinge in the world, upon an honorable pare of Crowtches, from hospitall to hospitall—fare ye well Sir. And yet do not you scorne us, for places in the Court, are but [like] beds in the hospitall, where this mans head lies at that mans foote, and so lower, and lower. [I.i.56-69][61]

One of the most pervasive sociopolitical issues in Caroline drama is the definition of accomplishments meriting elevated status. One way Davenant displayed disdain for social and economic climbing was to feature prominently the satiric motif of men trying to climb by marriage, as he did in *The Just Italian, The Wits,* and *News from Plymouth* (1635). More directly he offers commentaries such as the one by the virtuous warrior Oramont in *The Fair Favourite*: "I want / The skill how to grow great, the patience to / Permit those wrongs which they that rise / Must not alone endure, but praise" (II.i/220). Or the one by the courtier Saladine when he prods Oramont: "A little head may weigh enough, / When cozening fortune holds the scale, which she / Hath ever done in Court" (II.i/221).

Each of the Caroline professional playwrights—Shirley trying to restrict ranks to blood pedigree and Massinger trying to expand the ranks to honor achievement, Ford exalting the ideals and acts of born gentility and Brome denigrating them—presented a social hierarchy undergoing change. And each proposed a version of its supposed and desirable functions. An idea of what accomplishments each one considered worthy or unworthy of recognition can be gathered from what they variously deemed unworthy in their portrayals of "projectors." Each employed caricatures of these promoters to satirize accomplishments that he considered useless in the competition for clout and advancement. One telling estimate of social climbers, that is, of the others in the competition, implicates all Caroline aspirants to privilege, including the four professional playwrights. Agurtes, *"an Impostor"* in *Holland's Leaguer* (1631) by Shakerly Marmion, declares that

> one of [these projectors]
> Will undertake the making of bay salt
> For a penny a bushel to serve the State.
> Another dreams of building water-works,
> Drying of fens and marshes, like the Dutchmen.
> Another strives to raise his fortunes from
> Decayed bridges, and would exact a tribute
> From ale-houses and sign-posts; some there are
> Would make a thorowfare for the whole kingdom,
> And office, where nature should give account
> For all she took and sent into the world.   [I.v/25][62]

Each playwright places what he regards as worthless among seemingly countless absurd proposals made by contenders for sociopolitical rewards. And each persists in the attempt to appoint himself and his associates to higher, more privileged status.

Probably the sociopolitical issue that gained the greatest unanimity was that a court that continues to raise favorites and dump losers of favor is corrupt if not corrupting. Not that many argued against patronage as a system. They expressed disapproval of an extraordinary range of specific practices of patronage. While virtually everyone argued against abuses in particular cases, they could not agree on either the cases or the rationales; even the definition of gentility by birth or by merit and the amount of social mobility to be accepted remained at issue. This argument compounded the differences in the two other chief sociopolitical disagreements: first, over the ultimate sovereignty of king or parliament; and second, over allegiance to one of the value-laden terms, court or country.

A Social and Family Context

During the Caroline era sociopolitical hierarchy was inseparable from family hierarchy. Power in each is designated by the common Latin root for patriarchal and paternal. Ancient traditions from Aristotle and Seneca as well as from the Bible viewed the state as originating in and precisely analogous to family relationships. As Gordon J. Schochet has argued, the period's commentators interpreted fundamental paternalist principles founded in the Bible, in the classics, and in nature so as to buttress diverse social and political positions.[63] Apologists employed ceremonies and the arts as well as homilies, handbooks, and treatises to reinforce their views.[64]

Just as virtually all of those who participated in Caroline political determinations avowed monarchy, so virtually all of those who recorded their observations about Caroline society professed paternalism. But paternalists could disagree as fundamentally over the extent of a father's dominion as monarchists could over the site of ultimate sovereignty. And as the latter disagreements could lead to political factions, so the former could lead to contrary mores. Were the father's rights almighty prerogatives or dutiful responsibilities? The issue became especially vexed because there was a widespread perception among the privileged that the family was undergoing changes fundamental enough to threaten a revolution.[65]

Imperative for many was a new emphasis on the father's dominion, which was greater during this era than in those immediately before or after it.[66] This position was aligned with the absolute dominion sanctioned by all authorities—legal, political, religious, and moral: a father is endowed with complete control over his wife, children, householders, and holdings. Such advice was frequently restated in popular tracts such as Robert Cleaver's oft-reprinted *A Godly Form of Housholde Government* (1598) and his *A Plaine and Familiar Exposition of the Ten Commandments* (1604) with John Dod. These manuals reiterated the royal emphasis on patriarchalism as the foundation of order; they extended God's fifth commandment to "honor thy father" (with omission of "thy mother") to ecclesiastical, political, educational, and social authorities. This command formed one burden of several Elizabethan homilies that were required readings in Anglican pulpits. "An Exhortation to Obedience to Rulers and Magistrates" is founded on nature's hierarchy, Deuteronomy's code, and Paul's writings; "Against Contention" employs the same texts to exhort submission of parishioners, servants, and students; and "An Homily against Disobedience and wilful Rebellion" concludes that there can be no excuse for any uprising.[67] These homilies reinforce James's commission of himself as God's lieutenant on earth in the opening sonnet of *Basilikon Doron* and his reiteration of the analogy of himself as a husband to his wife or a head to his household in *The Trew Lawe of Free Monarchies*.

The attitude is epitomized in Sir Robert Filmer's *Patriarcha*. Filmer basically accepts the interpretation of Genesis that subordinates everything on earth to Adam and potently contends that through Adam the father's dominion in the family and in the state is an everlasting universal: "For as Kingly power is by the law of God, so it hath no inferior law to limit it. The Father of a family governs by no other law than his own will, not by the law or wills of his sons or servants. There is no nation that allows children any action or remedy for being unjustly governed."[68] Filmer's argument, despite the notoriety John Locke bestowed on it, was neither foolish nor unprecedented; it was supported by traditional interpretations of numerous Bible passages, classical references, and native laws. A wife and children had since time immemorial constituted the husband and father's economic and, most often, legal responsibility. In fact, a wife and children were often judged to be his attributes or properties. Absolute paternalism was a potent position sanctioned by tradition.

But the father's responsibility for his family's welfare, as a king's for his kingdom's, could be pressed to contrary claims. These followed from his duty to preserve the spiritual (hence psychological and social) well-being of his charges. Gordon J. Schochet and R.W.K. Hinton have demonstrated how patriarchalism was used as an analogy not only for absolutism but also for liberalization.[69] A handbook, such as the popular *Of Domesticall Duties* (1622) by the Puritan mentor William Gouge, could characterize a father's proper attitude as caring for his dependents and his appropriate role as leading mutual consideration, determination, and administration of family decisions.[70] Moreover, Gouge's ethic was encouraged by some religious advice and social custom. In the fifth and sixth chapters of his Epistle to the Ephesians Paul requires wives and children to submit to their husbands and fathers. But there too he admonishes husbands to love their wives as Christ loves the church or a head its body, and he advises fathers not to frustrate but to nurture their children. Gouge heeds Paul's advice on the obligations owed as well as the prerogatives held by the heads of families, just as by the heads of bodies, congregations, and states. His discipleship shows up even in the manual's arrangement. His first tract, on the scriptural foundation of Christian faith, leads immediately into tracts on "A *right Coniunction* of Man and Wife" and "*Common-mutuall Duties betwixt* Man and Wife"; then he devotes separate tracts to the particular duties of a husband, of a wife, of children, of children and parents *together,* and of servants and masters *together.* Repeatedly through the treatise he urges reciprocal obligations, shared concerns, and mutual gratitude. In sum, during the era there existed a strong sentiment in favor of mutual affection and duty in a hierarchical family, which featured consultations as well as orders and rights as well as obedience, just as there existed another powerful impulse in favor of absolute patriarchal authority.

Problems of paternalism extended throughout females' lives. Yet difficulties for them as well as for males intensified during adolescence, when choices are usually made about people's two most important social decisions, marriage and vocation. Any definition of adolescence for the early Stuart era is elusive, since some historians have questioned if the privileged considered it, or even childhood, to be distinct. These historians, following Philippe Aries' postulate by omission, surmise that before the nineteenth century adolescence was either submerged under a growing interest in childhood or sunk in the concerns of adulthood.[71] But the desire of patriarchs to disallow questions about a father's authority may account for a repression of comments on adolescence then and consequently hamper assessments by historians now. And Steven R. Smith seems right in saying that private advice to and about youth in religious manuals and sermons along with public statements about apprentices, recorded in the Statute of Artificers and the periodic expressions of alarm over rowdies, indicate consternation over adolescents.[72]

Historians tacitly admit some acknowledgment of adolescence by Stuarts whenever they recognize competing beliefs about who should choose spouses and professions. Stone and Flandrin have shown that a sizable contingent of fathers increased such control markedly during the era. A father well might compel his choices on his offspring, since he commanded all the legal and virtually all the economic power. Moreover, his direct powers were abetted by moral and religious imperatives, the most liberal of which assumed his prerogative to provide his children with callings and matches.[73] But a contrary view of a father's duties suggested shared decisions or even a child's choice. Although these attitudes do not appear in tracts on the family, they occasionally show up in diaries and personal accounts, such as the well-known record of the marriage quest of Simonds D'Ewes.[74] Stone and Christopher Hill have further suggested an affinity of children insisting on their marital choices with revolutionaries rebelling against the divine right of kings.[75]

Douglas Sedge has demonstrated an increase in the presentation of adolescent issues on the Caroline stage. The winning of mates and of

martial honor, together with the gain and maintenanance of status, remained popular topics in plays such as Davenant's. But presentations of
rebellious sons and daughters who put their personal honor and love
before their fathers' demands became increasingly popular.[76] The Caroline professional playwrights often focus on a youngster's problems
with his or her family. Shirley generally settles family conflicts in such a
way that rebellious children are penalized. Sometimes he concludes with
the sort of disastrous consequences that usually impend and transpire in
Ford's plays. Massinger consistently portrays forceful young women. The
anguish children feel over encounters with their fathers, their tortuous
evasions and debilitating rebellions, appear most often in Brome's plays.
Here strife spreads through families. Perhaps the most obvious example
is *The Weeding of Covent Garden,* which goes to great lengths to justify
several adolescent siblings who disobey their willful, irascible father.

One way the issue of adolescent male rights commonly appears in
Caroline drama is that a younger son challenges primogeniture. Joan
Thirsk considers commentators on inheritance, such as John ap Roberts
and John Selden, to be indicating that the popularity of primogeniture
among English gentry in the sixteenth century was giving way to more
concern for the plight of impoverished younger brothers in the seventeenth. Apparently in England as well as on the continent, establishing
trusts for younger sons while advancing the eldest was becoming a
favored mode of passing on family wealth.[77] Many of the privileged seem
to have felt the injustice that caused Sir Thomas Wilson to decry the "fever
hectick" of cutting off younger males.[78] In his discussion of parents'
duties Gouge mediates between biblical, western European, and English
legal traditions that guard the prerogatives of the first-born son, and a
general principle that parents should not show preferences among their
children. While the eldest son inherits the responsibility for, and so the
right to control, the continuity, status, and resources of the family, still he
should not be "a Gentleman, and all the other beggars": "In this respect
parents ought to be so much the more prouident for their other children,
in training them vp to callings, or laying vp portions, or setling estates
vpon them beside the maine inheritance, or in taking order that competent portions be raised out of the inheritance of the eldest son, in case God
take them away before they haue otherwise prouided for their children."[79]

Gouge was trying to forestall the ruin that threatened many a younger
brother on the early Stuart stage. The threat could be overcome by the
clever ploys of a Pallatine in Davenant's *The Wits* or evaded by the voluntary acquiescence of a Dorando in his *The Distresses.* Too often, though,
the burdens of acquiescence proved degrading and demoralizing. A
catalogue of grievances borne by younger brothers appears in the vir-

tuous Euphanes' denunciation of his villainous elder brother in Fletcher
and Massinger's *The Queen of Corinth:*

> May be you look'd I should petition to you
> As you went to your Horse; flatter your servants,
> To play the Brokers for my furtherance,
> Sooth your worst humors, act the Parasite
> On all occasions, write my name with theirs
> That are but one degree from slaves,
> Be drunk when you would have me, then wench with you,
> Or play the Pander; enter into Quarrels
> Although unjustly grounded, and defend them
> Because they were yours; these are the tyrannies
> Most younger Brothers groan beneath; yet bear them
> From the insulting Heir.   [I.ii][80]

Although the plight of younger brothers claimed attention on the
Caroline stage, paternalism over women commanded far greater interest.
As Sedge and others have shown, the social relations of women were
spotlighted on the Caroline stage as never before in England. The marked
increase in the number of forceful women characters has been taken as
one sign of an advancement of women and especially of married women,
most recently by Mary Beth Rose.[81] Few doubt that questions about the
status of women roused considerable interest, some ambivalence, and
perhaps a few fears. In terms of functionalism, there is some melioration
and rather more opportunity for women in somewhat less restricting
circumstances. In the increasingly popular terms of conflict favored by
Catherine Belsey, there is more contention over women's place.[82] Whatever, there seems to have been no more a gender than a family revolution;
the vast majority of women remained subject to men.[83] Davenant's plays
typically depict women under the sway of guardians, even if these guardians, such as Sir Tyrant Thrift in *The Wits* or Sir Solemn Trifle in *News from
Plymouth,* are satirized. Judging by the popularity of patient Griseldas on
stage, the queen in Davenant's *The Fair Favourite* seems likely to have won
the assent of a majority of its privileged audience. She is submissive when
her husband the king rushes to dismiss her: "You are too quickly weary of
our griefs! / I could endure 'em longer, sir, so I / Might tarry here. But 'tis
as hard for me / To disobey your will, as hinder fate" (I.i/210).

By native traditions, Christian tenets, and classical precepts, whether
promulgated by statutes and the common law, homilies and sermons, or
conduct books, the position of nearly all women, from their social rank
to their economic status, was subject to their fathers, husbands, guardians, and adult sons. The preeminent feminine virtues advocated in the
seventeenth century—obedience, chastity, and silence—were insepara-

ble from the universal assumption that no woman would have any vocation other than marriage.[84] The outstanding proof is that the virgin
queen, Elizabeth, was then, and remains now, honored for her marriage
to England. The homilies promulgated during Elizabeth's reign provide
ample testimony to the propriety of a wife's obedience to her husband.
They adhere to a revered tradition that extends from Paul's commandment in Ephesians (a woman should submit to her husband) through
the *Book of Common Prayer*'s admonition in the service for a solemn
marriage (wives are subordinates helpful for procreating and rearing
Christian children, avoiding fornication, and providing companionship).
In addition to Christian exemplars who helped make up for Eve's losses,
classical models of feminine subordination earned frequent mention: self-
sacrificing wives such as Portia, the wife of Brutus, and Cornelia, the wife
of Pompey, and self-sacrificing mothers such as Cornelia of the Gracchi.

Civil law unmistakably declared the lack of female rights outside of
criminal actions. T.E.'s *The Lawes Resolution of Womens Rights* generalizes
the account in Genesis of Eve's creation for the help of Adam, from whom
she was derived and to whom she remains attached; then it reinforces that
subjection by recalling Eve's penalty due to the fall. Because women are
considered with marriage in mind, politically and legally they lack rights
of advice, consent, or denial: "It is seldome, almost neuer that a marryed
woman can haue any action to use her writt onely in her owne name: her
husband is her sterne, her primus motor, without whom she cannot doe
much at home, and lesse abroad."[85] The very divisions of this legal
handbook repeat its bald opening premise of feminine obedience. Its five
treatises deal with preparations for marriage, pacts upon marriage, subject status during marriage, widowhood's difficulties, and questions of
remarriage.

It is unlikely that a daughter could forget her duty to obey the fifth
commandment or a wife hers to obey Paul's precepts and the nation's
laws. One constant reminder that she was a weaker vessel subject to a
man appeared in her social status. As Ruth Kelso realized, while a family
pedigree forever distinguished a gentleman from other men, no such
perpetual caste distinction set a lady apart from other women. A woman's
social status devolved from her father or her husband.[86] Unlike a gentleman, who could elevate a wife from a lower class, a born lady descended to her spouse's lower social rank. A set of signs constantly
reinforced feminine subordination and obedience.

Two other preeminent womanly virtues—chastity and silence—represent all-important signs of feminine obedience. As the male's hypersen-
sitivity to insults to his honor demonstrates his assertive superiority, so
the female's defense of her chaste honor proves her self-suppression
within the dual standard. In *Of Domesticall Duties* Gouge explains the two

familiar reasons why both Roman and Christian law value a woman's chastity more highly than a man's: "greater infamy before men, worse disturbance of the family, more mistaking of legitimate, or illegitimate children, with the like."[87] The first reason is the masculine dread of cuckoldry, the fear of a violation of a man's integrity when anyone else uses his property. The second is the masculine anxiety over maintaining patrilineage, the anxiety born of the coupling of social and legal sanction of the male line with recognition that only a female could be sure of her own offspring. To these reasons recent commentators, represented by Coppélia Kahn, have added a third, the misogynistic tradition that projects women as threateningly lustful and fickle.[88]

The elaborate tables of topics which customarily introduce the few ladies' conduct books proclaim their primary purpose: to exhort chastity. Richard Brathwait's mottos for his outline of the eight "prime subjects" of *The English Gentlewoman* (1631), the sequel to *The English Gentleman*, mainly treat chastity: (1) apparel is to be "Comely not gaudy"; (4) "Virgin-Decency, is Vertues Livery"; (5) estimation, "My prize, is her owne praise"; (6) fancy, "My Choice admits no Change." The climax, (8) "Honour is vertues Harbour," adds the motto "No passage to the Temple of Honour, but through the Temple of Vertue." His sections exhort the requisite feminine constancy, and his paragons are virgins, loyal matrons, and wary widows. The English translation of Jacques Du Bosc's *The Compleat Woman* (1639) corroborates Brathwait's advice that a woman should consciously adhere to one choice instead of errantly following her dissolute inclinations. Its topics urge women to maintain their reputations, virtue and devotion, chastity with courtesy, constancy and fidelity, and prudence and discretion. Such is the primacy of feminine chastity in manuals offering advice.

Feminine chastity played a central role in the era's drama. Revenge tragedies and problem plays, such as Davenant's early *Albovine* (1626-29) and *The Cruel Brother* (1627) and his late *The Fair Favourite* and *The Distresses*, are motivated by the dishonor dreaded by brothers as well as husbands of women who might be unchaste or unfaithful. Plays that feature testing patterns were enormously popular all the way through Ford's *The Lady's Trial*. In these a lover, a husband, a brother, or occasionally a father or family friend tests some woman's chastity or fidelity.[89] One standard motif of comedies based on testing patterns is a brother's compulsive warnings against and attempts to forestall his sister's apparent waywardness. Driven by the fear of dishonor, the brother in Thomas Nabbes's *Covent Garden: A Pleasant Comedie* (1632-33) proves comic because his sister emulates their young stepmother, a heroine who obediently endures her arranged marriage. Plays through the era were at least as preoccupied with cuckoldry as with these tests. A telling rejoinder suggesting why appears in Lording Barry's *Ram Alley* (1608), when Small-shanks answers the greedy Throte, who has just discovered that he has married Smallshanks' whore. The misogynistic victim protests the insult to his brotherhood of cuckolded lawyers, "Why should the harmlesse man be vext with hornes, when women most deserue them!" Small-shanks's punning response targets masculine vulnerability: "The husband is the wives head, and I pray / Where should the hornes stand but vpon the head?" (2584-87). There was no Caroline professional play-wright who was not preoccupied with representing concerns over fem-inine chastity and fidelity. Massinger exalts the virtue into feminine integrity; Ford often presents the tragic consequences of failures to abide by it; Shirley represents repulsion from violation of it; and Brome analyzes the angst that fixation on cuckoldry visits on families.

As a male's prerogatives of giving orders at home and speaking for the family in public assert his dominion, so the female's silence serves as the supreme outward sign of her submissive obedience. *The English Gen-tlewoman* repeatedly emphasizes a woman's "bashfull modesty." A major component of her reputation, "shamefastnesse," complements her ap-parel and behavior, especially since it helps her maintain chastity. Modest feminine silence is thus the last virtue in the triad. Although Brathwait acknowledges that "Without *Speech* can no society subsist," he imme-diately defines speech so as to confine women's conversation: "Truth is, their tongues are held their defensiue armour; but in no particular detract they more from their honour, than by giuing too free scope to that glibbery member." He emblemizes the ideal feminine mouth as a fortress doubly walled with ivory teeth hemming in the tongue's words and he specifies Ecclesiastes' admonition that no youth should talk much: "The direction is generall, but to none more consequently vsefull than to *young women;* whose bashfull silence is an ornament to their Sexe." [90]

The importance of silence as a feminine virtue is more often assumed than asserted on the early Stuart stage. Ben Jonson's *Epicoene, or The Silent Woman* (1609) turns on its desirability. But more typically, women, such as the brassily rebellious wife Alteza in Davenant's *The Just Italian,* are characterized by their violations of the restriction. The most eloquent evidence of feminine silence on the early Stuart stage is the paucity and poverty of lines delivered by women other than rebels or shrews or gossips, who epitomize "woman's last frailty." Even the Duchess of Malfi invokes this proverb against other women as she dies. Meanwhile on stage, faithful, obedient mothers and chaste, obedient daughters are rarely memorable. [91] One important trait of the Caroline professionals is that they gave a greater proportion of strong lines and great speeches to their women.

Male superiority was more than represented and institutionalized, exhorted and enforced under the early Stuarts. Through the campaigns of the era's Joseph Swetnams, James I's misogyny was promoted. A few advocates for women responded in kind, witness the Red Bull's staging of *Swetnam, the Woman-hater, Arraigned by Women* (1618).[92] More defenders of women, such as Daniel Tuvil in *Asylum Veneris* (1616), merely catalogued the culture's paragons of subserviently obedient, chaste, silent womanhood. Still others suggested that their society could afford to relax the restrictions on women. Consequently a popular observation reechoed across Europe: England was "the hell of horses, the purgatory of servants, and the paradise of women." In Massinger's *Renegado* Carazie pronounces the commonplace that "women in England / For the most part liue like *Queenes*" (I.ii.27-28). He goes on, however, to satirize the liberties of country, city, and court ladies.

Twentieth-century historians disagree over whether or not the status of women improved during the period. The most notable evidence of improvement is the apparently increasing recognition of wives' rights; more marriage manuals defended them. So, according to Stone and Chilton Latham Powell, sensibilities became more attuned to "affection": romantic love and companionship.[93] For whatever reasons— the Puritan respect for "holy matrimony," the charms of accomplished court ladies, the rise of platonizing courtly and literary love, the blessings and example of Charles and Henrietta Maria—many privileged members of Jacobean and Caroline society reevaluated the traditional considerations for choosing a helpmate. Procreating Christian families remained a strong motive. Providing comfort and companionship received more emphasis whereas avoiding fornication got less. Marriage manuals, particularly Puritan ones, indicate some shift from choosing a wife for her lineage and tangible assets toward choosing one for her personal and spiritual virtues.

Granted the universal demands for female obedience, some other signs indicate that requirements for women were becoming more liberal. Though no one apart from a few libertines advocated promiscuity, there was significant criticism of the double standard. While Gouge acknowledged tradition's force ("more inconuenience may follow vpon the womans default then vpon the mans"), he disapproved of its inconsistency: "Yet in the breach of wedlocke, and transgression against God, the sinne of either partie is alike." If any distinction is to be made, a hierarchy that grants sociopolitical superiority to males ought likewise to demand moral superiority from them: "[I]t is meet that adulterous husbands be so much the more seuerely punished, by how much the more it appertaineth to them to excell in vertue, and to gouerne their wiues by example."[94] During the Caroline era the double standard was also being questioned through calls for male fidelity after marriage.[95]

Presentations that at least implicitly questioned the double standard increased on the Caroline stage. The double standard remained in place, as it does in Sir William Davenant's presentation of the greater horrors of a wife's than a husband's adultery in *The Just Italian* and of the frequent reclamation of rakes by virtuous heroines, such as that of Cable by Carrack in *News from Plymouth* and that of Androlio by Amiana in *The Distresses*. Even so, Davenant's close parody of sexually abstinent love and sexual strictness in the courtly *The Platonic Lovers* indicates the growing importance of masculine sexual fidelity. The theme recurs forcefully through the plays of the Caroline professionals: Massinger repeatedly calls for male chastity; Ford punishes male as well as female adultery; Shirley reinforces postmarital male fidelity; and Brome presents the pain of a double standard by both inverting and juxtaposing relationships.

The evidence most commonly cited as advocating more opportunities for women comes from humanist teachers. But in a salutary warning against interpreting this evidence as univocal, Lisa Jardine has construed its effect as a moderation that insures female subordination.[96] One conclusion follows readily from Kelso's survey of Renaissance conduct books for women. The era's general assumption was that inculcating piety in women and training them to do household tasks provided all the education they needed.[97] So no one promoted women's education in the rigors of logic, rhetoric, and moral philosophy or in the professions. A few renowned schoolmasters, notably Vives, Elyot, Ascham, and Mulcaster, did advocate teaching women enough about language, reading, and writing that mothers could teach their children moral values and wives could make suitable companions for their husbands. Moreover, there had been a few remarkable pupils—a Queen Elizabeth, a Lady Jane Grey, a Mary Sidney, Countess of Pembroke, a Lady Mary Wroth, Countess of Montgomery—who proved that educating women could be important. Thus Du Bosc's *The Compleat Woman* urges women to read and praises "Learned Women" as it conventionally commends their quiet manner. Critics have long recognized that women represented on the Caroline stage, often Massinger's, to a lesser extent Shirley's, not infrequently Ford's and Brome's, are more eloquent, witty, and strongwilled than men. Typically they are more prominent and more likely to be dominant than in earlier plays.

The Caroline professional playwrights, and the privileged audience on whom they depended, unanimously held that society as well as politics was rightly founded on patriarchal traditions. But their consensus on fundamental principles here, as in politics, allowed considerable latitude for an array of diverging attitudes ranging from absolutism through appropriation or accommodation to reformation. Onstage as elsewhere, opposed poles of absolute command and obedience versus shared decisions and power appeared in social and family circles which were interlinked with sociopolitical spheres. In social and family circles disputes arose over a father's powers versus his children's rights (particularly during adolescence), over strict primogeniture versus inheritance by younger sons, and preeminently about the prerogatives of husbands and males versus the rights of wives and females. Inside this context of potential diversity within overarching agreement, the Caroline professional playwrights reflected a range of belief that helps characterize each writer, his primary audience, and presumably their era. Their concerns suggest an importance that has been ignored for too long.

Socialization

Massinger, Ford, Shirley, and Brome repeatedly presented to their privileged audience a common set of issues which they seem to have regarded as important. Yet because of their personal backgrounds, associations, and audiences, their individual social and political predilections, and their distinctive dramatic styles, they did not take a common stance toward these issues. Each subsequent chapter of this book features one playwright, and each follows the same pattern, scrutinizing ever closer a smaller sample. In the first part of each chapter I sketch what scholars have been able able to learn about the evolving heritage of the playwright, and I place him among the associates and patrons who have been identified. In the second I survey the views of politics, society, and the family that he consistently represented. (I do not intend to suggest by this useful generalization that any of the four held a fixed position throughout his career.) In the third I identify the developing dramatic techniques that he habitually employed and I posit connections to the views outlined in the second part. In the last I consider one play in detail as an example. By example I mean treating the play in a way that exemplifies a useful means of entry to many of the author's characteristic plays and also regarding the play as an exemplary work by that author.

My study further looks at each Caroline professional playwright from the perspective of a particular twentieth-century social hypothesis.[98] I use social reflexivity and reciprocity to frame Massinger's presentation of how characters define themselves, their roles, and their actions in accord with how they perceive others being affected by them and affecting them. This frame depends on theories of symbolic interactionism, role conformity, and situational definition. I use functionalist social theory to frame Ford's presentation of how ceremonials and rituals shape ideal roles. This frame relies on contemporary theories, corroborated by the practices of Renaissance monarchs and the perceptions of their subjects: rituals serve to enforce the discipline and reinforce the ideals of a cult, and ceremonies model behavior and promote social cohesion. I make the same assumptions that underlie the meaningful "accountability" of ethnomethodology to frame Shirley's presentation of how the hierarchy and norms of politeness associated with the court are reinforced when his characters learn, rehearse, and adapt prescribed role models. This frame takes to be accurate appraisals the self-conscious social sensitivity and explicit instructions promulgated in a play and in Renaissance handbooks of rhetoric and manuals of conduct. Finally, I use a revolutionary theory of the potential for innovation inherent in holiday revelry to frame Brome's presentation of how parody, inversion, and extemporaneous play can turn into vicarious social experiment. This frame coincides with recent theses by social anthropologists and historians of the era.

Within the constraints and possibilities granted by their setting, their audience, their medium, and their own talents and predilections, the Caroline professional playwrights reproduced a wide spectrum of views. Massinger often presented tragicomedies of reformation for a somewhat disaffected albeit privileged audience. His situations and characters become entangled and opposed; then, when his characters seem caught in inextricably destructive circumstances, some mediating miracle intervenes so they can discover loving contrition, forgiveness, and accommodating reconciliation. Ford generally offered tragedies of ritual suffering to idealistic aspirants to court. His characters work and endure to create ideal selves by playing to perfection roles that require them to embrace the penalties that societies often exact from adherents to absolutes; such heroes and heroines essentially are formed, or perhaps purified, through ceremonies that demand sacrifice to transcendental values. Shirley characteristically provided comedies of social codification for an elite, aspiring audience. His characters exemplify and thereby inculcate the identifying mores of the genteel; they display the lessons and rewards of knowing one's place by adapting gracefully to the assignments that maintain both the selves and the system. Brome seems to have approached a parodic comedy of types and inversions for a privileged yet venturesome audience. His characters and situations satirize dual contemporary vices, abuses of authority and abuses of ambition; and his plays ever more often proffer vicarious experiments in social reform.

In mode, the two earlier Caroline professional playwrights tended toward tragic seriousness, the two later ones toward comic play. In sociopolitical stance, one earlier and one later playwright maintained the status quo, the other two encouraged some change. Ford presented characters who, most concerned with maintaining the integrity of their essential selves, paradoxically turn out the most determined by rigid social modeling. But Massinger presented characters who convert near disaster to rebirth by learning to accommodate their interactions in the formation, maintenance, and reformation of themselves and their society. Shirley permitted characters to try on, play with, and then settle into roles within a rigorously restricted set. But Brome celebrated free, extemporaneous play with roles that promise potential personal and social reform.

2

Massinger's Tragicomedy of Reformation

The Disaffections of Massinger's Privileged Patrons

Massinger inherited from Shakespeare and from his master and collaborator Fletcher the role of chief playwright for the preeminent theatrical company in Renaissance England. Since the King's Men wore their monarch's livery and performed at court more often than any other company, many scholars have assumed that Massinger was a court reactionary.[1] And much in his early life confirms training for such a stance. Born in 1583 near Salisbury, he was the son of well-connected gentry through his mother's family, the Cromptons, and through his father's position with the powerful Herberts, who succeeded as earls of Pembroke. Likely prepared at Salisbury school, he entered his father's first college, St. Alban Hall, Oxford, in 1601 or 1602 but did not earn a degree. After a lapse of a dozen years, the record resumes with his prolific output of dramatic collaborations, first with Nathan Field and Robert Daborne, then with Thomas Dekker and, most importantly, with John Fletcher. In other ways, however, Massinger's record suggests training to be a mediating reformer rather than a nostalgic reactionary. For the Herberts, though members of the Privy Council, were disaffected from James's and Charles's favorites, particularly from Sir George Villiers, the Duke of Buckingham; so they made notable leaders of a politically Puritan circle.[2] Moreover, Massinger's father gained his position with the Herberts by merit, not inheritance. Just so, the son sought preferment with some reluctance and more than a little pride in his dramatic accomplishments.

When Massinger dedicated *The Picture* (1629) "To my Honored, and selected friends of the Noble society of the Inner Temple," he was thanking privileged associates. According to the title page this audience received *The Picture* "with good allowance, at the *Globe*, and *Blackefriers* play-houses, by the Kings Maiesties seruants." The title pages of most of Massinger's plays advertise performances by the King's Men at Blackfriars, London's elite company and playhouse, or by the Queen's at the Phoenix in Drury Lane, the next most prestigious. When he dedicated *The Roman Actor* (1629) he segregated his ideal, privileged audience from ignorant detractors *"onely affected with ligges, and ribaldrie."* A fuller understanding of the status of such privileged associates, patrons, and audiences to whom he presented his plays is important to the mediating social and political reformations that Massinger's plays suggest.

The primary evidence about Massinger's associates and potential patrons comes from his dedications.[3] He dedicated *The Roman Actor* to three of the lesser gentry, "my much Honoured, and most *true Friends, Sir Philip Knyvet*, Knight and Baronet. And to Sir Thomas Ieay, Knight. And Thomas Bellingham of *Newtimber* in *Sussex* Esquire." Two of the three were educated at a university; all three were trained at the inns of court; one was a member of Parliament. They seem representative of Massinger's associates aside from theater professionals. While these three proved the *"only Supporters"* during the *"composition of this Tragædie"* and the *"principall encouragement"* for its publication, others added their approval: *The Roman Actor "hath beene happie in the suffrage of some learned, and judicious Gentlemen when it was presented."* Massinger's verifiable patrons corroborate his characterization of a coterie made up of lesser gentry, most of whom were situated at the inns of court, many of whom had attended a university, and some of whom served in Parliament. These include Sir Aston Cokayne, who credited Massinger as a primary collaborator in the Beaumont and Fletcher canon, and such commenders as William Bagnall, George Donne, the son of John Donne, and John Selden, the noted jurist, scholar, and MP. Proven patrons include an early supporter, Sir Warham St. Leger, whom Massinger acknowledged in 1639 when he dedicated *The Unnatural Combat* to his son, Sir Anthony St. Leger. Other long-term supporters included Sir Francis Foljambe, baronet, and Sir Thomas Bland, to whom he dedicated *The Maid of Honour* in 1632. Both men, trained at the inns of court, were industrious gentry thriving on coal and lead mining. Apparently Foljambe, to whom Massinger presented a copy of *The Duke of Milan* in 1623, had long aided the dramatist. The last of Massinger's known friends and patrons among the lesser gentry is Sir Robert Wiseman, the son of a wealthy London goldsmith, to whom Massinger dedicated *The Great Duke of Florence* in 1636. Wiseman was related to Massinger's mother.

Frequently mentioned as a reluctant seeker of patronage, Massinger reveals a deep appreciation of his network of relatives and associates. This appreciation in turn suggests the considerable personal importance to him of the heritage of patronage that was psychologically, socially, politically, and economically invaluable to members of Caroline society, including playwrights who had to depend on patrons.[4] Apparently some time between 1615 and 1620 he sent a "Copie of a Letter written vpon occasion to the Earle of Pembrooke Lo: Chamberlaine." The journeyman dramatist "Scarce yet allowed one of the Company" (17) was driven by the dread that "Such as are Poets borne, are borne to need" (12). Yet even under economic pressure he worried about the disgrace of sycophancy, laying some of any potential guilt on those who corrupted an honorable system by buying rather than earning praise. So he makes his oft-quoted declaration of personal integrity:

> I would not for a pension or A place
> Part soe wth myne owne Candor; lett me rather
> Liue poorely on those toyes I would not father,
> Not knowne beyond A Player or A Man
> That does pursue the course that I haue ran,
> Ere soe grow famous.   [40-45]

In the lesser known continuation he makes his plea for a good patron:

> yet wth any paine
> Or honest industry could I obteyne
> A noble Fauorer, I might write and doe
> Like others of more name and gett one too.   [45-48]

Massinger's problem was gaining a patron worthy of an eternizing eulogy so that he would not bear the everlasting shame of offering praise to someone lacking merit. Consequently he praises the patrons of such poets as Jonson and Spenser, comparing these exemplars to Virgil's Maecaenas. He concludes with an extended plea that begins, "some worke I might frame / That should nor wrong my duty nor your Name, / Were but your Lo:^PP pleas'd to cast an eye / Of fauour on my trodd downe pouertie" (65-68). Massinger presents patronage as an honorable compact. Bonded by mutual gratitude, the patron offers security and provisions while the poet returns the loyal service of eternal praise.

This apparently unsuccessful appeal demonstrates Massinger's appreciation of the tradition he learned to revere through his family's allegiance to a noble Puritan family renowned for patronage. In appealing here to William Herbert, the third Earl of Pembroke, and later to his brother, Philip, the Earl of Montgomery, he was seeking support from the sons of Mary, that Duchess of Pembroke famous for her brother Sir Philip Sidney, her poetry, and particularly her patronage of poets.[5] In the dedication of Shakespeare's first folio Heminge and Condell called her sons "the most noble and incomparable paire of brethren. . . . our singular good LORDS." Moreover, he was applying through his father's long, faithful attendance on their father as confidential agent, overseer, adviser, and MP. As he attested in dedicating *The Bondman* to Philip Herbert in 1624, Massinger thereby won some support. He declared "a desire borne with me, to make tender of all duties, and seruice, to the Noble Family of the *Herberts,* descended to me as an inheritance from my dead Father, *Arthur Massinger.* Many years hee happily spent in the seruice of your Honourable House, and dyed a seruant to it; leauing his, to be euer most glad, and ready, to be at the command of al such, as deriue themselues from his most honour'd Master, your Lordships most noble Father." Claiming Herbert's previous approval of his play, Massinger pledges continued service and requests aid. He acknowledges the receipt in his dedication of "Sero, sed Serio" on the death of Charles, the son of Philip Herbert, by then the fourth Earl of Pembroke.[6] Finally, the Beaumont and Fletcher folio, containing much of Massinger's work, was dedicated to Philip Herbert in 1647, seven years after Massinger's death.

Just three years before "Sero, sed Serio," in 1633 Massinger dedicated *A New Way To Pay Old Debts* to a new Herbert ally, Robert Dormer, the Earl of Carnarvon, who was Philip Herbert's ward and son-in-law. Offering Italian princes and English peers as exemplars, Massinger again plies his claim through his father's faithful service: "I was borne a deuoted seruant, to the thrice noble Family of your incomparable Lady, and am most ambitious, but with a becomming distance, to be knowne to your Lordship, which if you please to admit, I shall embrace it as a bounty, that while I liue shall oblige me to acknowledge you for my noble Patron, and professe my selfe to be *Your Honours true seruant*." The plays Massinger chose to dedicate to the house of Pembroke do not seem coincidental. The family was prominent among the politically Puritan elite who criticized the crown favorite, Sir George Villiers the Duke of Buckingham, monopolists such as Sir Giles Mompesson, and the pro-Spanish insular and pacifist foreign policy. They were dominant among dissatisfied country and parliamentary nobility and gentry.[7] *The Bondman* has long been thought to adhere to the Herbert line. *A New Way To Pay Old Debts* should be seen similarly.

In order to gain patronage Massinger pursued professional as well as family connections. The second set of privileged patrons he sought were related to Lady Catherine Stanhope. This cousin of Mary the Countess of Pembroke was the sister of the Earl of Huntington, the chief patron of Fletcher, Massinger's primary collaborator.[8] Interest appeared as early as 1623, when Massinger dedicated *The Duke of Milan* to her; it continued until sometime after 1628, when her husband was created Lord Chesterfield. Then Massinger could present "A Newyeares Guift . . . to my Lady and M:rs the then Lady Katherine Stanhop now Countesse of Chesterfield." It is important that Massinger concentrates on her attributes and contributions to her family's heritage. These ennoble Lady Stanhope:

> Before I ow'd to you the name
> Of Seruant, to your birth, your worth your fame
> I was soe, and t'was fitt since all stand bound
> To honour Vertue in meane persons found,
> Much more in you, that as borne great, are good
> Wch is more then to come of noble blood
> Or be A Hastings.   [1-7]

Massinger persistently tried to forge such links into patronage. To win more friends like Sir Aston Cokayne, Lady Stanhope's grandson, he dedicated *The Renegado* (1630) to George Harding, Lord Berkeley, related by marriage to Lady Stanhope, and *The Emperor of the East* (1632) to John Lord Mahoun, Lady Stanhope's son-in-law, whom Massinger identifies as Cokayne's uncle. Both dedications reiterate two themes: the dedicatee contributes to his family's worthy heritage and part of the greatness of that family's tradition derives from its membership in a select fellowship of peers who support poetry. Just as important, like the heads of the house of Pembroke, Lady Stanhope's brother, Henry Hastings, the fifth Earl of Huntingdon, was the notable head of an influential, politically Puritan, anti-Buckingham, anti-Spanish family.[9]

These dedications embed a potential conflict. Looking to the past they honor and promote an ancient tradition of patronage in large part based on family lines, degree, ascription; but looking to the present and future they value and praise new contributions that claim rewards based on merit, achievement. This problem typifies the complex of sociopolitical quandaries that leaders of the era, some anguished, others unaware, faced as they tried to mediate between reaction and revolution. Their simultaneous allegiance to proven past heritages and pressing future requirements indicates a need for the mediating agency Massinger presented throughout his works: gratitude. Ingratitude was an infamous vice utterly condemned by many Elizabethan and early Stuart moral arbiters. When writers William Bullein, William Vaughan, and others condemned ingratitude they were extending a classical and medieval tradition traced by Catherine E. Dunn.[10] A damning label from ancient political arguments in favor of the status quo, ingratitude was opposed to the cosmic love presumed to unite the universe. From classical times ingratitude had been perceived as destroying the physical world and the social community. Destructive connotations were augmented by medieval authors who, promoting vassalage, pitted ingratitude against what they deemed to be honor. Largess on the part of the liege lord required gratitude on the part of the vassal. When in that hierarchy a servant or a child responded to a master or a father with ingratitude, he dishonored his lord and threatened all the society.

This tradition, however, could foster another emphasis: gratitude obliges responsibility on the part of masters and fathers. The protection and liberality of the guardians were at least as necessary as the loyalty and service of the dependents. From this perspective ingratitude could be regarded as a vice of the superior worse than that of the subordinate. Massinger needed only to reemphasize the requirement that superiors earn their status by fulfilling the obligations of their office in order to make gratitude an instrument of accommodation, the reformation he seems to have espoused. Gratitude could provide a device amenable to mediators like himself because of their era's characteristic yearning to discover their future in their past: in gratitude they could see a traditional mode for mediation between past mores and ideals and current necessities and promises; through it they could turn to the old order so as to justify present reforms. Massinger's profound commitment to the mutual bond of gratitude is embedded in the ideal of patronage he inherited from both his family and his profession.

Besides inheriting a traditional yet potentially reforming sociopolitical principle which could encourage accommodation, Massinger and his privileged associates had traditional training in managing conflicts. Having acquired techniques of rhetorical and forensic dispute, the privileged audience could appreciate the fact that Fletcher and particularly Massinger, whose plays are characterized by formal declamations and climactic court scenes, drew heavily upon the elder Seneca's *Controversiae*. These hypothetical cases offered Seneca's debaters the opportunity to demonstrate techniques of persuasive public argument while they provided showcases for virtuoso, recreative rhetorical displays.[11] Eugene M. Waith has demonstrated the importance of the *Controversiae* for plot, character, situation, and tone in Fletcher and Massinger's tragicomedies.[12] But Waith's emphasis on fantastic contrivance, imaginative fancy, and professional skill has effectively denied the practical power and moral nurturance of the *Controversiae*. Though many of the cases in the *Controversiae* are far-fetched, still they are founded on Roman law and magnify moral issues where law breaks down. Generally, at such junctures *jus* (legality and law) or *verborum vis* conflicts with *aequitas* (due process and fairness) or *voluntas* (will and intent). The cases put stress on legal points so that intricately crafted arguments are required in order to address grave moral questions. Speakers have to analyze ethical judgments so as to segregate what merely adheres to ordinance from what truly abides by piety.

These classical controversies seem to have remained popular among the early Stuarts because such models of form also made models of ethical questioning. For they address the same kinds of questions that lawyers, attempting to resolve fundamental discrepancies among competing social and political principles, were putting to English civil law. Massinger thus had two useful traditions: a model of patronage based on gratitude that offered potential reform of the commonwealth's domestic problems and a mode of entertaining presentation that offered reconciliation of divisive sociopolitical problems. Both were familiar to his privileged associates, patrons, and audience, who were searching for means of reconciling public and personal conflicts that augured consternation if not clash.

Within the mutually supporting constraints of state and family patriarchy the Caroline stage's privileged audience anguished over preferences across a spectrum of principles and practices public and personal. Those among Massinger's privileged audience who tended toward political reform (underemployed university graduates and lawyers, MPs seeking the preferment they lacked at court, out of power and out of pocket gentry, opponents of Buckingham and the monopolists) must have appreciated the potential social, political, and economic rewards of achieving relative dominance within some consensus of those who counted. Consequently they tended to favor the values of country more than those associated with court, to place ultimate sovereignty within a balanced constitution favoring Parliament's representative national voice more than the monarch's will, to promote social mobility based in reciprocal obligations of protection and maintenance for loyal and meritorious service to the commonweal, and to encourage civic uses of national resources rather than extravagant ostentation. Those among Massinger's privileged audience who preferred social reform generally suggested that fathers should ameliorate paternalistic absolutism by caring for their families and by sharing decisions about the callings and mates of their adolescent children, that men should forsake the double sexual standard and espouse joint fidelity, and that women should be prepared more as companions than as subjects. Their proposals seem aimed at achieving grateful love and mutual responsibility between superior fathers, husbands, and men and subordinate children, wives, and women. Moreover, this privileged group could support their tendencies to favor public and private reforms by calling on values present within traditions that supported the reigning hierarchy; all their reforms required was a renewed emphasis on what most privileged Carolines already professed.[13] Massinger presented the reforming sociopolitical tendencies in his era's heritage through a tragicomic mode he reformed out of his dramatic heritage. As he entertained his privileged associates he illuminated their problems and projected a vision of reforming patronage that accommodated present needs and future promises within past ideals and proven practices.

Social and Political Accommodation

Massinger's plays characteristically promote family, social, and political accommodation based on a reforming sense of patronage: gratitude for the old customs and values of traditional hierarchy combined with appreciation for the new responsibilities and promises of mobility based on merit. Thus his plays concentrate more on cohesion than on conflict, revealing less optimism about the possibility of political resolution than about the potential for personal and social reform. Distinctly more than any other Caroline professional playwright, Massinger presented some advance in women's status in courtships, in marriages, and in social politics. Beyond that, he suggested that his paradigm for reform in the extended family might be applicable to the affairs of state.[14]

Massinger presented reforms of inheritance patterns so as to secure the rights and finances of younger sons, particularly in such collaborations with Fletcher as *The Queen of Corinth* (1616-17), *The Spanish Curate* (1622), and *The Elder Brother* (1625?). Still, he primarily favored strong-willed women who stand up for their prerogatives.[15] One indication of this preference is that submissiveness by women usually compounds disaster in his plays. Theocrine's espousal of traditional feminine subjection augments the horror of *The Unnatural Combat* (1624-25?), and Athenais's declamation in favor of feminine subordination endangers the imperial family and the realm in *The Emperor of the East* (1631). Another indication that he favored strong-willed, active women is the number of plays in which he portrayed women who hold public power: the queen in *The Queen of Corinth*, Cleopatra in the collaborative *The False One* (1620?), the duchess Aurelia in *The Maid of Honour* (1621-22?), and the regent Pulcheria in *The Emperor of the East* all wield the might of their posts. Many of his women win influence or rights. Heroines such as Dorothea in his collaboration with Dekker, *The Virgin Martyr* (1620?), or Paulina in *The Renegado* (1624) are notable for gaining worthy victories, such as converting infidels to Christianity. Other women prove arrogant egoists; witness Paulina's counterpart Donusa before her conversion, the adulterous Beaumelle in Massinger's collaboration with Field, *The Fatal Dowry* (1617-19?), and especially the self-deifying empress Domitia in *The Roman Actor* (1626). Usually, strong-willed heroines in Massinger, as in his society, start as wards to a husband or a father or a guardian who serves as a public authority. Later, in contrast to the prevailing norms of his society, his wards evolve by a most significant way into women who wield power.

In a manner characteristic of his accommodations, Massinger's presentation of a reforming attitude toward the subordination of women depends on a western European tradition—the feminine *sine qua non*, chastity and marital fidelity. The extraordinarily high value Massinger's characters place on fidelity is suggested by the disastrous outcomes when the empress Domitia and the willful Beaumelle flaunt their infidelity, or by the tragic consequence when Sforza fails to trust his wife in *The Duke of Milan* (1621-22?), or the nearly tragic one when Theodosius vacillates between trusting and distrusting his wife in *The Emperor of the East*. Massinger's mode of reform emphasizes a potential in prevailing social values that was generally overlooked: raising the status of the women, not of their men, by exalting their chastity. This is intimated in the not uncommon way in which his plays consistently attack male philandering and in the less common way in which they advocate male sexual loyalty. Placket knights such as those in *The Parliament of Love* (1624), the courtly braggadocchio Eustace in *The Elder Brother,* and Adorio and his retinue in *The Guardian* (1633) become butts of curative satire for attempting to seduce wives or maidens. In contrast, faithful chaste lovers such as Eustace's older brother Charles, Adorio's rival Caldoro, and the title hero of *The Bashful Lover* (1636) eventually marry the women who inspire their loyal, ofttimes self-sacrificing love.

Even more notably, the personal integrity and strong wills of Massinger's women characters, sometimes for ill but especially for good, evolve from guarding and exalting their chastity and fidelity. This is as true of the arrogant Donusa inveighing against the double standard of the "Turk" as it is of her saintly counterpart, Paulina. Massinger's distinctive emphasis on chastity can turn tragic. In *The Duke of Milan* the duchess Marcelia overextends her marital fidelity into overweening pride and in Massinger and Fletcher's *The Double Marriage* (1621?) Juliana's weak husband fails to remain loyal to her fidelity, and her society fails to respect it. Counter to these tragic outcomes is Massinger's more characteristic presentation of the power of personal integrity gained by two maidens, who through their supreme virginity become advocates for significant women's rights and persuade their societies to recognize women.[16] Camiola, heroine of *The Maid of Honour,* converts her fickle fiancé, her native Sicily, and her nation's allies by the force of her chastity. Though she finally turns away from them and toward exaltation in the church, she offers them social reformation and reconciliation. Cleora, in *The Bondman* (1623), lives in stunning isolation by blindfolding herself and refusing to speak until her fiancé returns from the wars; she thereby embodies the powers of chastity she teaches Sicily. The possessive reaction of her fiancé Leosthenes earns her rejection whereas the understanding loyalty of the apparent slave Marullo/Pisander gains her love. Cleora's and Pisander's mutual goal, marriage, promotes respect for the personal integrity and marital choices of women within a reformed traditional hierarchy. However extreme the virtue Massinger required of his heroines, they achieve a status higher than his society was accustomed to allowing women; and in his plays' hyperbolic aura they are not so transcendent as this summary might make them seem.

Perhaps the most important sign of Massinger's reforming presentation of the traditional subordination of women lies not in their mutually faithful loves nor in their overpowering personalities, but in their effective speeches. His women do not exhibit the submissive feminine silence expected of them. Except for the chastening of Lady Frugal's vain chatter in *The City Madam* (1632) there is no hint that feminine silence is a virtue. In plays in which rhetorical setpieces comprise focal points, his women often make the greatest speeches. Besides defying the submissive silence usually assigned by his society, his women often address audiences in the two public arenas to which they were specifically denied access: councils of national policy and judicial hearings. Massinger thus extends humanist arguments for an education qualifying women to rear Christian children and help govern Christian households. He has women practice the rhetorical skills of demanding professions by debating public policies and arguing legal cases.

Massinger's women prove eloquent participants because many have been trained in making public decisions. In *The Great Duke of Florence* (1627) Carolo Charomonte has provided his daughter Lydia with the same princely education (save military discipline) he provided the heir apparent, Giovanni. She is thus prepared for her role as advocate in the play's climactic trial scene. There, with the duchess Fiorinda, she argues persuasively for amnesty for the duke's heir and the duke's favorite. In *The Emperor of the East* the regent Pulcheria proves a model for her sisters as well as for her brother by decreeing exemplary policies, administering an effective bureaucracy, and making wise judgments. Even more convincing are the eloquent speeches made by Camiola of *The Maid of Honour* and Cleora of *The Bondman*. Each exceeds her assigned station by persuading her society about significant sociopolitical reforms. All along Camiola demands that her guardian, the island's king, respect the rights of his subjects in his selection of magistrates and policies. In the concluding trial scene she proves an effective lawyer; she wins her cause and converts the play's rulers to making more responsible decisions. Cleora, serving as the voice of virtuous citizens, moves the populace to defend their island. But her public contribution threatens her traditionally possessive lover. Her reactions to the two responses earn her a greater sense of personal integrity and assertiveness; and she finally chooses a different husband. Her choice suggests the same possibilities for other women. In the integrity they derive from chastity, in their persuasive assertion of personal rights, and in their eloquent speech which affects public policies, Massinger's heroines indicate a more sanguine view of potential reform than appears in the plays of the other Caroline professionals. For his heroines do not seek to rebel against, but achieve the reformation of, the traditional hierarchy. This reformation emphasizes mutually grateful interactions up and down the scale, and it accommodates new demands and promises while it respects old successes and ideals.

Massinger's political inclinations parallel his preferences for mutually responsive personal, family, and social reform within accommodating patronage. At the same time his political observations offer a decidedly more pessimistic prospect; the few censored lines that remain of his last known political play, *The King and the Subject* (1638), question abuses of royal absolutism. Perhaps representing privileged associates, Massinger presented sociopolitical virtues that are linked to the traditional loyal,

hospitable, frugal country in contrast to vices attached to a selfish, wasteful court. The pattern appears from the early Fletcher collaboration,
Beggars Bush (1615-22), which extols an outlaw band restoring a reformed
commonwealth; and it extends to *The Guardian* (1632), in which a Robin
Hood rounds up the principals who restore order in Naples. Perhaps the
starkest contrasts between mutually supporting, simple country virtues
and contentious, extravagant court vices appear in *The Great Duke of
Florence* and *The City Madam*. The virtuous education at Carolo's country
estate stands against the affectations and scramble at court; and Sir John
Frugal and his steward Holdfast's former comfortable, generous household stands against their current modish, ostentatiously consuming one.
Such suggestive contrasts translate into a more urgent call for mutual
consideration between a ruler and his citizens than between a father and
his family or a husband and wife. They imply a higher valuation of equity
than of justice and a need to foster the public exchange of protection and
reward for service and loyalty instead of the willful exercise of prerogatives. Massinger's general sociopolitical principle is the necessity of
mutual gratitude within the body politic. This is demonstrated inversely
by the ingratitude that drives both Septimius, the traitorous assassin of
his commander Pompey, and the real title character of Massinger and
Fletcher's *The False One*, a selfish society that conforms to Caesar's and
Cleopatra's treacherous lust after sex, wealth, and power.

   Under compulsion, Massinger placed ultimate sovereignty in the law
and the relative dominance of Parliament. His dread of absolutism is
obvious in the disasters resulting from the deification of the emperor
Domitian in *The Roman Actor* or from the tyrannies of earls such as
Woolfort in *Beggars Bush* and Ferrand in *The Double Marriage*. More plausi-
ble problems with absolutism appear in Theodosius's oscillations in *The
Emperor of the East*, which may suggest Charles I's practical vacillations
from theoretical absolutism.[17] The emperor denies that he has absolute
prerogatives because these could lead to wrongful impositions and extor-
tions; but before he is disciplined he exerts virtually total control, granting
prodigal rewards and excessive powers to favorites and making extreme
edicts that threaten subjects and jeopardize the empire.

   Whether a consequence of his aiming for consensus or feeling ambivalent, the political implications of Massinger's presentations seem
ambiguous in application. Perhaps in this way he most reflected his
privileged audience. One kind of ambivalence appears in the politically
irresolute conclusions of tragicomedies, where royal absolutism is espoused but seems mitigated by leniency. In *The Maid of Honour* Roberto at
first rules as if he possesses absolute powers, and the duchess Aurelia
declares her absolutism. But Camiola, seeming to acknowledge that her
ruler's sovereignty is absolute, still refuses to obey her king's will when it

conflicts with her rights and conscience; she convinces Roberto that any true ruler should subordinate his prerogatives to just laws. *The Great Duke of Florence* presents a more perplexing political irresolution. Cozimo announces the necessity of his absolute prerogatives throughout the play and he frequently exercises them; at the same time he carefully listens to, even if he denies, his subjects' advice. The play's mediated conclusion in a court arraignment is complexly irresolute. Cozimo, serving as the supreme judge as well as the prosecutor, continues to declare his absolutism, his merciful grant of a reprieve, and his decision's lack of precedence. At the same time, his decision issues from bargaining rather than fiat, it bows to court opinion, it is constrained by earlier decrees and laws, and it perforce sets a precedent. Massinger's accommodating principle of mutual gratitude in a political hierarchy is more satisfactorily enunciated than analyzed or applied. But perhaps ambiguous irresolution represented the only outcome that could win general assent, as the elite in England seemed to agree only that sovereignty resided in the king-in-Parliament sitting as a legislative and judicial body.

Besides presenting the ambiguous resolution of a temperately administered absolute monarchy, Massinger later presented an ambivalent response to a different question: Could a legitimate, righteous monarch rule without machiavellian skill or contrary to some manifest destiny? *Believe As You List* poses the inquiry tragically—and bitterly. Although the morally vindicated true king, Antiochus, is sacrificially martyred and his manipulative, treacherous persecutor, Flaminius, is punished, political justice fails. Arrogant, machiavellian Roman imperialism is victorious. While Rome punishes its agent for unethical conduct, it never surrenders its proceeds and never disavows the methods he employs or the principles he invokes. Consequently, even if a few nations could achieve a reformed, grateful hierarchy, international reform seems remote.

Massinger was less ambivalent and more optimistic about the possibilities of reform within one state. Perhaps only he among the Caroline professional playwrights showed any faith that the traditional hierarchy could accommodate sociopolitical mobility based on achievement. While his plays reflect a hierarchy essentially based on ascription, they also reflect considerable mobility based on the redistribution of wealth and clout as apparently determined by merit. *The City Madam* rewards achievers by elevating them into the ruling ranks. Luke's avaricious climbing and Lady Frugal's ostentatious consumption and climbing are condemned. But Sir John Frugal and Master Jeffrey Plenty are acknowledged for their socioeconomic contributions to the common welfare; they are accepted by Lord Lacy and his heir. Although some critics have read reaction in *A New Way To Pay Old Debts* (1625), actually this play confirms social mobility by laying down principles for advancement.[18] It defines the criterion for sociopolitical elevation as service to the body politic; moreover, the contribution might very well be commercial, as in *The City Madam*. The condemnation of Overreach applies to his egoistic, destructive assault on all society, not just on its upper echelons. Furthermore, the others in the play recognize the necessity for mutual obligations of gratitude and service in interactions extending from marriage to national defense. It is not insignificant that in the only two extant plays he set in contemporary England Massinger presented the accommodation of social mobility based on contributions to the commonweal.

Two of Massinger's political plays are based on sociopolitical mobility: his and Fletcher's fanciful depiction of the Lowlands, *Beggars Bush*, and his quasi-ancient history of Syracuse, *The Bondman*. In *Beggars Bush* mobility is fostered by three groups—refugee courtiers in disguise, virtuous beggars, and Bruges burghers—who unite to overthrow a usurping tyrant and to create a reformed state. The outcome integrates loyalist begging brethren and, especially, city merchant venturers into a restored prince's ruling hierarchy. Until the play's concluding revelation all but the true heir's disguised father know him only as the most successful contributor to a community of entrepreneurs. So he follows his father's precedent of being elevated primarily for bettering the general social, economic, and political welfare. Sometimes narrowly construed as political propaganda for Pembroke, *The Bondman* has also been anachronistically hailed for whiggish speeches.[19] Though its ending seems uneasy over machiavellian means and its favorable presentation of meritorious advancement is hedged by a traditional revelation of blood degree, its hierarchy does accommodate elevation in rank for contributors to national well-being. The disguised Marullo/Pisander, however reckless or sinister in fomenting a slave rebellion, induces the repentant reformation of a vicious ruling class. Many reunite in an understanding, grateful, and dutiful hierarchy by renewing an old principle and raising an old practice into a new tenet: nobility and gentry by ascription must dedicate, even sacrifice themselves for the public good to maintain their status; and achievement, contribution to the public good, constitutes the main criterion for advancement into a hierarchy sustained by elevation of the worthy. Such is the accommodation of new promise within old forms that Massinger consistently presented.

A corollary to Massinger's favorable treatment of sociopolitical mobility is his frequent presentation of appropriate rewards for other public contributions besides military victory and his even more frequent opposition to arbitrary grants to favorites. Despite the occasional presence of favorites who have been promoted for merit, notably the exemplary Euphanes in *The Queen of Corinth* and the acclaimed Sanazarro of *The Great*

Duke of Florence, Massinger usually presented worthless courtiers scrambling for patronage. An arrogant, corrupt political pimp such as Fulgentio in *The Maid of Honour* or a vicious machiavel such as Francisco in *The Duke of Milan* come closer to his norm for royal favorites. This too has been generally attached to Massinger's and his patrons' displeasure over the corrupt Robert Carr, George Villiers, and other favorites whom James and then Charles promoted for personal gratification.[20] Characteristically, however, Massinger did not suggest destruction of the institution. Instead, he suggested the reform of traditional mores by a reemphasis on the legitimate rewards of patronage for genuine public service. In individual, social, and political matters, Massinger, and perhaps his privileged audience, thus invoked an accommodation of current needs and future promises within past successes and old ideals. Distinctively among the Caroline professional playwrights, his works maintain chastened optimism at the prospect of accommodation. His tragicomic artistic technique is founded on similar principles.

The Art of Redemptive Conversion

Massinger's dramatic craft conforms to his moral, social, and political inclinations: it pointedly both follows tradition and accommodates reform. Through his long apprenticeship in collaboration from at least his 1613 "Tripartite Letter" with Nathan Field and Robert Daborne, Massinger came to be the playwright who best exemplifies the self-conscious imitation and extension of Elizabethan and Jacobean techniques.[21] His privileged associate Aston Cokayne promoted recognition of him as the unsung partner in the Beaumont and Fletcher canon; and the prologues and epilogues to many of his collaborations honor his predecessors and modestly indicate his variations and extensions of them.[22] As he put it in the prologue to *A Very Woman*, he *"raise[d] new Piles upon an old Foundation."* That foundation consisted of what he learned mainly from his master, Fletcher, from his rare model, Jonson, and from the first dramatist for the King's Men, Shakespeare.

Massinger raised his art primarily upon Fletcher's techniques of tragicomedy. Thomas Jay's commendation before *A New Way To Pay Old Debts* suggests the specific bases for Massinger's achievement:

> You may remember how you chid me when
> I ranckt you equall with those glorious men;
> Beaumont, and Fletcher: if you loue not praise
> You must forbeare the publishing of playes.
> The craftie Mazes of the cunning plot;
> The polish'd phrase; the sweet expressions; got

Neither by theft, nor violence; the concept
Fresh, and vnsullied.   [1-8]

The premier Fletcherian technique identified by Jay and corroborated by many a critic is Massinger's highly intricate, continually surprising and reversing, symmetrically balanced and contrasted plotting. Second is his apt, decorous rhetorical polish; though his phrases echo and vary images, figures, and expressions from earlier works, these appear recreated with new or transformed power. Third, by extension, is his careful management of traditions of plot, scene, and character (as well as language) so that his plays evolve from past conventions. And fourth is his refocus on contemporaneous issues.

The compelling technique of Massinger's moral tragicomedy is the ingenious plotting he took beyond that of Fletcher. "Intricacy of plot" is not just another trait; it provides the impetus for the rest of Eugene M. Waith's justly familiar eight characteristics of *The Pattern of Tragicomedy in Beaumont and Fletcher.* [23] This impetus is compounded by Waith's "atmosphere of evil," more precisely, an anxiety over the testing of Massinger's characters that marks the development of a testing pattern prevalent throughout Tudor-Stuart drama. [24] The motivating constituent of moral tragicomedy's elaborate plotting and testing is the miraculous conversion of characters, which has been emphasized by Madeleine Doran. [25] If tragicomedy often relies on an initial "improbable hypothesis," its defining tenet is faith in the final charitable miracles of mutual self-discovery and contrition, forgiveness and reconciliation, reformation and reintegration of characters and societies. Thus tragicomedy's essential form of miraculous conversion, as well as its fundamental theme of community reintegration based on people's grateful charity, relies on Christian tenets. Massinger's plays exhibit this congruence of theme and form from his very early collaboration *The Queen of Corinth* to his last extant play *The Bashful Lover.*

Tragicomedy's somewhat disconcerting synthesis of the "imitation of the manners of the familiar world" with an aesthetic "remoteness from the familiar world" seems to derive from an elaborate stylization of stock dramatic traditions and commonplace social heritages during the Renaissance. These provide set situations, stereotyped characters, opposed character groupings, and a host of devices derived from metadrama (plays within a play). Other familiar types besides willful women troop by. They include the line of gruff, honestly blunt advisers from Romont in the early, collaborative *The Fatal Dowry* to the late title character Durazzo of *The Guardian,* and the set of machiavels from the tyrannical older brother Crates in *The Queen of Corinth* to Titus Flaminius of *Believe As You List* or the eunuch Chrysapius of *The Emperor of the East.* As these illustrations suggest, tragicomedy often counterpoints groups of stereotypes. Massinger habitually pits neglected virtuous contributors to society, most often heroic martialists, against ostentatiously wasteful preferment seekers and court favorites, often cowardly placket and trencher knights. From the folly of Onos's crew versus the public service of Euphanes and Conon in *The Queen of Corinth* to the decadent house of Cleon versus the capable slaves in *The Bondman* to the projectors versus the Countryman in *The Emperor of the East*, juxtaposed groupings seem to be formalized representations of moral and sociopolitical commonplaces.

Waith's "lively touches of passion" and "language of emotion" point to a stylized rhetorical poetry that is based on refinements of a treasury of domesticated topoi, imagery, and allusions. These characteristics fuse with the decorum of tragicomic plotting and convention. Massinger's declamatory style links long periods, encompassing extraordinary suspensions and parentheses, into flexible verse paragraphs. Through logical structure and hypotaxis, these periodic sentences hold in suspension the moral imperatives, legal requirements, practical conditions, and detailed evidence necessary for careful consideration of social and political equity. Moreover, Massinger's periods reintegrate accepted truths and long-tested images, illustrious witnesses from the past, traditional and reformulated comparisons, saws and precepts. All copiously amplify details necessary for an analysis of the conflict of old positions and new conditions that demand reform.[26] So Massinger's collaborations can be identified by his extraordinary repetition of formulae, particularly of incomparability topoi compressing allusions to his own work, to other dramatic predecessors, and to classical culture. But that fact does not indicate shallowness, insensitivity, or laziness. It testifies to artistic care with momentous issues.[27]

Massinger's frequent descriptions of art, from masques to emblematic jewelry, extend rhetorical poetry's moral and sociopolitical suasion. The Masque of Nilus that evokes Caesar's greed in *The False One* or the concluding masque that tests Luke for repentance in *The City Madam* are not as typical as the marriage masque that extols mutual marital fidelity in *The Guardian* or the dream masque that cures Don Martino Cardenes of combativeness in *A Very Woman*. Other important emblems in his plays include the wondrous apple that causes Theodosius's jealousy in *The Emperor of the East*, the curious "*Egyptian* Herogliphick" engraved on the transforming jewel in *The Guardian*, and *Beggars Bush* itself, a surprising symbol of an ordered commonweal. Massinger habitually synthesizes Caroline aesthetics and sociopolitics in such emblems.

Jay intimated that Massinger raised his art on Jonson's models as well as on Fletcher's tragicomedy. In a judgmental commendation introducing *The Picture*, Jay observes,

> I know you would take it for an iniury,
> (And 'tis a well becomming modesty)
> To be paraleld with *Beaumont*, or to heare
> Your name by some to partiall friend writt neere
> Vnequal'd *Ionson:* being men whose fire
> At distance, and with reuerence you admire.   [35-40]

Massinger seems to have learned from Jonson mainly how to employ a repertoire of techniques, including moral interludes, satires, and metadramatic extensions of masques and plays within plays into role playing and scene setting, so as to emphasize moral and sociopolitical issues.

More important than alluding to speeches from Jonson's plays, particularly in *The City Madam* and *The Roman Actor,* Massinger especially borrowed Jonson's refinements on estates morality plays for his satires, *The City Madam* and *A New Way To Pay Old Debts.*[28] He portrays social types based on Jonson's, the usurer and the climber in Luke and Sir Giles Overreach. And he employs societal estates to embody the clash of social relations; mutually grateful patronage is opposed to the arrogant greed that abuses tradition and promotes the new cash nexus.[29] Throughout his career Massinger portrayed antithetical social estates, characters, and attitudes so that these accentuate moral and social accommodation. This aspect of Jonson's influence most indicates the social bases of Massinger's work.

In another imitation of Jonson, Massinger uses a low, vicious satirical style. Both to lampoon and to undercut, he often employs a style that is swiftly dismissed as "prurience" or exploitative bawdry. More accurately, a low curt style of straightforward syntax and bawdy concrete diction creates vituperative, slangy flytings and self-revealing vices. Massinger's gruff counselors, such as Miramont in *The Elder Brother* or Durazzo in *The Guardian,* employ this style to attack others. His confidence men, parading as members of professions, flaunt it along with inflated jargon. Others, such as the members of Cleon's family in *The Bondman* or the "Empirick" in *The Emperor of the East*, satirize themselves by using it. Massinger's low, vicious style deserves to be seen as the counter that balances his style of rhetorical exaltation. The two reinforce each other and help establish the principle of mediation that prevails throughout Massinger's plays.

The last of Massinger's major emulations of Jonson is his exploitation and variation of the Renaissance metadramatic heritage: enclosed masques, dumb shows, plays within plays, manipulative role playing and scene setting, and the like. His curative masques, such as those near the end of *The City Madam* and *A Very Woman* have already been mentioned.[30] His most acclaimed metadrama appears in the succession whereby *The*

Roman Actor's Paris, Domitia, and Domitian presume to direct the inset plays and then the world of the play until Destiny exacts the penalty for their presumption. Such techniques mold the social politics throughout Massinger's plays. Sides vie for control by staging scenes and manipulating both their own roles and the roles of others, as do Flaminius and Antiochus competing for political and moral approval in the tragic *Believe As You List*. Characters produce and direct scenes to test each other and to teach repentance and charity as they move toward the reconciliations of tragicomedy, as first Durazzo and then the Neapolitan king Alphonso do in *The Guardian*. Alternatively, characters stage and manipulate settings, situations, and fake roles, and they employ masques in order to test and expel those who prove ungrateful and antisocial in satires; just so, Sir John Frugal tries, judges, and banishes Luke in *The City Madam*, and the whole society entraps Sir Giles Overreach in *A New Way to Pay Old Debts*. Most important, in his sophistication of all three of these techniques borrowed from Jonson—the refinements of the estates moralities plays, the satiric low style, and the devices of metadrama—Massinger followed his exemplar by creating plays intensely focused on social politics. In particular, when he employed the popular metadramatic and role playing tropes as devices to focus moral and social issues, Massinger was indicating the potency these tropes hold for the social sciences.

The final foundation on which Massinger raised his drama shows in his frequent borrowings from and allusions to Shakespeare. He affirms the continuity of the line of chief dramatists for the King's Men by tagging his predecessor's phrases and speeches, alluding to his situations and characters, and echoing his scenes. In doing so he imitates Shakespeare's exploitation of commonplaces.[31] But the effects are distinctly his own; they call attention to social more than psychological motifs. In the setting of *The Sea Voyage*, for example, he and Fletcher rely on *The Tempest* for reverberations, and in the opening situation of the collaborative *The Double Marriage* they depend on *Julius Caesar* for a foreboding mood. For his situation and his hinge in *The Duke of Milan* and *The Emperor of the East* Massinger is indebted to *Othello*. But in each case, besides working Shakespearean borrowings into his own intricately allusive tragedy and tragicomedy, Massinger enlarged Shakespeare's primary psychological focus to sociopolitical consequences: the need for reformation in an accommodating, reintegrated social order.

Like his privileged associates, Massinger sought mediation between a fundamental reaction and a revolutionary potential currently undergoing definition in his society. He explored some of the possibilities through a dramatic tradition he learned from a master craftsman and collaborator, Fletcher, a technical and moral exemplar, Jonson, and an incomparable predecessor, Shakespeare. The finest product of his craft is the moral tragicomedy, the form that most of his plays take, even when they function satirically and sometimes when they end tragically. The tragicomedy that Massinger developed out of elements in his rich heritage melds with his proposal for a charitable reformation of sociopolitical tradition to accommodate significant change. Both conclude in a miraculous reunion after extraordinary oppositions have clashed, twisted, and opened up ever more problems so that the situation seems irresolvable short of destruction.

Massinger constructed elaborately reversing plots and surprising recognitions that test absolute ideals and inflexibly willed people, thereby revealing the inevitable failings of frail humans and encouraging the kind of understanding that brings about conversion, repentance, forgiveness, and reconciliation. This movement can reform and reintegrate hierarchical society on the principle of mutual gratitude. Massinger made implicit social observations and judgments by juxtaposing groups of stereotyped characters and estates and presenting the working relations between them. He commented metadramatically through multiple plottings, masques, plays within plays, and character stagings. And he integrated elaborations on past allusive situations from classical culture and Renaissance drama so that they promote social understanding. He incorporated an extraordinarily dense texture of literary echoes in his janus-faced style of praise and blame. His extended judicial and rhetorical periods reintegrate frequently conflicting and qualifying traditional images, phrases, aphorisms, arguments, and tales into a reformed, mediating, and forgiving inclusiveness based on charity. And his curt, bawdy satire cures or cuts off whoever cannot reform and join a society that combines prospective needs with tested practices.

In sum, Massinger's highly wrought moral tragicomedy offers a comprehensive view and an integrated body politic based on a charitable mutual gratitude that, if improbable, may have seemed the primary hope for attaining the community he and his privileged audience sought. Moreover, his integration of artistic and sociopolitical vision calls for a synthesis of sociological and aesthetic interpretation. *The Picture* comprises an example at once representative and masterly.

Reflection and Reciprocity in THE PICTURE

In a reversal, recognition, and conversion that are characteristic of Massinger, a model knight named Mathias delivers a declamation that sums up the artistic and moral principles of *The Picture* (1629). Mathias has just salvaged his virtue by reneging on his earlier agreement to commit adultery with Queen Honoria. His momentary lapse was impelled by the change in a magical portrait of his exemplary wife Sophia. Because Sophia was tempted by two seducers sent by Honoria the reds and whites in Mathias's portrait of her had turned yellow, signifying her trial; then the lines had blackened, reflecting her willingness. So Mathias, believing that his wife was surrendering, agreed to an assignation. But when the portrait showed its original colors because Sophia reconfirmed her fidelity, Mathias recognized her essential integrity and so reaffirmed his. Consequently, at the designed assignation he seeks to convert Honoria to pride in virtue rather than vanity in adultery. His peroration:

> To slip once
> Is incident, and excusde by humane fraylty,
> But to fall euer damnable. We were both
> Guilty I grant in tendering our affection,
> But, as I hope you will doe, I repented.
> When we are growne vp to ripenesse, our life is
> Like to this picture. While we runne
> A constant race in goodnesse, it retaines
> The just proportion. But the iourneye being
> Tedious, and sweet temptations in the way,
> That may in some degree diuert vs from
> The rode that we put forth in, ere we end
> Our pilgrimage, it may like this turne yellow
> Or be with blacknesse clouded. But when we
> Finde we haue gone astray, and labour to
> Returne vnto our neuer fayling guide
> Vertue, contrition with vnfained teares,
> The spots of vice wash'd off, will soone restore it
> To the first purenesse.   [IV.iv.64-82]

Mathias reaffirms the primary artistic and moral tenet of tragicomedy: characters who recognize their inevitable human failures, repent, and thereby receive forgiveness from their loved ones and reintegration into their society demonstrate the miraculous power of conversion and reformation. Moved by Mathias's homily, Honoria kneels, confesses that she is repelled by her sins, and begs heaven's mercies. Then she promises that henceforth her beauty as a woman, a wife, and a queen will lie in her integrity and loyalty rather than in her physical endowments. Mathias's and Honoria's commitment suggests a general principle, since the speech employs a set of traditional metaphors for living: running a race, traveling a road, going on a journey, a pilgrimage, a voyage.[32]

Honoria is not the only one thunderstruck into self-recognition and recovery by Mathias's lightning reversal. So are her husband, Ladislaus, and his court, eavesdroppers who make up an audience. For Honoria did not intend to commit adultery, but rather to show off the might of her seductive beauty to the court by staging the spectacle of a pure husband's fall. Thus appears a second artistic and moral tenet of Massinger's tragicomedy: people, like Mathias and Honoria, set scenes and play roles to convince or convert audiences, who participate in the scenes they watch. When he hears Mathias's speech and sees Honoria's conversion from an upstart usurpation to a reformed marital order, Ladislaus reforms his uxoriousness. Their conversions signal a sycophantic court's return to hierarchy. Personal and family reform thereby extends through society to the state. This sociopolitical point is acclaimed when the society invites Sophia and Mathias to immigrate so as to become model Hungarian citizens as well as model mates.

An even more fundamental tenet of Massinger's Christian humanism, the union of art and morality, impels the whole performance: an orator can transform a hearer. Honoria, as she is being convinced of the self-destructiveness of her lusts and vanities, exclaims, "How [Mathias's] reasons / Worke on my Soule." And Ladislaus, who is moved from observation to participation in the lesson, declares, "I am rauished with / What I haue seene and hard." Both, responding to visual as well as verbal appeals, indicate the extension of rhetoric: art can convert an audience. Through Mathias's commonplace assertion that "our life is / Like to this picture" Massinger hints that both the magical picture of Sophia and the illusionist tragicomedy are emblems of the universe. The colors—of palette, of rhetoric, or of drama—are effected by and affect human intentions and mores. Thus Massinger's faith in *The Picture*.

The magical picture of Sophia is a moral emblem; it embodies the moral of *The Picture*. That moral is not the simplistic concluding aphorism that married men should beware "neither to dote to much nor doubt a wife." Nor is it to be found in Sophia's seeming resolve to maintain her ideal self, to be true to some eternal virtue or universal absolute (IV.ii).[33] Instead, the moral in Massinger's emblem emphasizes personal, social, and political needs for mirroring and giving, for mutual concern and accommodation. In terms familiar from the social sciences, as an emblem the picture suggests a human need for reflexivity and reciprocity or, as Anthony Giddens puts it, "the monitored character of the ongoing flow of social life."[34] It suggests how we see ourselves in others and their reactions to us, respond to each other in our actions and continuing self-creation, and continue mutually to create our society and the situations and roles it defines. To do so the magical picture refers to an analog for sociopolitical contracts common to both classical and Christian traditions—marriage as spousal fidelity.

The Picture seems to stage a casebook example of a symbolic interactionist version of three fundamental social principles: human identities and societies are mutually constituted and maintained; personal identities emerge from the roles we assume under given situations; we internalize such roles and situations as realities, that is, we interpret them and act on them. The play enacts these principles by dramatizing George Herbert Mead's famous abstraction: people produce "imaginative rehearsals" of daily actions, individuals think out various responses to an internalized sense of "generalized others," on whose opinions and acts, *as we construe them and our situations,* our opinions and acts depend.[35] It presents a less horrific because somewhat less deterministic scene than Philip G. Zimbardo's Stanford experiments on the way the staged situation enforced the roles of guard and prisoner or than his theories about *Influencing Attitudes and Changing Behavior.*[36] *The Picture* illustrates the potency of our manipulations of mental constructions of the world to consider and react to changing situations and stimuli, and thereby to produce the "Self-generated Attitude Change[s]" empirically tested by Abraham Tesser.[37] It presents the kind of situational definition pioneered by Mead, exemplified by Erving Goffman, and analyzed by Robert A. Stebbins.[38] For its characters, like the sociologists' subjects, soliloquize over who they are and how they should act in their settings. They explicitly consider how they perceive their commonly defined settings (their social situations), how they perceive each others' perceptions of them (their mutual reflection), and how they act in response to these perceptions of each other (their reciprocation). Obviously Massinger did not propose a set of "general statements about *classes* of definitions used by identifiable *groups* of men in particular but recurrent situations . . . [where] The groups of men to be studied are those in different *social identities,* the conventionally recognized categories in community iife into which human actors place themselves and others." Still, his characters think and feel and act through situations focused on precisely the same simultaneous self- and community-creation that social scientists investigate to test such general propositions.

The Picture portrays how Sophia reacts to her suspicions about her husband's cracked faithfulness, just as his lapse and recovery follow from his beliefs about her lapse and recovery of faithfulness. This exemplary lady and knight learn that human beings do not live by absolute tenets; they depend in their daily lives both on reinforcing each other and on having internalized such reinforcements. The lesson they learn and the way they learn it seem to exemplify the theories of symbolic interactionists: people live by the values they see in those they love; by perceiving reflections of themselves in their loved ones and by reflecting on their loved ones they evaluate themselves. The jealousy of each shows the need to see values reflected in the spouse as part of the self in order to reinforce personal integrity and behavior.

It is important that during this era the double standard was particularly questioned through calls for male chastity and loyalty, especially among the privileged Puritan circles whom Massinger served.[39] And it is just as important that this reform in some attitudes toward women was fostered inside the traditional patriarchy by incorporating within its structure more respect and love as conjugal duties the superior husband owes his subordinate wife. Among these mediators between reaction and revolution, a wife's status and rights, albeit still lesser, increased. *The Picture* represents Massinger's moderate reformation whereby the social hierarchy remains a patriarchy but one modified through gratitude so as to promote loving protection and maintenance as well as loving fidelity and service in marriage. Moreover, this marital principle can be applied to the extended family, as when Sophia compels Hilario to face his fantasies before she forgives and accepts him again. And it can be expanded into society and the state, as when Honoria and Ladislaus have to recognize their appropriate stations in the ruling hierarchy and when Ubaldo and Ricardo are forced to recognize their responsibilities before they are forgiven and reassimilated into the court. *The Picture* compels an awareness of the necessity for mutual understanding and charitable accommodation in creating and sustaining both the self and the community. Thus the play exemplifies Massinger's central principle that morality cannot be absolute, that since it must reflect human relationships that necessarily falter and occasionally fail, it needs to offer reciprocal loving contrition and forgiveness. This principle underlies all the plots, the relationships among characters, and the metadramatic and stylistic devices of *The Picture*.

During the course of the play Mathias learns about the reciprocity that Sophia realizes at the opening. Conversely, in his first speech Mathias indicates that he understands the reflexivity which Sophia learns about as the play goes by. Aware that their "mutuall consent of hearts as hands / Ioynde by true loue hath made vs one, and equall" (I.i.16-17), he recognizes that by marrying him his wife relinquished the superior station she was born to. So he knows that she sees herself in relation to him. His request that Baptista provide a monitor of her faithfulness, the magical picture which is the instrument of reflexivity, corroborates that he sees himself in relation to her. Also in his opening farewell Mathias reveals his shortsightedness. He has rewarded Sophia's obedience by having "beene euer an indulgent husband." His sense of granting her special favors indicates his lack of reciprocal trust, a failure likewise corroborated in his request for the magical picture.

Mathias's realization and failure appear as pride and seeming trust during his next scene. At his triumphal introduction to the Hungarian court the hero produces the picture, "my assurance she holdes out / And is impregnable" (II.ii.327-28). In order to remain loyal despite temptation,

Mathias needs to witness his wife's fidelity and to recognize that the integrity of each spouse depends on belief in the other:

>   if the King had tenderd
> Such fauours to my wife 'tis to be doubted
> They had not bene refus'd, but being a man
> I should not yeeld first, or proue an example
> For her defence of fraylty. By this sans question
> She's tempted too, and heere I may examine   *Lookes on the picture.*
> How shee holds out. She's still the same, the same
> Pure Christal rocke of chastity! perish all
> Allurements that may alter me, the snow
> Of her sweete coldnes, hath extinguished quite
> The fire that but euen now began to flame!
> And I by her confirm'd, rewards, nor titles,
> Nor certaine death from the refused Queene
> Shall shake my faith, since I resolue to be
> Loyall to her, as she is true to me.   [III.v.182-96]

Sophia's ability to resist temptation depends only slightly less on her belief in Mathias's fidelity. When, because of jealousy, she doubts her husband's faithfulness, she feels compelled to reconsider her own. "Strangely distracted with [her tempters'] various stories" suggesting that Mathias earned the riches she has just received by serving as a gigolo, she is goaded by "a curious iealousie" to arrange a private interview with each (III.vi.9, 20). Convinced by the stories, she feels dishonored. She momentarily agrees that chastity is nothing more than reputation because she believes Mathias has fallen. That is, she demonstrates what she has yet to learn, that her behavior reflects her husband's, as his does hers. Moreover, she plans a reciprocal vengeance, consent to adultery: Her tempters "shall be entertain'd, and if I stray / Let him condemne himselfe, that lead the way" (III.vi.160-61).

Sophia's intent immediately affects Mathias, who in turn reflects her and then reciprocates. As the next scene opens, he is replying to Baptista's request to save them by committing adultery with Honoria. Mathias affirms the righteousness of absolutes: his loyalty will be judged by God. Nevertheless, he considers his reflection in public opinion as more important. Since "To dye vntaynted in / Our fame, and reputation is the greatest" virtue, he questions that any honorable person would choose to survive after losing them. Then he is shocked to discover Sophia's reversal:

> Since my *Sophia* will go to her graue
> Vnspotted in her faith, I'll follow her

> With equall loyalty; but looke on this
> Your owne great worke, your masterpeese, and then
> She being still the same, teach me to alter.   *The picture altred.*
>
> [IV.i.23-27]

At once he forgoes moral absolutes and the ideal of the will's integrity. Both his words and his resolution demonstrate that morality and integrity depend on how they reflect and are reflected by others. His vituperation comes explicitly from the searing shame his era foisted on cuckolds, from his reaction to how he feels his wife's actions reflect on him:

> and this the figure of
> My Idoll few howers since, while she continued
> In her perfection, that was late a mirror
> In which I saw miracles, shapes of duty,
> Stayd manners, with all excellency a husband
> Could wish in a chast wife, is on the suddaine
> Turnd to a magicall glasse, and does present
> Nothing but hornes, and horror.   [IV.i.58-65]

Mathias's consternation is not to be allayed by ideals of personal integrity. When Baptista consoles, "You may yet / And 'tis the best foundation, build vp comfort / On your owne goodnes" (IV.i.65-67), Mathias thunders no, with a vengeance on Sophia. Because of her he now regards to be virtue what before he had scorned as vice. So now he begs from Honoria what the night before he had disdained. His reciprocal vengeance reflects Sophia's will; even more it is stimulated by his sense of how her actions reflect on him.

Mathias's utter dependence on reflexivity provides the scene's final impact. When Honoria shifts from a suppliant wooer to a disdainful lady, he is brought short. He does not know how to reciprocate because he is lost in conflicting reflections. Either choice he makes will damage his self-esteem:

> I am both waies lost; stormes of Contempt, and scorne
> Are ready to breake on me, and all hope
> Of shelter doubtfull. I can neither be
> Disloyall, nor yet honest, I stand guilty
> On either part.   [IV.i.163-67]

Mathias is overwrought precisely because of a dilemma predicated on reflexivity. He cannot know by whom to see and evaluate himself. Therefore he cannot know how to act, how to reciprocate.

In the immediately juxtaposed soliloquy Sophia, reconsidering her anticipated adultery, wants to imitate an ideal (IV.ii.1-24). But since she cannot claim perfect integrity, she has to rationalize circuitously. By evading acknowledgment of her imperfection she affirms her commitment to an absolute standard. At the same time, by tacitly confessing her contrition and faith in forgiveness she also confesses that she needs to be considered relatively. She opens by declaring a moral absolute she has apparently just read; she categorically denies that hordes of sinners can mitigate sin. But as she applies that moral she modifies it. First, she establishes that even though sinners may take comfort in communal wretchedness, each still suffers retribution. Next she considers her own case: "Howere my Lord offend, it is no warrant / For me to walke in his forbidden paths" (10-11). Denying reciprocity, she asks a leading question: "What penance then can expiate my guilte / For my consent (transported then with passion)?" She needs to allow for her actions within an ideal standard that judges all responses to be virtuous or vicious on the basis of the subject's will. So she answers evasively—in terms of reputation: "the woundes I giue my fame / Cannot recouer his." She further needs forgiveness of her lapse. So she provides another hedged answer that modifies even more any absolute. "Though" she has confirmed that she is guilty of willing adultery in ideal terms, she nevertheless claims "purity" for stopping short of any physical act. Then she declares faith that her wholehearted repentance and "loue to goodnes for it selfe" (19) will gain forgiveness from some unacknowledged agent, presumably God, who will purge her impure jealousy and receive her. Sophia has internalized reflexivity and reciprocity. She does not, however, acknowledge her need for the community based on them until the end of the play.

The reflection of Sophia's new resolve awakens her husband's reciprocal virtue. Having witnessed the restoration of reds and whites in her picture, Mathias enters the next scene "alterd . . . cheerefully." His own self-estimate is cleared. And because he can once again reflect on himself as he sees himself reflected in Sophia, he can now reciprocate with steadfast fidelity. Preparing his conversion sermon, he implies the play's social tenet: "I haue seene a vision / This morning makes it good, and neuer was / In such security" (IV.iv.3-5).

One scene more is required to convert Mathias to trust. Sophia compels his realization. Then a reformed society provides the reflection and commands the reciprocal love that effects her recognition and reintegration. In the last act the court, arriving at the couple's castle, discovers Sophia bent on avenging Mathias's distrust and testing him for repentance. When she opens her performance by refusing to appear for Mathias's welcome she is refusing to obey her husband so long as he fails to trust her. When she enters she interrupts Mathias, acts like a courtesan, and sarcastically indicts the queen and her court by declaring the service of the queen's two courtiers. She misleads all into suspecting the worst sort of reflexive reciprocity before Ricardo and Ubaldo confess that she has cured them of libertinism. She then turns on Mathias, repeating her refrain: "why doe you not againe, / Peruse your picture?" (V.iii.155-56). When she kissed Honoria she announced that "Without a magicall picture, in the touch, / I find your printe of close and wanton kisses"; when she responded to Mathias's jealousy, she declared that "you know / How to resolue your selfe what my intents are, / By the helpe of *Mephostophiles*, and your picture"; when she answered his accusations she punningly affirmed that "The truth is / We did not deale like you in speculations / On cheating pictures." Finally Mathias responds by "intreat[ing her] pardon": "I do renounce my error, and embrace you / As the great example to all after times" (V.iii.163-64).

Sophia does not make up readily. Since her marriage does not reflect mutual respect and trust, the loving consideration as well as the protection reciprocally owed by the traditionally superior husband, she seeks a separation and refuge in a convent. Because she trusted his fidelity she "set no spie vpon you to obserue / Which way you wandred: though our sex by nature / Is subiect to suspitions and feares." But he "did gainst your religion / With this inchanter to suruey my actions / [which] Was more then womans weaknes" (V.iii.172-74, 76-78). By embedding her society's misogyny in her accusation Sophia emphasizes reciprocal trust in marriage. So Mathias promises reform. And the court confirms his vow of penance, rehonors her example, and begs the couple to join their reformed commonweal. Finally, after Baptista abjures spying art, Mathias demonstrates his trust of Sophia by destroying the picture: "I will be / My owne security . . . . / I'll set no watch vpon you, and for proofe of't, / This cursed picture I surrender vp / To a consuming fire" (V.iii.210-15). "Vpon theis termes / I am reconcil'd" (V.iii.216-17). Sophia confesses her need for reconciliation and community by gaining pardons for Ubaldo and Ricardo. "So all ends in peace now" because reciprocity in human affairs is based not on absolute ideals but rather in the mutually grateful love that integrates insofar as all reflect each other.

The Picture's presentation of Sophia and Mathias's marriage suggests to a privileged Caroline audience that a husband and a wife need to reflect and reciprocate lovingly through inevitable failures as well as occasional successes. Massinger's artistry in *The Picture* depends on the same tenet. *The Picture* presents a plot in six movements wrought on the principle of reflexivity and reciprocity.[40] Its scenes alternate between Mathias and Sophia's country castle, where premises are set for their tests and where Sophia's temptation, momentary lapse, and recovery take place (I.i, II.i, III.i-ii, vi, IV.ii), and Ladislaus and Honoria's corrupt court, where Mathias's temporary fall and recovery occur (I.ii, II.ii, III.iii-v, IV.i, iii-iv); the resolution (V) brings the court to the country. Beyond presenting the emotional oscillations and reversals of moral position, recognition, and conversion Massinger is adept at, this alternation displays reciprocity: Mathias and Sophia alternately react to what each believes is reflected by the tale of the other's vacillating fidelity. In addition to this double test Massinger provides a parallel double test of Ladislaus's cringing and Honoria's arrogance. The alternations clarify moral locales by segregating the court from the country yet mediating betweeen the two, since country bumpkins and court fops come together to foreshadow the ultimate recognitions and reunions. And all the plot is framed by Mathias setting out on a pilgrimage of life and livelihood and by the court undertaking a pilgrimage to Mathias and Sophia's country castle.

Massinger's uses of metadrama accentuate patterns of reflexivity and reciprocity. As early Stuart drama approached Restoration drama, the easily segregated multiple plots (interrelated by geographic, social, and family proximity, by causation, by analogy, and by affect) become increasingly more complex and difficult to distinguish.[41] This sort of integration appears in the presentation of Mathias and Sophia's extended family, especially when Hilario's clowning makes up part of Sophia's cure of the corrupt courtiers.

The Picture's one formal play within a play is staged by Hilario to console Sophia's inordinate grief over Mathias's absence (II.i). Ready to enter *"with a long white hayre and beard, in an anticke armour"* at the call of a sowgelder's horn, Hilario rightly fears that his doggerel false report of good news will "make her howle for anger." In trying to play the servingman's faithful role the "dunder-head" replicates the failings of others in *The Picture*. As they fail to integrate their roles, so he fails to establish a coherent fiction and proves ridiculous. And as they engage in fabrication, so his reassuring news corresponds to nothing more than desire. As his baseless optimism fails, Sophia's oppressive illusions have even less grounding. Both, with the others, must be disabused of their fictions. At the same time the "dunder-head"'s inset also reflects achievement in *The Picture*. Although Hilario's art of cure and conversion fails, the inset's success demonstrates Massinger's faith in art, as the play within the play breaks out of its bounds into role playing. Because the infuriated Sophia recognizes Hilario's good intentions, she banishes him only until he reforms. For a while he plays the roles he created, fool and knight errant; then he turns Dolorio, weeping his eyes out and starving himself into the visage he sees as needing reform. Hilario recognizes his penitence reflected in the river and in a passing surgeon's comment that he appears to be a transparent anatomy. Gaining reentry into Sophia's presence to announce Ubaldo and Ricardo's arrival with factual news of Mathias, he is prepared to beg her pardon and she to forgive and restore him to his proper, reflecting and reciprocal post in the castle's extended family: "O comfortable wordes; eate, I forgiue thee" (III.ii.15). This paradigm of reciprocity reflects *The Picture*.

Hilario, who has taken the placket knights to be "no counterfaites" (III.ii.11) has been corrected beforehand by Corisca, "For such their outside spoke them" (III.ii.6). The two intersecting vantages focus the moral and enlarge the meanings of role playing to include a commentary on sociopolitics. The martial gigolos sent by Queen Honoria to tempt Sophia must be corrected into self-recognition, then repentance, and finally recovery. Their Christian cycle, analogous to social reflexivity, reciprocity, and reintegration, begins when they are taken into a fiction that encompasses their fabrication. When she resolves to maintain her fidelity rather than be infected by their lie, Sophia stages a curative counter-deception. She consigns each slandering seducer to a rendez-vous in a purgatorial cell where he is stripped and deprived for ungrateful betrayal of hospitality. Because "Ease and excesse in feeding made you wanton," she prescribes a "spare diet" of "the coursest bread, and water" earned by winding flax and spinning thread (IV.ii.176, 84). Afterwards Ubaldo admits that he has been castrated of lust and Ricardo pledges "not a doyte for a doxeie / After this hungry voyage." The direct relationship of sentences to sins and rewards to work (allowing for the era's gender devaluation) is so effective that Sophia claims that "Were all that studie the abuse of women / Vsd thus, the citty would not swarme with Cucchols / Nor so many trads-men breake" (V.i.105-6, 75-77). The commercial references and journey trope imply a reflexive and reciprocal sociopolitical principle, just as do Massinger's character clustering and plot, metadrama and role playing.

In *The Picture* problems with reflexivity and reciprocity in politics replicate the hierarchical inversion in King Ladislaus and Queen Honoria's marriage. Identifying *The Picture*'s secondary source, an anonymous translation of André Favyn's military and political history of Europe, *The Theater of Honour and Knighthood*, Colin Gibson proposes a quotation as Massinger's inspiration: "all men (euen by naturall instinct as it were) doe ill endure the commaund of a woman. For, they will be commaunded by their like, and not by a woman; whom all Lawes, both diuine and humaine haue subiected to Man." [42] But Massinger's reforming presentation of moral and sociopolitical interdependence contradicts Favyn's reliance on a tradition of universal absolutes. The end of the emblematic picture itself serves as a potent warning against absolutes: the unsurpassable "modell of *Sophia* / With more then humane skill limde to the life" must be destroyed for community to be restored. And Massinger's characteristic use of the incomparability topos and of frequent hyperbolic comparisons to classical myths, tales, and history undercut absolutes and support accommodating reflexive reciprocity. [43]

Sophia's search for the wisdom of her name and Honoria's vain quest for the reputation of hers diverge radically. So do Mathias's jealousy and Ladislaus's "Dotage." Though the royal couple mouth notions about reciprocity, they exchange roles and hence disrupt their marriage and their court. While Sophia may seem to be a "matchless wife" ("other ladies . . . in the harmonie / Of the soules rauishing musicke the same age / Not to be nam'd with thee" [I.i.46-49]), Honoria exhibits the vanity of "one that knowes her selfe" to be "Matchlesse": "as I am most eminent in place, / In all my actions I would appeere so" (I.ii.288-89). Claiming "in retribution to deserue / The grace conferd" (I.ii.150-51), Honoria depicts her status accurately and reveals her arrogant impulse deviously:

> I doe but act the Part you put vpon me,
> And though you make me personate a Queene,
> And you my subiect, when the play your pleasure
> Is at a period, I am what I was
> Before I enter'd, still your humble wife,
> And you my royal Soueraigne.   [I.ii.242-51]

Rather than resuming this avowed role, she assumes control. In an exchange notable for the formality with which Honoria inverts what she asserts, she seizes Ladislaus's prerogative to reward military heroes (II.ii.215-25). Supplanting her king's role even as she circumspectly addresses him in the third person, she labels each grant *"Honorias* guift" and she reiterates "I." Later she bars him from her chambers, lies that her doctor has confined her (III.iv), and confirms her power by describing his dotage (III.v.85-94). Her usurpation results from her distortion of reflexivity. She confesses her motive behind the double testing. She cannot abide anyone reflecting her (II.ii.400-3; IV.iii.13-18).

Even more than Mathias, Ladislaus is carried away by "overflowing" emotion. When "raped," "rapt," "ravished," "turned to a statue," he becomes more defective than ideal. Like Mathias, he must be shocked out of considering his beloved "transcendent," "above wonder," "beyond rivalry and envy." Because he is king, Ladislaus's inversion of the marital hierarchy damages all the state. Ubaldo introduces Ladislaus as the king who neglects policy for his wife: "At this very instant, / When both his life and Crowne are at the stake, / He onely studies her content" (I.ii.74-76). The good councillor Eubulus declares that *"Iuno's* plac'd / In *Ioues* Tribunall, and like *Mercurie*, / Forgetting his owne greatnesse, he attends" (I.ii.142-44). And on Honoria's entrance he points to the inverted reflection of the court by telling Ladislaus to doff his crown in deference.

This condemnation of inverting the traditional hierarchy does not constitute the advocacy of absolute superiority of males and monarchs to females and subjects common in the era's tracts. Although the legal justification of a ruler's absolute will is unequivocal, the justifications hedge criticisms of royal actions. The virtuous general, Ferdinand, observes that Honoria's temptation of Mathias is "a strange curiosity, but Queenes / Are priuiledgd aboue subiects, and tis fit" (IV.iii.27-28). And Eubulus adheres to his king's absolute prerogative amidst his criticism of Ladislaus's actions:

> You are a King, and that
> Concludes you wise. Your will a powerfull reason,
> Which we that are foolish Subiects must not argue.
> And what in a meane man I should call folly,
> Is in your Maiesty remarkable wisedome. [I.ii.120-26]

The problem both advisers foresee is that absolutism can foster a disastrous arrogance that destroys the reciprocity necessary in a nation, or a marriage. Only after Mathias compels Honoria to see how she is affected when she leads others to disaster does she recognize that she ought to act responsively, and responsibly. She begs forgiveness and reunion with a reformed society in which she owes reciprocal obedience to her considerate husband and king. Seeing his failings in her, Ladislaus responds to her change by forgiving her and reassuming his station. He will continue to trust and love her, but he will not again abdicate his place. And he will listen carefully rather than rule willfully. For monarchs too are members of society, with personal, sociopolitical, and economic obligations. Such reflexivity and reciprocity in the commonweal of patronage as in the private concerns of family could curb Caroline absolutists.

In a way topically current and artistically characteristic, Massinger in *The Picture* paid heed to the duties of and the maintenance due for military service until this concern emblemized the reflexive, reciprocal sociopolitics discovered by Ladislaus and Honoria. Moreover, he embedded the issue in distinctive, intensified image matrices implicit in his source, William Painter's version of Bandello's "The Lady of Boeme," the twentieth tale in *The Second Tome of the Palace of Pleasure*. Honorable military images, those of Mathias's profession and Hungary's salvation, frame the attempted seductions in Massinger's typical use of outworn metaphors of the battle of the sexes.[44] And the lady of Boeme's crafty vengeance on two villainous captains prompts Massinger's customary use of gormandizing to satirize lust and dressing for success to attack social climbing, since both waste valuable public resources.[45]

The Picture's socioeconomic proposal begins with a time-honored analogy that seemed urgent amid the failures of the early Stuart aristocracy: the extended family must maintain itself. Riding forth on a venture to enrich his estate with the rewards of military service, Mathias pleads need:

> 'tis for thee [Sophia]
> That I turne souldier, and put forth deerest
> Vpon this sea of action as a factor
> To trade for rich materialls to adorne
> Thy noble parts, and show 'em in full lustre.   [I.i.41-45]

Significantly for members of Massinger's audience who were clinging to their privileged status, Mathias incorporates the diction of wayfaring and commerce within warfare. He underscores economic, social, and political integration when he leaves to Sophia "the gouernment of my family / And our poore fortunes, and from these command / Obedience to you as to my selfe" (I.i.61-63). He delegates to Sophia the reflection of his reciprocal rule and care of the household as he reassures the servants about their expectations and obligations.

Thus Massinger begins by forging mutually reinforcing links between private obligations for maintaining an extended family and public duties for maintaining a commonwealth: household reciprocity and reflection project sound public policy. As the nation's defense against Catholicism dominated the interests of Massinger's politically Puritan privileged associates, so a nation's defense against the infidels dominates *The Picture*'s early imagery. Mathias seeks his fortune by saving a Christian nation from the Turks and the court celebrates the victory by tendering "Our Soules deuotions to his dread might, / Who edg'd our swords, and taught vs how to fight" (I.ii.317-18). This motif parallels the defense of chastity theme, which first appears when Baptista describes the signs of Sophia's magical portrait in warlike terms: so long as it is unblemished she remains "vnattempted"; if it begins to yellow "shees with all violence courted but vnconquerd"; "But if it turne all blacke 'tis an assurance / The fort by composition, or surprize / Is forc'd or with her free consent surrenderd" (I.i.179, 182, 183-85). Martial terms continue when Mathias brags about his besieged Penelope's defense of her fortress: "Though they raisd batteries by Prodigall guiftes . . . With all the Engins wanton appetite / Could mount to shake the fortresse of her honor" (II.ii.323-26), she would remain "impregnable." Mathias himself wins the great "encounter" (IV.iv) with Honoria, who had challenged, "Haue you fought so well / Among arm'd men, yet cannot ghesse what lists / You are to enter when you are in priuate / With a willing ladie" (III.v.104-7).

In *The Picture* Massinger establishes the value of these public and personal values, as he often did, in terms of the proper use of food and clothing. The court fasts for Christian victory (I.ii.8-9), then it celebrates with feasting. Precisely the recognition of a principle of adequately recompensing retainers wins what little praise Honoria merits. Her substantial grants to military heroes are doubly laudable. Eubulus melds prudential civic interest with ethical principle when he combines praise for royal generosity with anticipation of the state's profits. Honoria's "bountie should prouide" rich clothing and entertainment to officers: "Let men of armes be vsd thus, if they do not / Charge desperately vpon the Cannons mouth / Though the Diuell ror'd, and fight like dragons, hang me" (II.ii.245, 270-73). Similarly Mathias, declaring that Honoria owes Ladislaus sustaining love, refuses "to tast / The nectar of your kisses; or to feed / His appetite with that ambrosia, due / And proper to a prince, and what binds more, / A lawfull husband" (III.v.70-74). The submerged allusion to Tantalus's presumption threatens the punishment of any violation of hierarchy or marriage.

But the martial, food, and clothing imagery can also underscore failings at court akin to the notoriety of promiscuous English courtiers, such as Buckingham. The corrupted and corrupting Ricardo and Ubaldo deem "Court-warfare" superior because martial "bubble honour . . . is . . . Too deare a purchase" (I.ii.15, 17-20). On the home front, the campaign of the placket knights, to "approach," to "mine," and with sexually suggestive cannons to "batter" Sophia's "fort at the first assault" (III.i.27ff), repeats the degradation of their martial failures. This movement is further reflected in ostentatious court profligacy of the kind early Stuart favorites were commonly accused of. The court leeches Ubaldo and Ricardo recommend a courtiers' academy to reflect Hungary's magnificence. When Eubulus criticizes the idea because it would deprive soldiers of their rightful resources and recognition, he decries a recurring proposal in England: "Our court needs no aydes this way, since it is / A schoole of nothing else: there are some of you . . . haue donne / More hurt to the Kingdome by superfluous brauerie / Which the foolish gentry imitate then a war" (II.ii.28-33). The court trenchermen need restoratives after lechery (I.ii.32-34), assault Sophia as a dish (III.ii.68-69), and gorge on aphrodisiacs (IV.ii.25-33).

Sophia disciplines these placket knights, trenchermen, and clothes horses by depriving them. They must fast and freeze until they earn necessities by spinning and reeling. Massinger's satiric reversal from glut to curative fast is adumbrated in Hilario's reform through penitential austerity (II.i.160-71; III.i.1-21, 48-59; III.ii.10-19). Such dramatic ironies continue when Ubaldo alleges that Ricardo requires special fare to cure lechery, when he plans on a restorative caudle the morning after, and when Ricardo pops lozenges to ward off Ubaldo's alleged diseases. Sophia ministers their cure: "A plurisie of ill blood you must let out / By labour, and spare diet" (IV.ii.177-78). The same pattern is reflected in their initial excess of clothing and subsequent stripping. After the dandies lie that the jewels and gowns are Mathias's rewards for sexual conquests (III.vi.67-119), apparel imagery turns satiric. Ubaldo gives money to Corisca for clothing and to Hilario for a feast: "Pretty on, thers gould, / To buy thee a new gowne, and ther's for thee, / Grow fat" (IV.ii.41-43); and Sophia orders Corisca to provide him with "the wastcote I apointed / With the cambricq shirt perfumd, and the rich cappe" (IV.ii.76-77). The clothing Ricardo passes down to Hilario gets flaunted as the servingman "In stately Equipage" taunts the threadbare prisoners (V.i.31-32). It is fitting that wasteful fashion plates are consigned to freeze in petticoats, an old woman's cap, Hilario's rummage, and their undershirts, while they earn subsistence by producing thread.

As work replaces their indolence, starvation their surfeit, and austerity their indulgence, Ricardo and Ubaldo are trained to productive citizenship. They come to recognize that they must earn their maintenance by rendering sociopolitical service. Sophia draws the moral: "They haue learnd / Their seuerall trades to liue by, and payd nothing / But cold, and hunger for 'em, and may now / Set vp for them selues" (V.iii.151-54). Since these courtiers learn trades, good service seems to include making commercial contributions to the commonweal as well as providing it with defense and counsel. Once they understand the economics of a productive, reciprocal, and reflexive sociopolitical hierarchy they are reintegrated.

So in the last scenes of *The Picture* Massinger represents the correction of Hungary's ostentatious waste of resources and the restoration of proper maintenance of public servants by bringing the court to the country. He suggests national consequences when he returns to potent country associations at Sophia and Mathias's household, a model of wholesome personal ethics, family morality, and political principle. This motif Eubulus signals when he advises transplanting Sophia and Mathias to Hungary so as to reinvigorate the court: "Such a plante / Imported to your Kingdome, and heere grafted / Would yeeld more fruit then all the idle weedes / That sucke vp your raigne of fauour" (IV.iv.120-24). The motif is invoked in terms of classical hospitality and reverence when Mathias welcomes the court to his and Sophia's abode:

> Not *Ioue* attended on by *Hermes*, was
> More welcome to the cottage of *Philemon*,
> And his poore *Baucis*, then your gratious selfe,
> Your matchlesse Queene, and all your royall traine
> Are to your seruant and his wife.   [V.iii.3-7]

The reintegrations that conclude *The Picture* reflect the miraculous metamorphosis and semideification that reward the service of this mythological couple. Thus Massinger, by characteristically framing values in terms of virtuous country patronage, matched his country associates' desire for moderate reform of the monarchy through parliamentary and legal checks.

Finally, Massinger's characters employ epideictic's complementary styles of eulogy and vituperation for judicial and deliberative rhetoric, so that they reinforce human reflexivity and reciprocity. In *The Picture*, as is common in Massinger, they specify a Caroline issue contested by his politically Puritan associates. Eubulus eloquently analyzes, praises, and exhorts military service and bawdily attacks wasteful abuse of the system of favoritism. The reintegrated periods of Eubulus's formal oration supply *The Picture*'s most frequently quoted lines:

> [Soldiers] in a state
> Are but as chirurgions to wounded men
> Euen desperate in their hopes, while paine and anguish
> Make them blaspheme, and call in vaine for death;
> Their wiues and children kisse the chirurgions knees,
> Promise him mountaines, if his sauing hand
> Restore the tortur'd wretch to former strength.
> But when grimme death by *Æsculapius* art
> Is frighted from the house, and health appeares
> In sanguin colours on the sicke mans face,
> All is forgot, and asking his reward
> Hee's payd with curses, often receaues wounds
> From him whose woundes hee curde: so souldiers
> Though of more worth and vse, meete the same fate,
> As it is too apparent. I haue obseru'd
> When horrid *Mars* the touch of whose rough hand
> With Palsies shakes a kingdome, hath put on
> His dreadfull Helmet, and with terror fills
> The place where he like an vnwelcome guest
> Resolues to reuell, how the Lords of acres,
> The tradesman, marchant, and litigious pleader
> (And such like *Scarabes* bred 'ith dung of peace)
> In hope of their protection humbly offer
> Their daughters to their beds, heyres to their seruice,
> And wash with teares, their sweate, their dust, their scars;
> But when those clouds of war that menaced
> A bloudy deluge to th'affrighted state,
> Are by their breath dispers'd, and ouer blowne,
> And famine, bloud, and death, *Bellona's* pages,
> Whip'd from the quiet continent to Thrace,
> Souldiers, that like the foolish hedge sparrow
> To their owne ruine hatch this Cucckow peace,
> Are straight thought burdensome, since want of meanes
> Growing from want of action breedes contempt,

> And that the worst of ills fall to their lot,
> Their seruice with the danger soone forgot.   [II.ii.84-119]

This grand speech on the maintenance due retainers for their service offers a principle of reciprocal statesmanship applicable to Massinger's England. Eubulus demonstrates the principle through an elaborate argument that employs hypotaxis to reintegrate the diversity of his discourse; it thereby reflects the reciprocal hierarchy he extols. His use of the central moral image clusters of *The Picture* further unifies his speech, just as it does his projected society.

After introducing the thesis that the military are unusually dependent on society's immediate fears, Eubulus sets his governing extended simile of soldiers to doctors: promised everything when people are besieged by disease or enemies, after they have served to remove the danger they are denied sustenance. The body of the speech splits into two sentences, of 13 and 20 lines. The first, despite the period, forms a single sentence with a "but when" fulcrum; the second is parted by the same contradictive. Each contradictive sets up the antithesis of society's promises in need to its renegings once safe. Neither period can be closed until its last words; and the finale of the second is emphasized by a concluding couplet. This sentence is governed as well by a dependent "when" clause that delays entry of the compound multiple subject of the public behind "how" in the first half and the single subject soldier behind an elided "how" in the second; before the final predication this is trailed by the commonplace sparrow/cuckow simile. The series of descriptions of desperate need versus satisfied neglect are drawn out with details from family life, provision, and classical allusion. They are reinforced by repetitive and parallel figures such as "often receaues wounds / From him whose woundes hee curde" in the first sentence, balanced by "since want of meanes / Growing from want of action breedes contempt" in the second. Such devices as logical distribution of argument, balanced and compounded conjunctions that override modifying subordination, parallel constructions, and descriptive, allusive copiousness constitute only part of the artfulness. Eubulus reflects yet again the central moral of *The Picture*: a doctor cures the society in times of sickness, a knight protects it in times of danger; therefore the society owes its public servants reciprocal maintenance.

In contrast to his formal oratory Eubulus uses abrupt, sententious, bawdy vituperation to confront the moral inversions at court. He can counsel Ladislaus with satiric folk wisdom: "there is no such soker / As a yonge spongie wife; she keepes a thousand / Horseleches in her box" (III.iv.7-9). And he can comment caustically on Honoria's "strange inducements" of Mathias. His *double entendres* reflect perversions of maintenance in war and love:

the man sir being no souldier
Nor vsd to charge his pike when the breach is open
There was no danger in't: you must conceiue sir,
Being relligious, she chose him for a Chaplaine
To read old Homelies to her in the darke,
Shee's bound to it by her Cannons.   [IV.iii.7-12]

Massinger employs elaborately self-referential artifice—allusions to his literary heritage and his own works, repetitions of unifying image complexes, references to classical culture, verbal formulae, and commonplaces—in both his oratorical and his satirical modes. His comprehensively allusive art enforces personal and sociopolitical reform at the same time that it renews dramatic tradition. Moreover, it demonstrates aesthetically the very principle it inculcates: an accommodating tradition of reflexivity and reciprocity by which old ideals and proven techniques integrate new ideas and potential tools.

As Eubulus's lines illustrate the integration of Massinger's social and political preferences with his style, so Eubulus himself exemplifies the integration of Massinger's moral concerns with his dramatic art. Named for the notable early model in *Gorboduc*, Eubulus belongs to a Tudor-Stuart stage heritage of wise counselors, which includes Massinger's own series of gruff advisers from Romont in *The Fatal Dowry* to Durazzo in *The Guardian*. As such he provides a traditional choric commentary that has shortsightedly been indicted for its datedness and its mistrust of actors.[46] Eubulus opens by envisioning a righteous state opposed to current perversions. He cheers comments such as Ferdinand's rebuff of the courtiers, "As I liue, / Answer'd as I could wish. How the fops gape now!" (II.ii.74-75). He encourages rewards for warriors by applauding Ferdinand's honesty (146-49), by explaining the necessity of military maintenance to Honoria (241-44), and by praising her reciprocal maintenance. He punctuates the reforming promise of Mathias's conversion speech (IV.iv). He closes by establishing the general principle of a properly reintegrated sociopolitical hierarchy, calling to mind the predilections of Massinger's politically Puritan privileged associates.

But by playing the role of the traditional gruff counselor and commentator, Eubulus represents an imitation that can rouse the ire of twentieth-century critics. His initial oscillation between opposed absolute principles recalls York in Shakespeare's *Richard II*. Both men espouse and desert: each advises a king to foster hierarchy by rendering a monarch's reciprocal obligations but then each supports that king's absolute, willful rule. Eubulus, however, also marks Massinger's refinement of tradition in his distinct difference from York. Instead of ending a weak, vacillating commentator whom others scarcely accept, Eubulus learns to accommodate opposing values. He is converted to the extent that he counsels a reformed, reciprocal, personal love that reflects his politics. Eubulus progresses through sudden changes and revelations, ending in self-discovery, penance, and forgiven reintegration. His progress reflects the elaborately ingenious and surprisingly twisting plots by which Massinger's tragicomedies come to reformed resolutions. Both exemplify Massinger's extensions of the dramatic and behavioral potential of his models.

Just as Eubulus's case displays technical and moral refinement, so it demonstrates faith in the power of rhetoric and art to convert an audience. At their inaugural appearance Eubulus tells Ladislaus and Honoria a parable to teach them appropriate roles (I.ii.188-231): granted absolute control by the "impotent louing King" Ninus, the courtesan Semiramis secured her position by having Ninus decapitated. Facetious in offering the model as "worth your imitation Madam," Eubulus suggests that "This [story] is a patterne" from which Honoria and Ladislaus can learn reciprocal roles by revulsion. But art in itself no more sustains Eubulus than art by itself converts others in *The Picture*. Real cures come through role playing artist teachers. Eubulus employs two styles to play two roles aimed at the same end. As an orator/adviser he tells the parable and as a satirist he banters Ladislaus.

Eubulus's own transformation (recognizing his failings, committing contrite penance, begging and receiving forgiveness, and gaining readmission into a society reformed by reflexive reciprocal charity) replicates Massinger's governing principle of the reintegration of society by way of miraculous conversion. So he achieves the final stage of Massinger's development of another type, the stage misogynist.[47] Early in the play he opposes Honoria's rule because of his sense of invariable female inferiority. When Acanthe repels Ladislaus's approach to Honoria, Eubulus wonders how marriage differs from prostitution if a husband must purchase his wife's favors. His answer for sexual relations: a conqueror forces his will on the weaker vessel:

> Be as you are sir
> An absolute monarch, it did show more Kinglike
> In those libidinous Cæsars that compeld
> Matrons, and virgins of all rankes to bow
> Vnto their rauenous lusts, and did admit
> Of more excuses then I can vrge for you.   [III.iv.43-48]

But Eubulus's gender politics is at odds with his politics. Though his advocacy of willful force in the family is inconsistent with the debt of love, honor, and protection he counsels for a king responding to a subject's service, he remains "bitter / Against the Sex" (V.iii.32-35). He prejudges

Sophia: "Ther's no climate / On the world I thinke where one iades tricke or other / Raignes not in women." But her reversing "ijggobobs" miraculously bring about his climactic recognitions and instantaneous conversion. Approving the lessons Sophia has meted out to Ricardo and Ubaldo, Mathias and the court, he suddenly feels two needs. One is for this "good woman" to replenish society. The more important is for his masculine society to practice reciprocity by cherishing and respecting wives, lovers, and women, so that it reflects a reformed, reintegrated sociopolitics. Thus Eubulus admits his flaws and begs forgiveness by joking about the need for love:

> 'Tis not alone enough that you are good,
> We must haue some of the breed of you; will you destroy
> The kind, and race of goodnesse? I am conuerted
> And aske your pardon Madam for my ill opinion
> Against the sex, and show me but two such more,
> I'll marry yet, and loue em.

Any study of *The Picture* must conclude with the magical portrait. The miraculous metamorphoses of the colors signifying Sophia's fidelity in reds and whites, her temptations in yellow, her fall in black, and her restoration in reds and whites, do more than reflect a human pattern of inevitable fall, potential conversion, and forgiven reintegration into a reformed order. They reinforce that pattern's promise of reciprocal charity. Moreover, in the probing pun on colors, the picture displays Massinger's abiding esthetic tenet—the power of rhetorical art to effect reformation. For its colors illustrate the emotional and moral status of the person portrayed, just as colors constitute the fundamental figures in Seneca the Rhetorician's *Controversiae*. Such rhetoricians were showing off their skills and ingenuity in fantasy and displaying their abilities to argue any side of an issue. But mainly they were intent on describing the attitudes, the motives, the wills of litigants. Moreover, by delineating these intentions they were searching out the ways of charitable equity, of understanding what is just under flawed human conditions where legal ideals and absolutes often clash and remain unattainable. Massinger's sociopolitical theater led Caroline drama in presenting his society's crucial concern with failures within the achievements of traditional ideals and absolutes. Perhaps for many of his privileged audience it suggested their desire for grateful, charitable reform of their heritage so as to accommodate new promises and demands. In short, its significance may derive from his exhorting his society to recognize the values of reflexive reciprocity.

Massinger, the earliest master among the Caroline professional playwrights, offers their most accommodating view of self-creation through the interaction between some presumed interior self and a society, within the constraints and potentials of a community undergoing constant self-redefinition. His fellow elder offers a contrary view; Ford insists on the essential self of his characters. Paradoxically his characters end up the least adaptable and most determined by society. Perhaps that is why Massinger's characteristic dramatic form is the tragicomedy of reformation, whereas Ford's is the tragedy of ritual suffering.

3

Ford's Tragedy
of Ritual Suffering

The Gentility of John Ford

The second son of parents whose lines went back almost a century as gentry around Ilsington, Devonshire, John Ford was the only unqualified member of the gentry among the Caroline professional playwrights.[1] From both families he inherited a tradition of membership in the Middle Temple. There he apparently remained (save for one brief lapse) after admission, 16 November 1602, at the age of sixteen. "TO MY WORTHILY RESPECTED FRIENDS, Nathaniel Finch, Iohn Ford [his cousin], Esquires; Mr. Henry Blvnt, Mr. Robert Ellice, and all the rest of the Noble Society of *Grayes* Inne" he dedicated the first published of his unassisted plays, *The Lover's Melancholy* (1629).[2] To his identically named cousin, esquire, and bencher, he dedicated *Love's Sacrifice* (1633), conventionally lauding kinship, friendship, and virtue. More significantly this dedication implicitly repeats a claim he pressed in his first dedication. He is appealing only to an elite of personal and literary peers: "*As plurality hath reference to a Multitude, so, I care not to please Many: but where there is a Parity of condition, there the freedom of construction, makes the best musicke. This concord hath equally held betweene* Yov The Patrones, *and* Me The Presentor."

Ford courted nobility long before he showed any plays. He composed *Fame's Memorial* (1606) to seek the patronage of the widow Penelope Devereaux Rich, the noble sister of the late ill-fated Earl of Essex and celebrated Stella of Sir Philip Sidney's sonnet sequence, as well as to elegize the death and eulogize the life of Charles Blount, Lord Mountjoy and the Earl of Devonshire. The twenty-year-old poet seems doubly drawn to the accomplishments and nobility of this military leader and lord of his native county. In the face of considerable disapproval at court Mountjoy had remained honorably faithful to his lover, who divorced her husband to marry him and legitimize their five children. That same year (1606) Ford exhibited his interest in court ceremonies and his aspirations for connections to the nobility. His *Honour Triumphant, or The Peers' Challenge* presents the amatory theses defended by four prominent lords at a tournament celebrating the king of Denmark's visit. The Duke of Lennox, the Earl of Arundel, the Earl of Pembroke, and the Earl of Montgomery were all influential patrons. Lennox, a Scottish and an English peer, was noted for generosity. Arundel provided a model of noble connoisseurship. Pembroke and Montgomery were the brothers who carried on the Sidney tradition of Puritan political leadership and patronage that Massinger served. To the countesses of Pembroke and Montgomery, Ford dedicated this work. And he is likely the author of the anonymous *Christ's Bloody Sweat* (1613), which was dedicated to Pembroke.

In 1613 Ford certainly authored the anonymous prose *The Golden Mean,* which he enlarged and reprinted in 1614. This tract, which honors nobly patient endurance under duress, he addressed to the Earl of Northumberland, who had been confined in the Tower since 1605 for being a close relative of the leader of the Gunpowder Plot. In 1620 Ford presented a complementary tract on the rewards of noble sufferance, *A Line of Life,* to Northumberland's son-in-law, Lord Haye, the Viscount Doncaster and a member of James's Privy Council, who finally procured Northumberland's release. One more early nondramatic work, no longer extant, piques curiosity. In 1615 Ford produced *Sir Thomas Overbury's Ghost, contayneigne the history of his life and vntimely death;* this presumably recounted the vengeful poisoning of the upright if arrogant knight who opposed the immorality and abuse of position by James's favorite, Robert Carr, the Viscount Rochester and Earl of Somerset. In addition, Ford wrote a commendatory verse on Overbury, *"that man of virtue,"* for the eighth impression of *Sir Thomas Overbury His Wife.* In sum, through fifteen years of nondramatic literary production Ford sought to identify with nobility. Were his addressees noble in title only he would have been merely pursuing the patronage required for survival then. But Ford seems to have presented works specifically honoring and exhorting noble actions, particularly sufferance, to titled patrons renowned for their nobility.

When, after about a decade of dramatic collaboration, Ford began publishing unassisted plays he resumed his search for noble patronage. As he paid his first respects to his compeers at Gray's Inn in 1629, so he paid his last, with *The Lady's Trial* in 1639, to another gentleman associated with Gray's Inn, the "Deservingly-honoured, IOHN WYRLEY Esquire, and to the vertuous and right worthy Gentlewoman, Mrs MARY WYRLEY his wife."[3] In between he dedicated his plays to oft-commended patrons. Lord Mordaunt, the Earl of Peterborough and Baron of Turvey, to whom Ford dedicated *'Tis Pity She's a Whore* in 1633, had apparently made "Noble allowance of *These First Fruites* of my leasure in the Action"; so the poet claimed a "particular duty to your Fauours, by a particular Ingagement." Ford's other offerings indicate hopes more than achievements of noble recognition. Lord Craven, to whom he dedicated *The Broken Heart* in 1633, was famous for his virtuous attendance on Elizabeth of Bohemia and his Protestant military accomplishments. Lord Randell Macdonell, the eccentric Earl of Antrim, was an appropriate dedicatee of *The Fancies* in 1638. And William Cavendish, the Earl of Newcastle, to whom Ford dedicated *The Chronicle History of Perkin Warbeck* in 1634, was well known for literary patronage, especially of Jonson and Shirley.[4]

Ford's recognition of his audience of barristers and his dedications seeking noble support were not mere afterthoughts. He wrote for a genteel, noble, and sometimes courtly audience. Both his collaborations and his solo dramas were produced by the succession of companies managed by the impresario Christopher Beeston at a private theater, the Phoenix or Cockpit in Drury Lane. Beeston's troupe, whose productions catered to a privileged clientele, achieved a prestige second only to the King's Men. *The Sun's Darling*, Ford's moral masque with Dekker, was presented at Whitehall as well as at the Phoenix. The only exceptions to the Phoenix performances are his unaided *The Lover's Melancholy* and *The Broken Heart*, both performed by the King's Men, the first at the Globe and at Blackfriars, the second advertised at Blackfriars only. Thus Ford presented plays generally characterized by courtly formality to the elite.[5]

Ford's propensities and dramatic career seem to have been based, more than those of any other Caroline professional playwright, on values and ideals characterized by courtliness. A historian could comfortably predict from Ford's life and dedications that he would adhere to monarchical absolutism and familial patriarchy, to status in the hierarchy based on ascription or favor to bred nobility, and to traditional gender roles— that is, to attitudes in contrast to those of Massinger. The historian might predict that among the Caroline professional playwrights Ford's dramas would seem to be removed furthest from their time and that his major characters would be valued for holding faith with what they perceive to be their essential selves. It would be harder to predict that this ideal earns glorification not from these souls' victories but from their sufferings caused by their pursuit of integral noble selves. Their struggles to maintain ideal selves turn out to be the most socially deterministic and the most tragic presentations on the Caroline stage. Consequently Ford's dramas, most often considered moral and psychological, turn out to be sociological.

Political and Social Resignation

Even if they come to confront moral despair or relativity, many critics concur with Thelma N. Greenfield's recent working assumption that Ford's dramas are essentially moral.[6] Our disagreements over *'Tis Pity She's a Whore*'s empathetic presentation of brother-sister incest are atypical only in their vehemence. George F. Sensabaugh portrays a modern Ford whose young lovers' individualism challenges a decadent, deterministic world, whereas Mark Stavig depicts a traditional Ford whose young lovers' immoral sex and their society's perversions both get undercut.[7]

Similarly Sensabaugh sees in *Love's Sacrifice* an adulterous Fernando and Bianca confronted with the problem of how to consummate their love despite their conventional society, whereas Stavig perceives an immoral triangle of "passionate sinners" and "rationalizing fools."[8] These representative moral poles can be inferred indirectly from opposed conceptions of Ford's attitude toward Queen Henrietta Maria's courtly love cult. They can be taken directly from opposed interpretations of Ford's recurring presentation of obsessed lovers, or seekers of absolutes, who challenge but do not question the barriers posed by their societies.[9] Despite their attention to moral psychology in Ford's plays, then, many critics evidently concur with Greenfield's focus on "the ineluctable confrontation between private values and the impossibility of translating those values intact into action in the Fordian stage-world."[10] Ford's dramas, in short, do not turn so much on moral issues that result in psychological insights.[11] Rather, I am going to argue on the basis of the focus of both critical response and Ford's works themselves that Ford's dramas, like those of his fellow Caroline professionals, turn on social questions about how people play roles in given situations.

The primary focus of Ford's plays is not moral because, apart from Giovanni's arguments that nature accepts incestuous love contra western taboo, Ford's characters do not think through either their own moral premises or those of their societies. They adhere to unexamined, usually disastrous, absolute positions. In his search for *The Moral Vision of Jacobean Tragedy* Robert Ornstein implicitly recognizes Ford's social basis when he confines Ford's concerns to immediate ethical experience.[12] So does Tucker Orbison when he begins with the most morally laden tragedy, *'Tis Pity,* progresses through the less morally condemnatory *Love's Sacrifice* and *The Broken Heart,* and concludes with the morally distanced *Perkin Warbeck.*[13] The primary focus of Ford's plays is not psychological because his protagonists prove passive disobedients. They are resigned to defying, then patiently submitting to the inevitable levy of social penalties. Both T.S. Eliot's condemnation of the lack of "inner significance" in Ford's drama and Una Ellis-Fermor's praise of its universal psychology tacitly acknowledge that they are considering not personal psyches but social types.[14] Others suggest similar acknowledgments when they note that Ford's characters are revealed through glimpses into states of mind rather than self-examining soliloquys.[15] The dominant critical consensus is that recognizably Fordian characters commit themselves to noble social roles of the greatest integrity they can achieve. Therefore, in contrast to Massinger's or his own tragicomic characters, they cannot accommodate and reform but must, because of their total commitment, suffer the tragic consequences meted out.[16]

Viewing Ford's plays as tragic social dramas (that is, tragedies focused on characters coping with their circumstances by playing out roles) helps account for the critical usefulness of considering *Perkin Warbeck* a meta-drama concerned with illusion and reality. Jonas A. Barish, extrapolating from responses to *Richard II*, concludes that Perkin Warbeck's performance, whether fraudulent or self-deluded, wins audience identification.[17] Michael Neill concentrates on performances wherein Warbeck and other Ford protagonists, all consummate mannerist players, create neo-stoic nobles out of nothing more nor less than style.[18] And Joseph Candido, influenced by Greenblatt's Renaissance self-fashioning, subsumes Neill's aesthetically moral action under self-creation.[19] They thereby arrive at Clifford Leech's description of Ford's presentations of an aristocratic code of endurance or at Anderson and Kaufmann's "tragedy of manners" or at Sharon Hamilton's "communal tragedy."[20] Ford's social tragedies of ritual suffering present situations wherein characters defy socially received norms that thwart their self-realization. His characters commit themselves to absolutes that embody their society's highest ideals, with as little examination as their society conforms to norms that compromise these same ideals; they create selves of extraordinary integrity by playing roles demanding self-sacrifice.

Ford did not find his highest value in any set of ideals but instead in a code of honorable conduct. From his earliest publications he promoted noble resolve to achieve self-fulfilment, that is, the sublimated victory of playing one's role honorably at the cost of martyrdom to sociopolitical demands. In the verse elegy *Fame's Memorial* and the prose defense *Honour Triumphant: or the Peeres Challenge*, Ford values nobility as distinct from and superior to ascribed degree (albeit closely knit to it). Though he offers conventional praise of Lord Mountjoy, what he emphasizes from the opening through the concluding "tombs" is the belief that, whatever base contemporary opinion says, perdurable fame rewards noble behavior. His elaborate defenses of the distinguished lords' propositions (*"Knights in Ladies service haue no free-will," "Beauty is the mainteiner of valour," "Faire Lady was neuer false,"* and *"Perfect lovers are onely wise"*) may be either laboriously playful or facilely ironic. In either case they demonstrate a real interest in the manners and attitudes of courtly paragons.[21]

Ford's poem of affective worship, thanksgiving, and homily, *Christ's Bloody Sweat*, and his ethical prose tracts, *The Golden Mean* and *A Line of Life*, suggest the essential virtue that the dramatist came to represent. *Christ's Bloody Sweat* mingles pathetic descriptions of the sacrifice of an innocent Christ, fierce condemnations of humanity's sins that required his suffering, and moving exhortations to imitate Christ by avoiding sins while enduring sins' penalties. It thus initiates two prevalent Ford concerns. First, as Stavig has noted, the sins that Ford attacks result from excess after loss of rational control, whereas the virtues he promotes reduce desires. Second, as Leech has pointed out, the endurance that wins salvation for the elect is related to the endurance that wins honor for virtuous nobles.[22]

The noble morals that Ford extols in his paired prose tracts are stoic endurance on behalf of ideals and faith in ultimate honor. An exhortation that the Earl of Northumberland patiently bear his monarch's neglect, *The Golden Mean*, "Discoursing *The Noblenesse of perfect Virtue in extreames*," dwells on the ennoblement someone can achieve through adversity. Whoever faces calamity with inner temperance and outer control demonstrates the wisdom of the quest for that providential constancy which is inseparable from nobility. Citing classical, traditional English, and contemporary models as well as hypothetical situations, Ford calls for nobles to preserve honorable integrity by accepting sufferings: Disfavor, neglect, forfeiture of one's estate, banishment, and imprisonment are due a prince. Death is owed to Providence. Relief comes with noble death. *A Line of Life. Pointing at the Immortalitie of a Vertuous Name* presents complementary means and ends. More resolute and less resigned than the earlier tract, this sequel focuses on lives lived so as to attain perpetual life and glory: "Action, perseverance in action, sufferance in perseverance, are the three golden links that furnish-up the richest chain wherewith a good man can be adorned" (388). This triad of virtues appears in a deserver's triple role: he is a reasonable, self-controlled microcosm, a private man; a magnanimous, modest governor of the body politic, a public man; and a generous contributor to humanity, a good man. Ford employs negative exempla, warning against the arrogance that displaced sufferance in leaders such as the Duke of Byron, Sir John van Olden Barnevelt, and Sir Walter Ralegh. Both Ford's text and his marginal notes repeatedly cite Seneca, Cicero, and Aristotle among a host of witnesses. His concluding exaltation of "James the Good" as "James the Peaceable" and "James the Learned" (414-15) further supports the supreme virtue of internal peace earned through a life of wise acceptance issuing from unqualified commitment to unquestioned absolutes.

A character's commitment to absolutes despite suffering provides the supreme noble integrity Ford lauds in his plays. It thus governs such contributing noble values as obeying one's monarch, submitting to one's assigned station in the hierarchy, and playing out the child, gender, and occupational roles for creating one's identity as these have been allotted by society. Despite his protagonists' characteristic defiance of sociopolitical authority there is almost no questioning of authority, of a king, a father, or a male. Part of this lack of questioning may result from Ford's little notice of politics, in contrast to his fellow Caroline professionals. Alone among these playwrights, all of Ford's solo plays, except for *Perkin Warbeck* set in English history more than a century old, take place in Italy, in Greece and its possessions, or in Spain. Moreover, the pretender Warbeck's challenge to Henry VII reinforces absolute royal rights.

All three representatives of royalty in *Perkin Warbeck* reinforce Ford's presentation of the absolute rights of a monarch. Henry VII plays a machiavellian prince, investing resources with political acumen, promoting effective advisers, maintaining excellent intelligence, maneuvering secretly, and marshalling manifold martial and political force. But unlike Bolingbroke in *Richard II*, he also claims the divine right held by Richard. As his kingdom's anointed body, Henry's cheek pales and his strength suffers when his subjects are hurt or must be removed for the state's health. His advisers, particularly the Bishop of Durham, lay claim to the divinity of his post and the absoluteness of his prerogatives. Thus the play's mood remains one of "turmoyles past / Like some vnquiet dreame, [that] haue rather busied / [Henry's] fansie, then affrighted rest of State" (V.ii/202).[23] Warbeck also lays claim to the supreme rights of royalty, since the prerogatives need to remain absolute and divine for his pretension to be potent. The great admiration won by the "Imposter beyond president" derives from his superb manifestation of both of the king's two bodies without ever breaking role—not in court, not in private with his wife, not in covert scheming with his personal adviser who acknowledges the plot, not in conference with a confessed pretender, not in soliloquy. Warbeck's speech acts of regal self-presentation and self-anointment are committed with the Fordian personal integrity of utter dedication in "Action, perseverance in action, sufferance in perseverance" that verifies divine absolutism. Though vacillating, outmaneuvered, and acquiescent, James still declares his royal prerogatives and retains his sovereignty inside Scotland. His desire that Katherine marry Warbeck instead of her father's choice countermands her filial obedience. Acceding to the "rape done on mine honor," Huntley's commentary is telling: "Kings are earthly gods, there is no medling / With their annoynted bodies, for their actions, / They only are accountable to Heaven" (III.ii/163).

Elsewhere in Ford royal absolutism is taken for granted. The platonic lovers Fernando and Bianca in *Love's Sacrifice* personally defy the Duke of Pavia, who elevated them to favorite and wife, but they submit to his authority as a betrayed friend, husband, and lord. After the title character of *The Queen* dutifully transfers her realm and person to her husband, the former rebel, Alphonso, she remains unresisting despite demotion to ignoble status, banishment from court, and condemnation to death. In Ford's plays a monarch can continue to sway after his death as he ruled absolutely during his life. In *The Lover's Melancholy* not only do Palador's councillors seem fretfully powerless at the potential dissolution of the kingdom of Cyprus because of their young ruler's malady, but the personal situation he cannot control was bequeathed him by his father. Once cured, the prince's orders direct the cures of others. Even rule that is unjust and corrupt goes unchallenged in Ford's works. The resolution of *'Tis Pity* is left to the Cardinal. Although he has already caused unrest by harboring the murderer of an innocent because the murderer has royal relatives, he nevertheless remains unresisted when he confiscates wealth and rule in Parma. Contrary to Massinger's legal and parliamentary checks on monarchy, Ford's plays assume royal absolutism.

Interlocked with their unquestioning obedience to divine monarchy, Ford's characters make commitments to their assigned social status that are unmatched by the characters of any other Caroline professional playwright. His ridicule, generally regarded to be "disgusting" comic satire of ignobility, stings anyone trying to climb to a higher station. Sedge's claim that *Love's Sacrifice* criticizes court preferment needs qualification, but he accurately discerns that *The Fancies Chaste and Noble* condemns social aspiration.[24] Juliet Sutton has perceived that critics' disapproval of this play derives partly from guilt over being trapped into recognizing their pruriently voyeuristic fancies about innocent platonic love.[25] What aggravates their ire is that the play further convicts them of ignoble scandal-mongering.[26] For scandal-mongering, according to Ford's tracts, is the characteristic vice of avariciously ambitious social aspirants. Just so, the next to last couplet of the young ladies' epilogue accusingly observes that "*Distrust is base*, presumption *urgeth* wrongs; / *But* noble thoughts *must prompt as* noble tongues."

One pincer of *The Fancies'* movement impedes the audience from discovering that in his "bower" the old Marquis of Siena sequesters three nieces and an initiate, aptly named Castamela, from social corruption. The other takes advantage of dramatic and social conventions that encourage the audience to assume an attitude of knowing cynicism and leap to infer scandal: we listen to Juvenalian diatribes against a society that panders for preferment; we overhear rampant slander about a harem of "Fancies"; and we witness the Fancies' witty courtliness (seemingly an "infected tongue" that indicates debased mores) and the bawdry of servants who imitate them. So the play not only depicts Ford's ideal of living with integrity despite society's envious slander, it also ridicules society's majority for hustling preferment. The play's effect depends on a virtuous stage Machiavel. Troylo-Savelli, rather than recruiting the audience as accomplices, manipulates three characters and us into a humbling self-knowledge which requires that we repudiate our overeager slander. First Castamela discovers innocence in the marquis's bower. Next her brother Livio, who has vacillated between exultation and guilt over winning preferment by jeopardizing her, confesses his error. Finally her prospective bridegroom, Romanello, who suspects her of dishonor, is convicted of proprietary presumption. The revelation that Romanello's satire and courtship disguise envy and preferment-seeking proves him unchaste and ignoble, unworthy of Castamela. So he loses her to the loving, trusting Troylo-Savelli.

Ford's castigation of envious prurience and ignoble scandal-mongering, two facets of inordinate status pursuit, is sustained in *The Fancies'* other plots. In the high-caste plot, Romanello's sister, Flavia, has been disowned for being pandered by her former husband to her current one, old Lord Julio. She has had to assume hauteur in order to conceal her suffering and to preserve herself from defamation and from the sexual advances of Julio's retainers. Everyone discovers, however, that her apparently ignoble quest for status is actually obedience to her first husband, a former climber whose repentance she supports, and to her current lord, whom she honors and loves. In the low-caste plot a satirically foul-mouthed, sly servant, Spandello, gulls a pretentious young barber, Secco, into suspecting that his old wife and guardian of the Fancies is cuckolding him. Attacking self-promotion, this plot also condemns the dual manifestations of an ignoble pursuit of preferment—envy and slander.

Love's Sacrifice suggests that while climbing is damnable, the occasional preferment of inferiors by their superiors is acceptable. Chaos comes when Bianca, advanced for her beauty and virtue to the status of duchess of Pavia, and Fernando, advanced for his courtly accomplishments and good looks to the status of favorite of the duke, fall in love and challenge the court's hierarchy of perquisites. Yet this tragedy does not simply condemn social mobility. First, the "chaste" lovers exhibit the superlative personal integrity that Ford represents as the noblest virtue: Bianca, declaring her physical fidelity to her husband, sacrifices her life to his jealousy, and Fernando commits suicide to prove the purity of his love of Bianca. Second, the play condemns the other characters for strife over status. The duke (Othello's descendant) is goaded into fatal action by his jealous widowed sister, who manipulates his pride in the "honor" of his house and court. That "honor" seems to result not from role integrity but instead from an egoistic grasping for prerogatives and reputation. The duke's secretary (his Iago), D'Avolos, is tortured to death because of his quest for advancement as the spy, operative, and sexual broker of the duke's sister. Mauruccio, an ancient laughingstock vain enough to seek the preferment of court ladies, is banished from the court and married to a widow with a bastard. All are condemned for chasing status.

The rest of Ford's scramblers for advancement follow either of two ridiculous patterns from *The Fancies*—the sycophants hang onto the coattails of power (like Julio's followers Camillo and Vespuccio), the commoners imitate the court (like Secco and Morosa's circle)—or a compound of both. Ridiculous retainers seeking favor include the mayor, mercer, tailor, and scrivener who cling to Perkin Warbeck, and the captain and astronomer of Alphonso's party in *The Queen*. Absurd commoners aping courtiers include Pelias and Cuculus (with his transvestite page Grilla) in *The Lover's Melancholy*. *The Lady's Trial* presents three vainly pretentious compounds. Two national stereotypes, the upstart Italian courtier manque, Fulgoso, and the cowardly Spanish *miles gloriosus*, Guzman, court the *"fantastick"* lisping maiden, Amoretta. Unlike Massinger's promotion of social elevation for achievement, Ford's plays repeatedly reduce preferment seeking to contempt.

Katherine's suffering obedience as a subject, a daughter, and a wife in *Perkin Warbeck*, Flavia's enduring obedience to both of her husbands in *The Fancies*, and Bianca's self-sacrificing fidelity to both her husband and her beloved in *Love's Sacrifice* all indicate Ford's acceptance of his era's traditional gender roles: women are subordinate; their supreme virtue is chaste obedience. The universal praise bestowed on Katherine makes an obvious case. An exemplary subject daughter, even as Warbeck's appointed queen she drops to her knees to beg her father's blessing. At her betrothal, submitting to the absolute rule of a husband bestowed by her erstwhile king, she vows that time "shall not stagger, / Or constancie, or dutie in a wife. / You must be *King of me*" (III.ii/168). When Warbeck's cause fails she is exiled, forced to flee, and captured, yet still she pledges to remain a regal widow (the historical lady remarried several times), since "No humane power, can or [does] divorce / [Her] faith from dutie" (IV.iii/187). For the suffering that results from her absolute feminine obedience, this "Great miracle of Constancie" earns the admiration of Henry's court. A choric tribute is provided by her father, who "glorie[s] in [her] constancie" during "these tryalls of a patience" whereby she has been proved "In every dutie of a wife, and daughter" (V.iii/215).

A paragon of Ford's supreme virtue (the integrity of unquestioning commitment to an assigned role), Katherine also seems typical of his women's obedience to the absolute prerogatives of male, father, and husband. Prevailing feminine roles are repeatedly reinforced through such plays as *The Lady's Trial*, which is preoccupied from its opening lines with the familiar masculine horror over the possibility of a young wife's infidelity. When Old Auria ventures in the wars to win fortune, fame, and office, he leaves Spinella home to gain the only prize available to women. She earns her honor from her husband and his circle by maintaining her obedient, quiet fidelity despite the temptations of rakish young lord Adurni and the slanderous condemnations of a self-appointed, overzealous guardian, Auria's closest friend. This central theme is echoed when Auria rewards Adurni's conversion with betrothal to Spinella's compliant young sister. It is reechoed when Adurni's "wanton" mistress is converted to a renewed fidelity to her soldier-of-fortune husband.

Ford may uphold mutual marital trust when in *The Lady's Trial* Spinella finally suggests that her husband's faith in her ought to match her faith in him. And Ford may condemn the double standard when in *Love's Sacrifice* Ferentes is ceremonially murdered by three women he has abandoned with bastards. But these episodes hardly offset society's tacit approval and Putana's explicit praise of Soranzo's experience in *'Tis Pity.* Nor can they meet Ford's repeated presentations of the virtue of a wife who plays her role of acquiescent obedience and fidelity in spite of enduring whatever arbitrary and possessive commands her husband imposes, whatever indignities and scandals her society requires, whatever privations her conscience demands. So a lasciviously adulterous, jealously vengeful Hippolita is condemned in *'Tis Pity;* so a Thamasta is happily converted from vain mistress to obedient wife in *The Lover's Melancholy;* so a Penthea wins praise for obediently suffering the "miseries of enforced marriage" in *The Broken Heart.*

The value of feminine subservience is epitomized in the declarations of *The Queen, or the Excellency of her Sex.* The Queen of Aragon proves her virtue by surrendering "my Crown, my Heart, / My People, My Obedience" (I.646-47) for marriage to a rebel.[27] Even though Alphonso essentially reneges and though his mania jeopardizes the country, she remains obedient and protective despite suffering sequestration from his bed, her household, and her court because he slanderously accuses her of adultery. She repeatedly demonstrates that "A Wife must bear / Withal what likes her Lord t'upbraid her with, / And yet 'tis no injustice" (II.1251-53) until she finally gains a reconciliation wherein he retains monarchy and mastery. Humble feminine obedience is confirmed to be a virtue in the second plot. In it a proud widow has to repent doubly her former scorn of a valiant suitor: on the scaffold she warns vain beauties before he saves, then rejects her; at the end he saves her from a penitential pilgrimage and a cloister by marrying her once she agrees to be his subject. In contrast to Massinger's characteristically paternalist accommodation of the integrity of women and children who exercise personal choice, Ford's plays typically honor the integrity of a wife who submits wholly to the authority of her husband. She serves as an exemplum for social relations that comply strictly with the dominant ideals of the Caroline court: families maintain their roles with honorable suffering, female wards obey guardians, daughters accept subordination to sons, women give way to men.

From his first solo play, *The Lover's Melancholy,* Ford represented the virtuous obedience of daughters, female wards, and householders. The loyalty of Eroclea and especially of Cleophila to their melancholy mad father, Meleander, provides one model; the fidelity of the "reduced courtier" Rhetias provides another. The filial virtue of unquestioning obedience by female wards to patriarchal authority is reaffirmed by the nieces in *The Fancies* and by Castanna with her brother-in-law in *The Lady's Trial*. The outstanding counter-example is *'Tis Pity She's a Whore*'s Annabella, who evades and violates her father's desires and moral standards. But she is condemned and repents. Moreover, she obeys her brother; their incest can be interpreted as the tabooed excess of an obedient loyalty to the family praised by Ford's society. In *The Fancies*, for instance, Flavia is troubled most by the disapproval of her brother Romanello.

Perhaps because he was a younger brother from the gentry, Ford's plays are ambiguous about the obedience due from sons. Since Palador's loyalty to his dead father in *The Lover's Melancholy* may be primarily allegiance to his king, Ford's only certain approval of a strict obedience due from sons appears in Daliell's loyalty to his prospective father-in-law Huntley in *Perkin Warbeck*. Though Giovanni infamously defies his father in *'Tis Pity*, such situations rarely arise in Ford. So, perhaps the status of sons and male wards in Ford represents a point of conflict over power among males, where women warrant little consideration. Ford consistently portrays the tests and victories of masculine friendship: Amethus remains more loyal to Menaphon than to his own sister in *The Lover's Melancholy*; Fernando remains loyal to the duke regardless of his love for the duchess in *Love's Sacrifice*; Auria remains loyal despite his old friend's insulting presumption about his wife in *The Lady's Trial*. Among women, however, except for leering nurses or bawds from Morosa in *The Fancies* to Putana in *'Tis Pity* or Shaparoon in *The Queen*, Ford's plays ignore feminine companionship; women remain adjuncts of their men. Maybe these instances confirm the female subjection apparent throughout Ford's plays.

When Ford exalts the virtue of those victims of society who play their assigned roles without examination and with unsurpassed integrity despite heavy penalties, he does not challenge his courtiers' pieties. The absolute dominion of monarchs over subjects, of husbands over wives, of fathers or guardians over daughters and (less likely) over sons, of men and friendship over women and love, remains unquestioned in his works. Moreover, the suffering Ford's heroes and heroines patiently endure often results from loyalty to the court's noble professions as opposed to the courtiers' common practices. Ford's frequent condemnation of the ignoble envy and slander of those who are truly noble unites with his condemnation of ambitious strife over preferment. Ford's cluster of values is embodied in the connotations of his universally recognized mode, a characteristically subdued spectacle notable even among the elaborate stagings of his fellow Caroline professional playwrights for its preeminently formal, ceremonial manner.

Ceremonial Style

At least since Sargeaunt assessed the restrained formality of Ford's verse and Leech appraised the distanced universality and static spatialization of the plays, critics have agreed that Ford polished the refinement characteristic of the Caroline professionals into a ritualistic style. Scholars have identified traits, discovered sources, and analyzed forms which contribute to Ford's singular style—Ornstein's ceremonialism, Stavig's emblematic masque symbolism, Anderson's emotive iconography and pageantry, Neill's moral aestheticism.[28] Like his fellow Carolines, Ford employs situations and roles from the familiar topoi of English dramatic tradition.[29] Ford's paragons of suffering integrity play out their roles as distinctive extensions of a heritage of decorously restrained ceremonies and emblematic masques emulating one line and of formal rhetorical figures, images, and tropes emulating another. Anderson has noted that Ford's manner is not invariably refined.[30] But Ford's alternative style, often scored as a lapse into vulgar comedy, provides the foil for his essential decorum; moreover, his clamor and violence are stylized and ritualistic.

Since Antonin Artaud chose *'Tis Pity She's a Whore* to exemplify his "theater of cruelty" (the formal objectification of compelling, latent human viciousness), the play's ritualistic presentation of horror has seemed paradigmatic.[31] Its foci are three stylized rituals that celebrate an incestuous love affair, a murderous betrayal, and a sacrificial execution: Giovanni and Annabella pledge troth near the opening (I.ii), Hippolita presents a vengeful marriage masque in the late middle (IV.i), and Giovanni makes a grand and bloody entry to the treacherous banquet at the end. To promise sexual fidelity, the brother and sister mirror each other in a ceremony wherein they kneel in mutual obedience, pledge their faith, and kiss twice. As in a wedding, each repeats the formal vow, "On my knees, / Brother [Sister], euen by our [my] Mothers dust, I charge you, / Doe not betray mee to your mirth or hate, / Loue mee, or kill me Brother [Sister]." To avenge the betrayal by her former lover, Hippolita comes to Soranzo and Annabella's wedding feast accompanied by music and *"Ladies in [masks and] white Roabes with Garlands of Willowes."* After the ladies dance she releases Soranzo from any promise, then she pledges the newlyweds with a cup of wine which she poisons and passes to Soranzo; but Vasques, Soranzo's loyal retainer, reveals her crime and his earlier poisoning of the wine, so she utters a death curse. To make a triumphant entry to the final family banquet of mutual destruction, Giovanni impales Annabella's heart on his upthrust dagger.

Throughout his dramatic career Ford seems taken with the ceremonial form of his early masque, or "moral mirror," written with Dekker (licensed 1624). In *The Sun's Darling* Raybright dances a progress through the seasons; distracted by the antimasquers, clown Folly and Lady Humour, he fails to appreciate nature's moderate pleasures. Except for the brief entertainment in *Perkin Warbeck*, Ford continued to employ his masques for dramatic and moral ends, as he did with Hippolita's in *'Tis Pity*. Vengeance and morality are united in the masque in *Love's Sacrifice* wherein three women execute Ferentes for betraying them. By means of Ford's most efficacious masque, Corax cures Palador in *The Lover's Melancholy*. And a reconciliatory masque, featuring representatives from the various estates, makes the conclusion of *The Fancies* festive.

The focal scenes of ritualized horror in *'Tis Pity*, observes Carol C. Rosen, crown a host of language stylizations.[32] One of the most obvious is *'Tis Pity*'s reliance on allusions to *Doctor Faustus*, *Othello*, *The Atheist's Tragedy*, *The Duchess of Malfi*, and particularly *Romeo and Juliet*.[33] *'Tis Pity* presents Ford's star-crossed lovers, from a single home in Parma rather than from rival houses of Verona. In the love scenes Giovanni and Annabella echo Romeo and Juliet's courtly love lyrics through duets and soliloquies; their framing mutual vow and kisses particularly recall the framing pilgrimage and kissing sonnet at Capulet's ball. Moreover, the opening scenes, when Giovanni moons over Annabella before factions of her suitors brawl over her, reverse Shakespeare's opening, and similar extreme oscillations of mood dominate both plays; the bawdy nurse Putana and the well-meaning but failing and fleeing Friar Bonaventura play off Shakespeare's nurse and Friar Lawrence; the recurring challenges to fate and the marriage-deathbed and womb-tomb complex also follow Shakespeare. English dramatic tradition provides both *'Tis Pity*'s setting in a stereotypically hot-blooded Italy and also its revenge tragedy motives and motifs, as Hippolita pursues her vendetta against Soranzo, her husband Richardetto pursues his against both, Soranzo and Vasques pursue Soranzo's against Annabella's unidentified lover, and Grimaldi mistakes his when he waylays Bergetto.

Critics have shown that, true to the professionalism of these Caroline playwrights, Ford conspicuously varied literary precedents in his ceremonial style of noble suffering. From the collaboration with Barnabe Barnes on his first nondramatic work Ford maintained active relations with other authors. He did more than write a long, critically appreciative elegy on John Fletcher[34] and commend John Webster on *The Duchess of Malfi*, Henry Cockram on his dictionary, Ben Jonson, Massinger on *The Roman Actor* and *The Great Duke of Florence*, Brome on *The Northern Lass*, and Shirley on *The Wedding* (Shirley returning the compliment before *Love's Sacrifice*). He wrote his earliest plays with others: *The Witch of Edmonton* with at least Dekker and Rowley, the lost *A Late Murther of the Son upon the Mother* with Dekker, Rowley, and Webster, and *The Sun's Darling* plus two missing plays, *The Fairy Knight* and *The Bristowe Mer-*

chant, with Dekker. In the prologue to *The Lover's Melancholy* he delineated his attitude toward the imitation of sources:

> *Our Writer, for himselfe would haue yee know,*
> *That in his following Sceanes, he doth not owe*
> *To others Fancies, nor hath layne in wait*
> *For any stolne Inuention, from whose height*
> *He might commend his owne, more then the right*
> *A Scholer claimes, may warrant for delight.*

Ford assumes two artistic principles common to the Caroline professionals: an author imitates models, and an author makes the imitation his own.

In his formal ritualistic style Ford both conspicuously follows models and converts them to individual ends.[35] Fletcher's disguises become significant to Ford, as in *The Lover's Melancholy;* so do his mistaken identities and surprising reversals and revelations, as in *The Fancies*. *Richard II* is important for *Perkin Warbeck*, *Othello* for D'Avolos and the Duke in *Love's Sacrifice* and Muretto and Alphonso in *The Queen*. Othello and Iago's importance likely derives from Ford's repetition in *'Tis Pity*, *Love's Sacrifice*, *The Lady's Trial*, *The Queen*, and *The Fancies* of the popular stage situation of a close friend rousing a husband's vengeful wrath. *The Fancies'* Romanello offers the repeated variant of a suspicious brother or presumptuous guardian testing a woman.[36] Maybe because of Ford's predominant revenge structure only *Perkin Warbeck* among Ford's plays is set in England. *The Lover's Melancholy* takes place on Cyprus, *The Broken Heart* in Greece, *The Queen* in Spain; the rest occur in Italy. All present variations on the national stereotypes that abound in Ford's predecessors and that he catalogs in the descriptions of European courts near the opening of *Love's Sacrifice*.

Balanced plotting augments the formal elegance of Ford's stylized traditional topoi. *'Tis Pity* displays a three-level hierarchy in its tragic brother-sister incest plot, its family vengeance plot around Hippolita, and its comico-pathetic wooing and murder plot centered on Bergetto; these interlock complexly through parallel love-hate triangles.[37] Moreover, *'Tis Pity*'s formality is increased by its hierarchy of dramatic and social stereotypes. It presents a familiar collection of vicious personages, starting from the arrogantly rapacious cardinal and descending through Grimaldi, the treacherously ambitious gentleman soldier of fortune; Soranzo, the worldly noble; Bergetto, the loutish suitor and "white boy" nephew of a rich merchant; and Vasques, the gentleman retainer and machiavellian Spanish avenger. Socially lower come several characters with dual roles: a lascivious adulteress and lewd widow to a supposedly dead citizen; a female adviser and bawd; and a sheltered tutor and shattered friar.

Concentrating on *The Lover's Melancholy* but noting triplings in *Love's Sacrifice* and *The Lady's Trial*, Juliet McMaster points out how often and how formulaically Ford returned to the three-level hierarchy of a tragic main plot, a subordinate serious or partly comic plot, and a comic relief plot.[38] *The Fancies* (with a comic main plot), *Perkin Warbeck* (if the treason among Henry's councillors and the antics of Warbeck's entourage are considered plots), and *The Queen* also fit. Just as each example indicates that Ford uses stereotypical characters as foils, so all suggest Ford's dependence on stylized clusters of stereotyped roles, a major consideration in Jeanne A. Roberts's "John Ford's Passionate Abstractions." Ford fills his stage with types, effecting symbolic distance, allegory, ritual. There are state authority figures, such as the two kinds of ideal sovereign represented by Perkin Warbeck and Henry VII. There are eccentric fathers, such as Meleander in *The Lover's Melancholy* and Huntley in *Perkin Warbeck*, who domineer over love-struck adolescent children and wards, threaten and fear jealous wooers and vengeful mates. There are machiavellian Iagos and manipulative bawds. And there are crowds of court apes—presumptuous, sycophantic courtiers and upwardly striving, ineptly ambitious commoners. Moreover, Ford labels more characters and groups than do the other Caroline professionals. In *The Lover's Melancholy* appear the deceased Agenor (wise), Amethus (sober), and Sophronos (reasonable); Parthenophil (lover of chastity), the pseudonym chosen by Eroclea (honored love) with her sister Cleophila (lover of honor); Cuculus (cuckoo) and Grilla (grasshopper). Most casts include some woman labeled for her corruption or imbecility, such as Putana (a variant of whore) in *'Tis Pity*, Shaparoon in *The Queen*, and Morona in *Love's Sacrifice*.

Character labeling relates to the dominant element of Ford's ritualized style—the masquelike artifice when characters set scenes in which others act. Often this involves eavesdropping on comic characters practicing fantasies of social success, as when Cuculus rehearses with his page Grilla disguised as a lady usher in *The Lover's Melancholy*, when Mauruccio rehearses with his servant Giacopo in *Love's Sacrifice*, or when Guzman and Fulgoso plan advances on Amoretta in *The Lady's Trial*. Serious scenes can also take this form; for example, the duke and his sister eavesdrop to entrap the platonic lovers, his wife and favorite, in *Love's Sacrifice*. Significantly, in these instances, as when the duke responds to his sister's pressure to play the avenging Italian husband and lord, Ford's characters self-consciously act out roles. The level of their self-awareness ranges from the public confessions of melancholics (which can be as forthright as Corax's descriptions in his masque at the heart of *The Lover's Melancholy*) to the private glee of Ferentes over his lechery and of D'Avolos over his treachery in *Love's Sacrifice*. Moreover, Ford's scenes often seem formally staged to a degree usually reserved for inset masques. Witness the ritualized sequence of the three messengers who bring Meleander the honors prescribed for his cure at the end of *The Lover's Melancholy* or the trial by combat Muretto stages for the climax of *The Queen* or Ferentes' formulaic rejections of the three women before his fatal masque. Perhaps the most obvious role playing is carried out by the Fancies in Octavo's bower and by Secco in his mocking revenge on Spadone in the barber chair. Self-advertising, masquelike, ritualized role playing and stagings constitute the dominating spectacle of Ford's style. His other characteristics enhance its effects.

In his formalized ceremonials, pointed dramatic allusions, conspicuously elaborate multilevel plots, and stereotypical character clusters, Ford maintained a rigorous decorum of two styles of language. The speech norm of the noble is a restrained and refined, languorously rhythmical, and sparsely but analytically figurative poetry. A range of variations on the noble norm can be illustrated by *'Tis Pity*. Giovanni and Annabella alternate between his conflicted declamations on natural and platonic love and their elevated courtly parlance; meanwhile the friar interjects laments, homilies, and diatribes. All their talk is replete with life-giving images of heart, blood, and sustenance which get rent, spilled, and poisoned. The deviant speech of the ignoble is an indecorous, mimicking, exaggerated, generally bawdy prose. In *'Tis Pity* Putana's vicious bawdry and Bergetto's witless, nonsensical ribaldry provide a foil to the polite decorum and undercut the hypocritically vicious politesse of Parma's elite.

As virtually all critics have realized, Ford, from the early *Christ's Bloody Sweat* on, relied primarily on rhetorical schemes of balance and repetition. These he refined into what are usually designated the languid rhythms and loose parallels of his dramatic verse. Less often remarked is the recurrence in the early poem of affective blood and water imagery and evocative types of Christian sacrifice. Also less noted, until such studies as Anderson's and Kaufmann's, is Ford's use of subdued but sustained images and tropes that emphasize dramatic themes. Finally unnoticed in the early poem is Ford's alternation of speakers and forms of address. These range from a withdrawn narrator, who tells, through a believer, who meditates, to a homilist, who explains significances, draws morals, and directs emotional affects. Just so, Ford's dramatic characters display a wide spectrum of stereotyped roles, which counter and balance each others' styles and conform to social situations.

Mid-twentieth century critics accepted and modified Bradbrook's description of an image-poor Ford style and a "generalized" Ford emotion.[39] Then Thelma N. Greenfield made a more precise analysis of the ritualistic, decorous style employed by Ford's elite.[40] She describes a style that analyzes and explains the actions, reactions, and emotions of characters who earn their labels, that searches ambivalent responses and refines thought and sensibility through qualifying periphrases and ambiguous connections, that employs causative and resultive verbals to modify and make abstract nouns concrete, and that balances short clauses against long ones so as to provide formal yet not schematic rhythms. This Ford style intimates more than it explicates. Ronald Huebert adds to Greenfield's description by emphasizing Ford's employment of catechretic tropes; these embody the dilemmas of characters committed to ideal roles that have to be sacrificed to pragmatic demands.[41] The language of Ford's nobility is infused with their vocation. They perpetually practice courtly arts, play the ideal ceremonial roles and speak the ideal ceremonial lines of a monarch or a warrior, a noble father or husband or lover, a humble and loyal lady. At the same time their ceremonial language embeds its own violation.

The style of noble ceremonial ritual in Ford is relieved by mimicry. Ignoble follies erupt satirically, marking the failures of some characters to achieve enobling formality. Courtly apes such as Cuculus or Mauruccio or Guzman and Fulgoso ineptly imitate their betters in a language of ostentatiously mixed and senseless figures. Guzman's silly love-war troping presents but one of many variations that undercut pretentious preferment seekers. The most vicious of Ford's characters who make nearly legitimate courtly claims is Ferentes, who is marked by his cynicism and demeaning insults. Ford frequently satirizes pretentious commoners through their use of occupational jargons instead of courtly professions. Warbeck's entourage invite ridicule by phrasing their state counsel in the terms of a mercer, a tailor, a scrivener, and a local politico; and Alphonso's followers, a bombast soldier and a pretentious starcaster, consistently undercut themselves. Still more debased are commoners who employ figurative foolishness and bawdy nonsequiturs; such include Bergetto in 'Tis Pity or Morosa and most of her associates in *The Fancies*. The most vicious of these practitioners besmirch the integrity of others, whether by the slander of a Spadone in *The Fancies* or the temptation of a Putana in 'Tis Pity or a Shaparoon in *The Queen*. The mixed figurative nonsense, calculatedly ambitious but inane mimicry, and inept bawdry of the ignoble style sets off Ford's dominant, distinctively noble style of restrained, ceremonial decorum.

No one element nor any sum of elements constituting Ford's ceremonial style segregates it from his fellow Caroline professional playwrights—not his perpetual allusiveness to a dramatic legacy from masters in characterization, situation, and setting; his repeated presentation of remote situations and locales for avenging adultery and enduring suffering; his elaborate, thematically linked, hierarchical plots; his juxtaposition of clusters of dramatically and socially stereotyped roles; his dual lan-

guage of an idealized courtly discourse versus a debased imitative jab-
ber; his focused, sustained image complexes. Rather, what distinguishes
Ford's style is the consistent subduing of each element so that it contributes to the whole, cumulative affect: a decorously exalted, highly formal,
ritualistic tragic suffering. Just as the elements of his style are subordinated to the formal presentation of the tragedy of noble suffering, so
Ford's characters and themes are subordinated to the presentation of a
caste of paragons who maintain their integrity by committing themselves
with unquestioning adherence, despite penalties and suffering, to the
ideal roles assigned them by their society. The social is thus essential to
Ford; both his exemplars and his style exalt the noble society that presses
characters to conform to its rituals. *The Broken Heart* is Ford's quintessen-
tial presentation. Its characters achieve dutiful moral integrity by living
the role of honorable suffering that has been fashioned by their courtly
society, and by employing the ceremonial mode of allusive decorum,
ritualistic action, and stylized language that meets the idealizing predilections of Ford's fit audience.

Ritual Roles in THE BROKEN HEART

Ford signaled his interest in a privileged, especially a noble, audience by
dedicating *The Broken Heart* to Lord Craven, a renowned military commander on the continent. In the prologue he forthrightly describes his
role and end, thereby suggesting his audience's appropriate stance. The
play's title and its Spartan setting imply his serious aim; its lack of low
jesting indicates his disregard for "brothel courts applause" roused from
the "vulgar admiration" of "unchaste ears." He seeks the discriminating
approval of courtiers and barristers. Because he adheres to the heritage of
moral aesthetics he promises the approval of virtue and the castigation of
vice. So his audience "may partake a pity with delight." In his epilogue,
besides characterizing his audience and insinuating their response, Ford
places conditions on them: "Where noble judgments and clear eyes are
fix'd / To grace endeavor, there sits truth not mix'd / With ignorance.
Those censures may command / Belief which talk not till they understand." [42] Because he seeks an understanding, privileged audience who
can discern nobility, Ford shows little interest beyond the most privileged
audience of the best company, the King's Men, at the finest private
playhouse, Blackfriars: "Our writer's aim was in the whole address'd /
Well to deserve of *all*, but please the *best*."

    The interests of Ford's noble audience have led most critics to consider
"true honor" the focus of *The Broken Heart*. Mid-play its "moral authority,"
Tecnicus, royal tutor and interpreter of Apollo's oracle, delivers an oft-
quoted homily. It begins with "Honor consists not in a bare opinion,"

declares that "real honor / Is the reward of virtue, and acquir'd / By justice or by valor," and concludes by assigning a lesson: "I leave thee to the fit consideration / Of what becomes the grace of real honor" (III.i.32-50). Tecnicus counsels the audience as well as his student to contemplate an apparently moral definition of honor.

But the professor proffers so general an exhortation that virtually everyone brought up in Western culture has to agree to its tautology. His argument goes: since honor follows virtuous and just behavior, anyone who seeks greedy or vengeful goals by violating just laws cannot be honorable. One decides whether goals are wrongfully self-seeking and vengeful instead of virtuous and just, and apparently whether or not laws are just, by deciding whether or not they can be rationalized. If they can be they thereby earn sanction as absolute truth rather than as arbitrary opinion and desire. Since any choice can be rationalized, Tecnicus offers any, or every, basis for judgment. The social practice in Ford's plays, however, forbids such anarchic tendencies. Because throughout Ford's plays almost everyone, especially the ones who defy authority, accept suffering as the rightful consequence of violating current norms, Tecnicus's homily upholds the naturalization of traditional authority as the moral norm: obey your monarch, accept your social status unless you are elevated by superiors, and follow your father and other males.

Tecnicus further requires that unquestioned honor be adhered to with courage, despite potentially damaging consequences. If by chance, then, inherited authority makes a mistake or commits a violation, a protagonist can challenge that act. By embracing his or her society's penalties while she or he is verbally defying the society's moral judgment, the protagonist demonstrates a nobler, higher morality. What finally defines morality for Tecnicus is not the rationale for a moral decision. Instead, morality is the commitment to living a given role with integrity, if need be by defying social authority and accepting its penalties.

Thus, critics who approach *The Broken Heart* through the consideration of good and evil end up honoring a character for the very same trait, perceived differently, for which they also blame that character. What they find both culpable and admirable is not the moral stance but the role integrity. In answering the wrong question, an Irving Ribner who finds humanity displaced or a Roger T. Burbridge who senses evil's illusiveness interprets *The Broken Heart* as morally irresolute.[43] In misplacing the problem of evil near the play's center, they create a host of reading problems: Eliot discovers evil inextricably compounded with good; Ornstein condemns Penthea's betrayal by ambition, psychosis, and seduction; Sensabaugh diagnoses "Burtonian love madness"; Stavig reveals "irrational behavior" and inconsistent principles; McDonald ranks characters on a *scala imperfectionis* graded by the degree to which their passions disrupt their reason, their injustices overturn justice, their opinions defeat knowledge; the Kistners report strife over dominance in love.[44]

Peter Ure and Glenn H. Blayney more usefully focus on the social violation closer to the play's center. They place *The Broken Heart* in the historical context of social and literary interest in the miseries of enforced marriage, intensified here by a guardian's refusal to abide by two powerful conventions, the betrothal contract and romantic love.[45] Yet this focus too seems somewhat off center. Penthea's marriage to the jealous Bassanes was neither more nor less arranged than her earlier betrothal to the avenging Orgilus; both were family alliances, the earlier agreed to by her father to stop a feud, the later designed by her brother to gain status. Moreover, Orgilus's insistence on controlling his sister's marriage and her acquiescence lead to the play's only successful marriage, whereas Calantha's freely chosen love match with Ithocles ends in disastrous death. Still, all the characters reiterate that violations of the custom of betrothal have tragic consequences for the lovers, Penthea and Orgilus, for the jealous husband Bassanes, and for the perpetrator, Ithocles.

The imperative here, and of *The Broken Heart* generally, is: *abide by custom.* The characters obey without question the customary hierarchical order. Crotolon, yielding to the king's request to send for his son, makes a representative statement: "Kings may command; their wills / Are laws not to be questioned" (II.ii.29-30). The neighboring prince, Nearchus, reaffirms the mandate when Calantha assumes the crown on her father's death: "Royal lady, / Your law is in your will" (V.iii.15-16). Patriarchs come next, followed by brothers. Penthea's madness and death are manifestly brought on by her strict obedience to the desires of her brother and then her husband. Euphranea tells her beloved that she will marry whomever her father and brother choose. Calantha chooses her own husband only after her father grants the privilege. At the opening Orgilus feels compelled to justify to his father his apparent departure. Later, on hearing that the king favors his sister's marriage to their enemy's close friend, he takes the sole near-exception to the established order in the play:

> His will [the king] hath,
> But were it lawful to hold plea against
> The power of greatness, not the reason, haply
> Such undershrubs as subjects sometimes might
> Borrow of nature justice, to inform
> That license sovereignty holds without check
> Over a meek obedience.   [III.iv.2-7]

The brevity and lack of force in this demur indicate the power of social sanction in *The Broken Heart*. The only permissible disobedience is passive and vocal—complaint registered in compliance.

Attempts to advance in status are also forbidden. Ithocles's former drive for rank, wealth, and power now grieves him, humbles him before his accusers, compels him to try penitently to compensate those he surpassed, and so distorts his love for Calantha that his sister Penthea has to reassure the princess that it is not "ambition." Moreover, social climbing is satirized in the brief plot's bumptious and presumptuous curriers of favor. Hemophil and Groneas are ridiculed for ineptly miming the manners and the military, political, and personal courtship of their betters (particularly in the triumphal return [I.ii.106ff]). Whatever promotion for merit is allowable gets granted by superiors. Thus, Orgilus's half-concealed accusation when the princess Calantha chooses Ithocles for her husband (IV.iii.105-9).

The Broken Heart's setting, ancient Sparta, more than suggests a society that militantly demands a rigid code of citizen obedience.[46] Spartan society so dominates as to disallow any protagonist and, as Leech has shown, commands its nobles to obey its code.[47] For many critics, including both Sensabaugh and Stavig, custom bears the blame for the tragedy. For others, impressed by the pervasive references to oracles or the unfathomable quality of events, the responsibility devolves on fate.[48] But any conclusive judgment about the final dominion of custom or fate cannot be answered from what is within the play. For the play focuses on another issue: the characters' universally unexamined commitment to playing out their assigned roles with integrity, regardless of the personal consequences.[49] Ford effectively denies the miraculous charity of social accommodation that underlies Massinger's tragicomedy of reformation. He exalts the admirable undeviating commitment of playing absolute roles seemingly destined for tragedy. The self-awareness of playing such roles and the anguish of fulfilling them seem just as inevitably presented through decorously stylized, fatalistically ritualized social ceremonies.

As Massinger's *The Picture* exemplifies a moderating symbolic interaction theory of personality maintenance, so Ford's *The Broken Heart* exemplifies an extreme functional theory of ritual ceremony, of the sort outlined by sociologist Émile Durkheim and corroborated by anthropologist Marcel Mauss. The play suggests a secular extension of Durkheim's functional analysis of sacred ritual in Book III of *The Elementary Forms of the Religious Life: A Study in Religious Sociology.* Herein Durkheim argues that ritual, or ceremony, performs negative cult functions of inculcating discipline (training members in abnegation, self-denial, obedience to a cult's prohibitions and constraints) and positive cult functions of promoting social cohesion, revitalization, and euphoria. Two points seem particularly important for Durkheim's overall theory and Ford's ceremonial forms. First, "In all [of "the religious life" 's] forms, its object is to raise man above himself and to make him lead a life superior to that which he would lead, if he followed only his own individual whims: beliefs express this life in representations; rites organize it and regulate its working." This would seem to describe accurately the workings of both characters and ceremonies in Ford, if Durkheim's rituals are viewed as secular. Second, "before all, rites are means by which the social group reaffirms itself periodically."[50] Extension beyond the sacred, as confirmed by Mauss's studies of the opposite pole of magic, leads to the conclusion that rituals perform these functions for a whole society or some subgroup of a society, without any need for Durkheim's teleology (or his and Ford's transcendental values).[51] So sociologists have substituted for Durkheim's terms "negative cult," "positive cult," and "religion," the more general terms, "social rule," "social life," and "society."[52]

Ford had before him both promotional practices that substantiate Durkheim's theory and witnesses who perceived the same effects from those practices that Durkheim saw. The progresses, pageants, and masques of the Tudor and Stuart monarchs and other bodies that represented the elite have spawned numerous interpretations of their usefulness in motivating and directing community allegiance, ideals, norms, and policies.[53] Moreover, a spectrum ranging from practitioners such as King Charles and Archbishop Laud to astute observers such as John Selden realized that popular ceremonies could prove helpful in containing community disorder, reinforcing and promulgating communal standards, and supporting policies.[54]

The Broken Heart focuses on ceremonials that define and sustain identities and communities. Moreover, its characters make a commitment to roles and to rituals that is all the more conspicuous because of a dual self-awareness: they perfect and their audiences appreciate performances. The play's first scene, in which Orgilus lies to his father Crotolon about leaving Athens, begins by outlining family roles. But at Euphranea's entrance, the necessary exposition of the family's relationships becomes instead an insistence on their roles. Crotolon introduces Euphranea as Orgilus's sister. She then designates her brother. And Orgilus replies: "Euphranea, thus upon thy cheeks I print / A brother's kiss . . . in presence of our father / I must prefer a suit to 'ee." She responds, "You may style it, / My brother, a command" (I.i.86-91). Such a presentation reinforces the ideal decorum of obedience in a hierarchical family. The second scene, Ithocles' triumphant return, ostentatiously attends to role performance. When the harbinger arrives the princess Calantha does not inquire about the army's welfare; instead she wants to hear "How doth the youthful general demean / His actions in these fortunes?" (I.ii.33-34). The answer by Ithocles' best friend, Prophilus, is soon corroborated by Ithocles: he "thinks but 'twas his duty" to serve his country (I.ii.47, 97-98). As each dignitary speaks, he partly sets relationships: Armostes is an uncle, Crotolon a public spokesman. Mainly each insistently describes his or her role. The sequence reaches a formal climax when Calantha declares to the conqueror that "I myself, with mine own hands, have wrought / To crown thy temples this provincial garland" (I.ii.65-66). Then both Ithocles and king Amyclas laud her dutifully exemplary role playing: "Y'are a royal maid." "She is in all our daughter." The scene dissolves amid the comic ineptitudes of Ithocles' retinue trying to resume their roles at court after playing others in camp.

These first two scenes set a pattern of self-aware role playing and appreciative audience response that is sustained throughout *The Broken Heart*. The acutely self-conscious Calantha plays her role flawlessly; and the title honors her performance. Whatever the cicumstance she never forgets she is the heir apparent who represents ideal Spartan society. Moreover, she leads the admiration of performances given by others, such as the crown prince of Argos, Nearchus, who has come to negotiate a marital and political alliance:

> CALANTHA.   Princely sir,
> So well you know how to profess observance
> That you instruct your hearers to become
> Practitioners in duty, of which number
> I'll study to be chief.   [III.iii.21-25]

Calantha not only proves aware of her royalty; she makes her auditors aware of it. When Penthea woos Calantha for her brother Ithocles, they conclude with a display of keen sensitivity to the roles of loyal princess and obedient sister: "You have forgot, Penthea, / How still I have a father." "But remember / I am a sister" (III.v.103-5). Calantha proves her magnificence by the way she plays her greatest scene. She does not break off the formal dance despite the succession of messages that reveal the deaths of her father by age, of Penthea by starvation, and of her betrothed Ithocles by the vengeful Orgilus. After all three deaths have been announced to the assembly and Calantha, having sentenced Orgilus to die, has swept out regally, the rest admire her performance. "'Tis strange these tragedies should never touch on / Her female pity." At the same time they recognize that her duty to office is not unique in kind but heroically exemplary: "She has a masculine spirit. / And wherefore should I pule . . . . Let's be all toughness / Without distinction betwixt sex and sex" (V.ii.94-98). So Penthea's bereft husband. And so Calantha sustains her magnificent performance through the concluding ceremonies (the dedication of her coronation, the negotiation of an alliance of succession with Nearchus, the funeral of Ithocles, and her marriage to Ithocles) before her heartstrings at last unravel from their initial rupture at the news of the triple deaths.

Just as witnesses admire Calantha's exemplary role playing, so the central characters esteem each other precisely for maintaining role integrity. Penthea sets her pathetic role simply and effectively by echoing a biblical term that signifies womanly obedience. Her first lines reply to her enforced husband's repeated offer of splendid clothing to impress a courtly audience: "Alas my lord, this language to your handmaid / Sounds as would music to the deaf. I need / No braveries . . . . my attires / Shall suit the inward fashion of my mind . . . . I am no mistress" (II.i.91-107). For designating her role as a handmaid and rejecting one as a mistress she is approved by her husband. For sustaining it she is applauded by all.

Penthea submits to a lord so extreme in his role of jealous husband that his introduction (II.i) alludes to Corvino imprisoning and threatening Celia in *Volpone.* Bassanes is intent on barring Penthea from a role of adulterous wife. He overacts until others label him a Jonson "humour" (II.iii.135, III.ii.136ff); then he overmeddles with his servants' roles. Beyond scorning his histrionics ("You dote, / You are beside yourself"), Penthea's guardian also warns him, "teach not me my trade; I know my cue" (II.i.149-52). Bassanes is compelled to play his humor because he is torn between two parts; his public asseverations at court of the joys of being a husband versus his private fantasies at home of being a cuckold provide poignant satire. He is the one character in the play admired for changing his role, as he turns from raving "cuckold in conceit" to penitent supplicant: "And wherein I have heretofore been faulty / Let your constructions mildly pass it over. / Henceforth I'll study reformation" (IV.ii.10-12). His conversion comes too late to save his wife from going mad and starving herself to death. And her mad role leads to the noblest commitments to roles by her forbidden lover Orgilus and her brother Ithocles.

Orgilus's execution of Ithocles (by trapping him in the "engine" and stabbing him to death in front of Penthea's seated corpse) and Orgilus's execution of himself (by letting his own blood in front of the assembled court) provide a dual testament to committed role playing. Each character is admired by his audience for acting out his role with consummate integrity. Ithocles, when he realizes that Orgilus's vengeance is not so treacherous as sacrificial, meets execution with extraordinary courage:

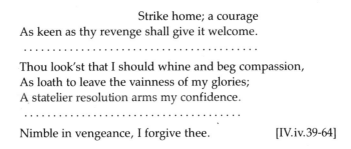

> Strike home; a courage
> As keen as thy revenge shall give it welcome.
> . . . .
> Thou look'st that I should whine and beg compassion,
> As loath to leave the vainness of my glories;
> A statelier resolution arms my confidence.
> . . . .
> Nimble in vengeance, I forgive thee.   [IV.iv.39-64]

In Orgilus's estimation Ithocles flawlessly gives up his life in payment to righteous retribution for his former ambitions, which destroyed his sister. As early in his performance he expresses appreciation for Orgilus's dedication to the role of avenger, so in the end he wins honor from Orgilus:

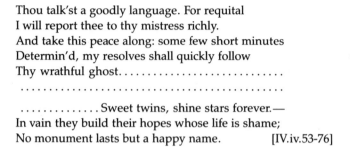

> Thou talk'st a goodly language. For requital
> I will report thee to thy mistress richly.
> And take this peace along: some few short minutes
> Determin'd, my resolves shall quickly follow
> Thy wrathful ghost. . . . .
> . . . .
>
> . . . . Sweet twins, shine stars forever.—
> In vain they build their hopes whose life is shame;
> No monument lasts but a happy name.   [IV.iv.53-76]

After these nobles admire each other's performance, Orgilus proceeds to self-accusation and suicide, fulfilling his role before an awestruck audience.

At court Orgilus honors his victim and himself. By his account Ithocles had been "butcher'd, had not bravery / Of an undaunted spirit, conquering terror, / Proclaim'd his last act triumph over ruin" [V.ii.41-43]. Afterward, opening his vein, he directs his audience to applaud his own performance:

> If a proneness
> Or custom in my nature, from my cradle,
> Had been inclin'd to fierce and eager bloodshed,
> A coward guilt, hid in a coward quaking,
> Would have betray'd fame to ignoble flight
> And vagabond pursuit of dreadful safety.
> But look upon my steadiness.   [V.ii.112-18]

The Spartan court admires with awe. "Desperate courage!" "Honorable infamy!"

The potent affect produced by the dedicated role-players in *The Broken Heart* derives only in part from their paying the ultimate external penalty. It derives mainly from the internal penalty exacted during their struggles to maintain full commitment to ideal roles despite their other drives. Euphranea poses everyone's dilemma when she has to answer, before her family can approve it, a marriage proposal from Prophilus, the worthy whom she loves yet the best friend of her family's nemesis, Ithocles: "What can you look for / In answer to your noble protestations, / From an unskillful maid, but language suited / To a divided mind?" (I.iii.64-67). Both her eavesdropping brother Orgilus and the audience anticipate Euphranea's promise: total commitment to her obedient role. Though she loves Prophilus, Euphranea remains steadfast to marrying only with her father's and brother's consent. The pathos of *The Broken Heart* derives from the agonies characters endure as a result of dedicating themselves to roles. So does the admiring wonder they earn.

Orgilus and Penthea suffer the most rending roles in the play. Orgilus's split occurs mainly near the opening, Penthea's mainly near the end. At the beginning Orgilus faces role conflicts in meeting the world and in committing himself. The rationale he offers his father for going away (to relieve Bassanes of jealousy, to release Penthea from confinement, and to free himself of sorrow) is not inaccurate, nor is his hiding at home instead maliciously dishonest. But his disguise so as to spy on "Penthea's usage and Euphranea's faith" indicates to Tecnicus a dangerous duplicity:

> This change
> Of habit, and disguise in outward view,
> Hides not the secrets of thy soul within thee
> From [the stars'] quick-piercing eyes, which dive at all times
> Down to thy thoughts. In thy aspect I note
> A consequence of danger.   [I.iii.2-7]

Orgilus himself confesses to a disastrous internal fissure, the "unsettled mind" of an incurable "lover's wound." Since his love for Penthea can be manifested in many ways, physical or spiritual, conciliatory or vindictive, he must learn more about the role she chooses before he can commit himself to anything further. Their poignant garden conference determines his future role.

Because Penthea does not see through Orgilus's disguise in scholars' robes, she considers his praise of the communion of lovers' souls a learned abstraction. When his lament for a "divided heart" calls to her mind her own afflictions, she asks and then commands him to leave. When instead he disrobes, she warns that her role forbids him the role of her physical lover:

> Rash man, thou layest
> A blemish on mine honor with the hazard
> Of thy too desperate life. Yet I profess,
> By all the laws of ceremonious wedlock,
> I have not given admittance to one thought
> Of female change since cruelty enforc'd
> Divorce betwixt my body and my heart.   [II.iii.51-57]

Her accusation and oath seal her command. Her blame requires that if he loves her he must not violate her role; and her oath calls on the wedding ritual that includes her vow to fulfil that role, however enforced. When he claims the rights of their sanctifying betrothal, she responds with signs of love but requires that he resume his disguise before she explains why she lives up to the role forced on her. Thus Orgilus is sundered in a role psychologically and physically closest and furthest from Penthea when she declares that, despite her love, she "never shall nor will" be "wife to Orgilus" because another has possessed her "virgin dowry," the physical sign of her integrity. To enforce her all-or-nothing commitment Penthea banishes Orgilus from her presence. In doing so she compels him, looking "not like the ruins of his youth, / But like the ruins of those ruins" (II.iii.129-30), to intensify his duplicitous role. To integrate his will and deeds he becomes an avenger. Though his tutor and his father are appeased by his deceptive truce with Ithocles, Tecnicus fears violence from Orgilus, and Crotolon diagnoses an "Infection of [Orgilus's] mind" (III.iv.44). Both react to the inner division revealed in Orgilus's commitment to the stage-honored tradition of a revenger's concealing duplicity. This split he endures until he has witnessed Penthea's dissolution under the burdens of her role as dutiful wife and sister.

Penthea's inner rift issues from the impossible goal of becoming reconciled to her assigned role as the obedient wife to Bassanes and sister to Ithocles, despite their violation of her betrothal to her beloved Orgilus. After Orgilus leaves, she and her husband vow to make independent pilgrimages to death. Bassanes can then begin to give over bestial, doting envy and resume his role as a sound Spartan councillor, albeit one owing a lifetime of penitent service.

It is much harder to repair the family rift caused when Ithocles, to further his patriarchal ambitions, commanded Penthea's rending role. When he laments that "We had one father, in one womb took life / Were brought up twins together, yet have liv'd / At distance," she accuses him of forfeiting his right to invoke patriarchy by "forfeiting the last will of the dead, / From whom you had your being" (III.ii.34-36, 41-42). But even though she demands retribution for his violation of her betrothal and her integrity, she accepts his contrite confession of guilt and grants her sisterly support of his unpromising courtship of princess Calantha. Penthea restores Ithocles by mending the family tree: "being children, but two branches / Of one stock, 'tis not fit we should divide" (III.ii.112-13). While he occasionally reverts to his adolescent arrogant folly and viprous ambition, he regains control of his role through doing penance for his past and seeking alliances for his future. But Penthea's role of handmaid to her brother and her husband, in violation of her bond with her beloved, tears her until she comes apart in a scene that recalls Ophelia and the literary tradition of prophetic truth being uttered in madness: she predicts her death, bewails her barrenness, accuses Ithocles of cruelty and Bassanes of jealousy, declares her love for Orgilus, mourns his distraction, and finally sees her role exploded. For Penthea wholeness comes through suicidal starvation.

What finally proves the importance of the integrity but rarely the happiness of roles is Calantha's performance. She neither falters nor needs to reform. Nonetheless she must endure the anguish of her part. Implicating her society of not a little sexism, she describes her duty's burden:

> Now tell me, you whose loyalties pays tribute
> To us your lawful sovereign, how unskillful
> Your duties or obedience is, to render
> Subjection to the scepter of a virgin,
> Who have been ever fortunate in princes
> Of masculine and stirring composition.
> A woman has enough to govern wisely
> Her own demeanors, passions, and divisions.
> A nation warlike and inur'd to practice
> Of policy and labor cannot brook
> A feminine authority.   [V.iii.2-12]

She carries on by negotiating with Nearchus of Argos for Sparta's sovereignty when he succeeds to the crown; only then can she carry out her posthumous ring exchange with Ithocles and allow her heart to fragment, unable to bear her role any longer. Bassanes' elegiac eulogy invokes a social interpretation: "Her heart is broke indeed. O, royal maid, would thou hadst miss'd this part; / Yet 'twas a brave one."

The listing of "THE SPEAKERS' NAMES" before *The Broken Heart* makes explicit the thematic and formal centrality of integrity in role playing. For as this heading puts it, characters' names have been "fitted to their qualities." Greenfield has observed that the fit comes not from abstract humors or typical traits, but rather from "states of being evolving from action and situation."[55] That is, the characters gain their identities by the ways in which they perform their roles in their social relations. Except for functionaries, a Christalla *"Crystal"* and a Philema *"Kiss"* or a Hemophil *"Glutton"* and a Groneas *"Tavern-haunter,"* characters earn their names. The uncle Armostes' mediation as *"an Appeaser"* and the father Crotolon's *"Noise"* designate the roles councillor of the state and head of a clan. The central characters become their roles. Ithocles reforms from an arrogant arriviste into the *"Honor of Loveliness"* as Calantha grows into the *"Flower of Beauty."* Orgilus waxes *"Angry"* because of Penthea's *"Complaint,"* which results from Ithocles' erstwhile ambition and Bassanes' jealous *"Vexation."*

The sole consummation of love is signalled when Prophilus is *"Dear"* to both Ithocles and Orgilus's sister Euphranea, *"Joy."*

The interlock of cliques and the complex plotting in *The Broken Heart* make apparent that identities in the play are created through the characters' dedication to situating and performing their social roles. A little arbitrarily, stereotypical characters can be distributed in hierarchical clusters representing national politics around Amyclas (*"common to the kings of Laconia"*), courtly society around Calantha and Ithocles, and household service around Bassanes.[56] Character groups can also be juxtaposed in terms of whether they impede or aid loving couples. Ithocles and Bassanes block Orgilus from Penthea; in contrast Nearchus temporarily hinders Ithocles and Calantha but finally helps Amyclas further their romance; similarly Orgilus blocks then blesses Prophilus and Euphranea while Armostes, Crotolon, and Ithocles advance their match. The distinction between impediments and aids to love could serve to layer the plots. Either the first or the second plot would be primary, the other secondary, the third contextual. Intermittent comic underplotting also integrates the aspiring courtiers in Ithocles' entourage, the witty maids of honor in Calantha's, and the miming commoners in Bassanes' household. Such demarcations reveal not only *The Broken Heart*'s complex cohesion but also its extensive overlaps. Thus they suggest that the play focuses not on analogies between the stereotypes and the several plots but instead on characters playing the roles that make them. Their highly disciplined, ceremonial society inculcates and appreciates above all the commitment to roles despite suffering and the performance of roles in a decorous, ritualized manner. For the committed, stylized performance of courtly roles molds the noble integrity that Ford extolled and his elite audience applauded.

The masquelike namings and intricate coherence of *The Broken Heart* indicate the formal ritualistic stylization that most distinguishes Ford's tragedy of suffering from the plays of the other Caroline professionals. And that ceremonial spectacle powerfully reinforces and exalts the society's role requirements. The importance granted ceremonies in *The Broken Heart* is obvious from the reiteration of references to Ithocles' initial violation of Orgilus and Penthea's betrothal.[57] And the extent of ceremonial in the play is extraordinary. Besides scenes representing ceremonies, there are scenes that become ritualistic through dramatic allusions and reworkings of settings, actions, and gestures; there are interpolated songs that sustain and celebrate emotion; and there are refrainlike references to Delphic oracles. Moreover, the incidence and duration of these ritualistic elements increase markedly from early in the third act. Then Orgilus commits himself to action by resuming his identity, Penthea becomes increasingly torn by the demands of her beloved and her brother and her enforced husband, Nearchus arrives to complicate Ithocles' and Calantha's courtship, the king hears the prophecies, and the first song wafts across the stage.

Flourishes announce the first two ceremonies, the triumph honoring the Spartan troops (I.ii.51) and its mirror, the marital and political negotiations between Sparta and Argos (III.iii). More significant is the private ceremony that opens the wooing of Calantha (III.v) just after Crotolon and Orgilus bless Prophilus and Euphranea's betrothal "till a greater ceremony perfect" it (III.iv). Penthea's last will and testament to Calantha becomes a ritual through triplings. After renouncing youthful enjoyment of the three "vanities" of beauty, pomp, and sensuousness, Penthea makes three bequests: she petitions her executrix to distribute her youth to chaste and faithful women, to render her fame to history, and to receive her brother Ithocles "in holiest rites of love." This leads to the ceremonial betrothal of Calantha and Ithocles (IV.iii.47-97), which is announced during the celebration of Prophilus and Euphranea's nuptial preparations. At the end of the procession of the three messengers of death during the next-to-last ceremony of the play, this couple's wedding dance, Calantha proclaims the paramount importance of ceremonial:

> 'tis, methinks, a rare presumption
> In any who prefers our lawful pleasures
> Before their own sour censure, to interrupt
> The custom of this ceremony bluntly.   [V.ii.24-27]

The final scene of *The Broken Heart* brings together the earlier ceremonies that shape society's roles. It comprises a cumulative ritual of Calantha's coronation dedication, her delivery of the treaty that guarantees Sparta's future with her testament that installs its political hierarchy, her marriage to Ithocles' corpse, and her initiation of her own last rites. Ceremonies of passage for body politic and microcosm, for union and separation, are synthesized in this culminating reinforcement of social roles. Incorporated too are a ritualistic funeral hymn and an oracular fulfilment.

Until this climax, ritualized performances—which allude to stage traditions, elaborate on gestures, and repeat settings and actions—achieve greater formality than do ceremonies. The simplest of these techniques is the use of dramatic allusions to heighten scenes. The threats that Orgilus makes as he eavesdrops on Prophilus and Euphranea's somewhat stichomythic garden wooing evoke the threats Bel-imperia's brother Lorenzo and Horatio's rival Balthazar make as they watch the stylized garden wooing of Horatio and Bel-imperia in *The Spanish Tragedy;* and the way pathetic, fragmented Penthea passes out blessings echoes the way sad, mad Ophelia passes out flowers. The paramount value of

ceremonious decorum in custom-laden gestures is foregrounded in Ithocles' and Nearchus's contention over Calantha's ring. When Calantha
tosses the ring to Ithocles, the suitors insist on the significance of this
"cheap" "toy." Ithocles, offering it to her on his knees, challenges her
trailing "spaniel"; Nearchus and his royal retainers upbraid the "mushroom" for presumption. Their vehement argument issues in accusations
of lack of breeding and manners atop violations of decorum and status;
these in turn almost provoke challenges to a duel (IV.i.20-116). In exhorting Ithocles, Orgilus clarifies what is at stake in a courtly society that
demands and scrutinizes the due observation of the manners, perquisites, and other signs of status that fashion its members' roles: "In point of
honor / Discretion knows no bounds" (IV.i.105-6). But so formal and
public a forum functions as well to curb aberrant excesses in role performance. So, when Nearchus returns as the messenger of Calantha's love, he
reestablishes regal prudence and restores ceremonial pomp (IV.ii.181ff).

Ritualistic devices reinforce and elaborate on characters' roles
through variations played out in ritualized scenes. Ford often juxtaposes
ceremonies in contrasting moods. The festive dance celebrating Euphranea and Prophilus's marriage accedes to the sobering triple messages of
death that give way to Orgilus's horrifying suicide-execution (V.ii). He also
pairs off rituals. The penultimate scene's dissolution of a marriage in
death adumbrates the final scene's synthesis of both rites of passage.
"New marry[ing] him whose wife I am" and preparing to die, Calantha
remembers when she threw Ithocles her ring: "Bear witness all, / I put
my mother's wedding ring upon / [Ithocles'] finger" (V.iii.63-66).

As Anderson has shown, Ford's central ritualizations insistently re-
cycle sets, props, and gestures.[58] One begins with the role pledge when
Penthea grasps Orgilus's hand, kisses it, and kneels to him, a sequence
Orgilus imitates (II.iii.64-67). When they repeat the actions (without
kneeling) in front of her husband and brother, the ritual confirms Penthea's disintegration before it erupts in Orgilus's flight (IV.ii.110-33).
Another ceremony knots the roles of brother, handmaid, and beloved
mid-play and unties them after Penthea's death. At their reconciliation
Ithocles and Penthea draw their chairs closer together at his request and
again at her agreement (III.ii.33-117). In death, brother and sister are
drawn closer still since Orgilus puts a coffin seat for Penthea between his
seat of judgment and Ithocles' chair of execution (IV.iv). As this setting
provides the closing frame for two roles, it also provides the opening
frame for the ceremony ending Orgilus's role. Attended by Bassanes and
an admiring court, Orgilus lets his blood with the same dagger he used to
kill Ithocles, presumably seated in another chair of execution (V.ii.99-157).
Such ritualistic observances initiate, form, and dissolve the roles and the
identities dedicated to them. And they reinforce the response of woe and
wonder characters earn from spectators on stage and off.

Four songs deepen the ceremonials of loss in this play scored for trumpet flourishes, incidental music, dances, and dirges. The first soft, mysteriously sourceless song is heard by the companions arranging Ithocles and Penthea's reconciliation. Yet it opens with allusions to Ithocles' violation of his sister's betrothal to Orgilus. Its three initial couplets pose a series of rhetorical questions: "Can you" represent or calculate or analyze the impossible, or "rob a virgin's honor chastely" (III.ii.6)? But these deeds, which are declared impossible with "No, O, No," can sooner be achieved than "Beauty's beauty" can be expressed. So in its close the song emphasizes Ithocles' compound violation of his sister's role. It thereby underscores both the role of family patriarch and the role that earns his name, "Honor of Loveliness." Sister and brother echo the song's burden in the rest of the scene. The second song introduces notes of apparent resolution through roles and ceremonies. In front of gathered attendants Orgilus sings a bridal blessing for his sister Euphranea and Prophilus (III.iv.70). His song petitions custom-honored rewards (comfort and love, peace and plenty, "fruitful issue") in perpetuity; its rimes and images repeat the theme of "lasting," "increasing," "never ceasing," "fruitful," "budding," and "spring." But the promise of ceremonial suture for roles other than husband and wife for "Dear" and "Joy" is evanescent. The third song, immediately following Ithocles' and Orgilus's apparent reconciliation, removes any tone of resolution. Floating from Penthea's rooms, it announces her dissolution, which severs the men's potential friendship and brings them together only in death. Beginning with negation, *"O no more, no more,"* ending with love and love's martyrs *"ever, ever dying,"* it intertwines *nos* and *dies* because of the disintegration of Penthea's role and the end of the roles of avenger and martyr (IV.iii.142-52). *The Broken Heart's* final song provides a choral summary as Calantha dies. It recalls that nothing of value lasts unless the mind that embraces it is *"not untroubled."* The doubled negation indicates that all things, crowns, beauty, worldly honors—are transient except for the integrity of formal, suffering role playing.

If *The Broken Heart's* songs are melancholy, its oracles are dire. While optimistic interpretations are available, the hopes seem false in the offering. Just before the first song and just after Orgilus shucks his master and his disguise, Armostes delivers oracles newly arrived from "Delphos" to Tecnicus. This "grave man" is needed to interpret the message of the "seal'd box," "the health of Sparta, the king's life, / Sinews and safety of the commonwealth" (III.i.61-67). The coffin of the king's two bodies bodes such ills that Tecnicus's divination is delivered in fragments; before his national prophecies reach the council, Tecnicus segments his personal warnings. Fleeing, he warns Ithocles (*"When youth is ripe and age from time doth part, / The lifeless trunk shall wed the broken heart"*) and Orgilus (*"Let craft with courtesy a while confer, / Revenge proves its own executioner"*)

(IV.i.117-43). When Armostes receives the prediction he recognizes that "we might construe / [Tecnicus's] words to fatal sense" (IV.i.144-45); he would thus agree with the brooding young men. But instead he and Crotolon evade the obvious reading of Apollo's oracle for Sparta (the plot), the king (the stock), and the princess (the grape):

> *The plot in which the vine takes root*
> *Begins to dry from head to foot;*
> *The stock soon withering, want of sap*
> *Doth cause to quail the budding grape.*
> *But from the neighboring elm a dew*
> *Shall drop and feed the plot anew.*   [IV.iii.11-16]

Eager to reassure the king, the councillors claim that Amyclas wrongly predicts his own death and Calantha's. They offer a comforting but palpable misconstrual.

Before events fulfill the king's forebodings, Bassanes' meditations on fate and Apollo (V.i.1ff), Orgilus's recollections at his suicide (V.ii.145-47), and Armostes' remarks on Calantha's death (V.iii.98-101) keep recalling the prophecies of disaster. Reiterations of the oracle's images reecho ominously through *The Broken Heart*'s role-playing ceremonies, allusive ritualized situations, and concluding songs. They reinforce Ford's stylized tragedy of suffering by which characters create themselves and their fates, exhibiting from one perspective the pathetic failures that follow from compulsions to play absolute roles unquestioningly and from another the admirable achievements that issue from dedication to roles integrating identities.

As *The Broken Heart* is marked by ever greater pressure on increasingly restricted role playing, so Ford's style is unique among the Caroline professional playwrights for its compression of ritualistic ceremony and linguistic decorum. Greenfield's sensitivity to Ford's stylization supplies an entry into the ritually formal language Ford created to portray the dignified, integrated roles that constitute his elite society. She begins with Brian Morris's articulation of the traditional critical impression of Ford's distinctively wrought "periphrastic manner" and rarefied abstraction: a mode of dignified "direct utterance," violated occasionally by shocking outbursts, signals the "ornate good manners" of an aristocratic sensibility.[59] She then describes Ford's formal, analytic speeches: in extensions sometimes mistaken for repetitive tautologies, these speeches delineate links of causation and propose alternatives that qualify and refine. Greenfield does not describe the ritualism derived in part from patterns of triplets that are related to the prominent triplets in Ford's ceremonial scenes. These triplets—which, for example, form Orgilus's summation of the reasons for his "voluntary exile" (I.i.76-82), his list of reasons for reappearing (III.i.12-21), his conditions for Bassanes' oath (V.i.29-57), and his salutation of the dead before his suicide (V.ii.136-39)—accumulate until they endow the analyses with an incantatory quality that reaffirms determinism and reinforces roles.

Another extension of Greenfield's description follows the fact that most of the periphrastic passages appear early in *The Broken Heart*, while Ford's fusions of concrete to universal, which she persuasively describes as rendering his style elevated and abstract, dominate toward the end. The reiterations that refine points, the causative verbals that modify generalizations, and the increase of elisions become possible later because of the context established in earlier extended analyses. Thus even her example of a grammatical and semantic ambiguity in Bassanes' recollection ("I have seal'd a covenant with sadness, / And enter'd into bonds without condition / To stand these tempests calmly" [V.ii.62-64]) is more usefully considered a radical compression. Its context has been set by Bassanes' pledges in the immediately preceding scene. He has made a vow to himself and to the gods to suffer in patience, and he has promised Orgilus to practice obedient patience. Moreover, these pledges reiterate his conversion soliloquy (IV.ii.34-39). As Greenfield may imply by concluding with Ford's crystalizing ceremonies, Ford's style builds incrementally through the ritualistic incantatory repetition of images, ideas, patterns of discourse, and themes. His style thus represents the same kind of accretion that, through the repetition of gestures, language, attitudes, actions and reactions, forms identity, especially in nobly committed, integrated role playing.

Ford's style is epitomized in the incantational variation of image clusters that, toward the end of *The Broken Heart*, are condensed into abstract yet moving paradoxes, oxymora, and catechreses.[60] This element seems behind Eliot's well-known comment that Ford wrote his best lines for a lunatic unfettered by any need for relevance or sense: "The quite irrelevant and apparently meaningless lines '*Remember, / When we last gathered roses in the garden, / I found my wits; but truly you lost yours.*' are perhaps the purest poetry to be found in the whole of Ford's writings."[61] Actually, Penthea's mad lines to distraught Orgilus derive their very beauty and power from a relevance and a sense that have been refined through ritual repetition. At their previous garden meeting Orgilus threw off his disguise to claim his role as Penthea's betrothed, and she, despite her love, compelled him to assume the role of a platonic lover because she had surrendered herself to the role of a faithful wife, however enforced. By the time these lines are uttered, this role and the one of reconciled sister have given her means to establish integrity; but they have also constrained her to madness and starvation. By the time these lines are uttered, Orgilus has committed himself fully to the role of avenger; but to maintain that role he has had to assume duplicitous guises that are undermining his integrity and will finally betray him into self-execution. By the time these lines are uttered, both are near the end of their dedication to the integrated roles that are their glory and disaster. Penthea's lines, then, project and condense the clarifications of her reconstituted sanity and Orgilus's mounting madness. Their poetic power derives from uncommon relevance and deep sense compressed by formal, ritual repetitions into a simple, elegant image and utterance.

The most potent creation of *The Broken Heart* is the compressed imagery that delineates Ford's central characters. Critics universally note the imagery associated with Ithocles' apparent change, particularly in his soliloquy before the reconciliation with Penthea and in his attendants' criticism after the altercation with Nearchus. Birds and gods soaring to heights emblemize his old ambition, while plunging to oblivion describes his new contrition. Orgilus cuts Ithocles down from the "lord ascendant / Of [Calantha's] devotions" to the *"lifeless trunk"* sacrificed to Penthea (IV.ii.200-201). Critics also note Bassanes' projection of a world of wanton females, lecherous males, and mulish servants. From his opening tirades through his distracted interruption of his wife and brother-in-law's reconciliation, this self-perceived horned beast supplies the play's harshest language. Bassanes' vow to reform is pervaded by images of conversion:

> Men, endow'd with reason, and the use
> Of reason, to distinguish from the chaff
> Of abject scarcity the quintessence,
> Soul, and elixir of the earth's abundance,
> The treasures of the sea, the air, nay, heaven,
> Repining at these glories of creation,
> Are verier beasts than beasts. And of those beasts
> The worst am I: I who was made a monarch
> Of what a heart could wish for, a chaste wife.   [IV.ii.22-30]

The most powerful of Ford's characterizing images derive from gradual compression through ritualistic repetition into fusions of ruptures, such as Calantha's broken heart. Several rent emblems begin in a torn dialogue that initiates not only the images but also the incantatory repetitions that progressively crystallize them. Typically these images get mentioned, then analyzed, and finally condensed. When Orgilus speaks to Penthea about the harmony between lovers' souls, the holiness of innocence, and the glories of beauty, he employs the aureate Petrarchisms of Aplotes (*"Simplicity"*) that suggest the play's dominant flawed images:

the broken heart, the dishonored wife/desecrated temple, and the insub-
stantial banquet. Penthea cannot parse his "troublesome" "school terms"
and needs him to "Set [his] wits in a less wild proportion." His terms
seem empty until the accretion of repetitions and analogies grants them
meaning. It is yet too soon for Penthea to recognize herself as a "white
table of unguilty faith" on which "Time can never . . . Write counterfeit
dishonor" or to imagine her transformation into a violated temple, her
eyes dropping incense at Vesta's altar (II.iii.25-33). Nor can she fathom
Orgilus's figurative fatal banquet until it is implicated with the sundered
heart and associated with the violated betrothal:

> All pleasures are but mere imagination,
> Feeding the hungry appetite with steam
> And sight of banquet, whilst the body pines,
> Not relishing the real taste of food.
> Such is the leanness of a heart divided
> From intercourse of troth-contracted loves;
> No horror should deface that precious figure
> Seal'd with the lively stamp of equal souls.   [II.iii.34-41]

As with much unsituated and therefore apparently meaningless discourse, this gains coherence and cohesion as Penthea begins to derive a
context, empathize with the speaker, and identify him. Likewise, as the
paradoxes of rendering are chanted through the play, the images gather
significance. This passage only initiates the image complex which
through ritual accretion becomes *"The lifeless trunk shall wed the broken
heart"* and *"The stock soon withering, want of sap / Doth cause to quail the
budding grape."*

Similar ritualistic accretions refine the image cluster that Penthea
chooses for herself. Countering Orgilus's "rash" claim if not her society's
misogynistic presumption of female inconstancy, Penthea asserts her
marital fidelity in images that will emblemize her: "I have not given
admittance to one thought / Of female change since cruelty enforc'd /
Divorce betwixt my body and my heart" (II.iii.55-57). She continues
describing the "rape done on my truth" when Ithocles violated her earlier
betrothal, her "virgin dowry . . . ravish'd by" her enforced husband.
Later she compounds the image when she explains that Ithocles has made
her "A spotted whore. . . . For she that's wife to Orgilus and lives / In
known adultery with Bassanes / Is at best a whore" (III.ii.70-75). The
raped wife complex, which embodies the rupture in Penthea's role,
reappears in her accusation of her brother and her husband, who have
"Widow'd [her] by a lawless marriage," "strumpeted" her name, corrupted her blood, and compounded her "noble shame" with "mixtures of

pollution" (IV.ii.146-50). Because of her inner rift she refuses to "taste of sustenance." Further implications in Penthea's image complex also get compressed and refined through chanted references to correlative images. Moreover, the central image complex is overlaid by another of virtually divine integrity. She is, for Orgilus, Ithocles, Bassanes, and perhaps herself, the violated inviolate shrine of the play's first song. Orgilus describes her as a "shrine of beauty" and a "heaven of perfections" subjected to the "barbarous thralldom" of a possessive husband (I.i.49-65). Bassanes repents having to "redeem a sacrilege so impious" as brutishly trying "to pull down / That temple built for adoration only, / And level't in the dust of causeless scandal" (IV.ii.31-34). And Ithocles repents martyring a deity: "Wrong'd maids / And married wives shall to thy hallowed shrine / Offer their orisons" (III.ii.82-85). He becomes the sacrifice on the altar he mistakes for a throne when Orgilus, Penthea's priest, severs his trunk in the engine.

Orgilus's image as the cloaked avenger is the most obvious one in the play. His split role derives from a cold, "straying heart" bled empty of life, whose "every drop / Of blood" Penthea madly calls "an amethyst, / Which married bachelors hang in their ears" (IV.ii.129-31). Tecnicus first discerns that Orgilus, *"Angry"* over being barred from his role of lover, has donned ever more treacherous disguises, put away his old "borrowed shape," a "shadow," so as to "fly upon / A new-hatched execution." He has "Shrouded unlawful plots" (III.i.4-10). The tutor's pun on disguising describes Orgilus's perfidious role-playing as a shroud; in that role Orgilus's sacrificial execution of Ithocles and his retributive self-execution end their roles. This image complex is pressed through verbal and visual repetition into the oracle's condensed yet analytic *"Let craft with courtesy a while confer, / Revenge proves its own executioner."*

Ford's ritualized, incantatory style begins with abstract, periphrastic analyses of causation and response, accumulates through intensifying repetitions, and compresses until ruptures of paradox become catechreses of sundering. This characteristic style comes to seem an inevitable medium for *The Broken Heart*. It maintains Ford's expressive decorum of masquelike namings and character groupings that are elegantly plotted through ceremonial situations and acts. All these together provide more than a means of presenting characters who create roles of suffering integrity that ennoble them. Together these provide as well the means whereby a courtly society creates its identity and its noble members theirs by playing out roles so dedicated to maintaining individuality and achieving glorious self-assertion that the noblest embrace penalties of disastrous suffering and destruction. *The Broken Heart* constitutes a tragedy imaged by a flawed crystal. Formed under extreme pressure, then cut and re-polished until it gains iridescence, it shatters. Just so, the roles to which the play's characters conform harden under a noble society's pressures and within its refining rituals until the characters achieve purified, elegant integrity and flawed, woeful self-destruction.

By the same irony Ford, the Caroline professional playwright who most insists on the essential selves of his characters, most often insists on the destruction of his characters. In his lack of reconciling accommodation he differs greatly from his fellow senior, Massinger; and in his adherence to old ideals instead of new experiments he differs most from his junior, Brome. Though like his junior, Shirley, in calling for courtly ideals, unlike Shirley, whose characters are rewarded for playing appropriate roles, Ford presents characters broken for trying to live the roles others profess but evade.

4

Shirley's Social Comedy
of Adaptation to Degree

Shirley's Reverence for Degree

"I never affected the ways of flattery: some say I have lost my preferment, by not practising that Court sin." [1] So claimed Shirley in 1639, finally dedicating his second play and first tragedy, *The Maid's Revenge* (1626), *"come late to the impression."* This oft-noted asseveration was made by a poet-playwright who could make some claim to privilege (far more than Brome, perhaps more than Massinger, distinctly less than Ford), enough to display a coat of arms. One wondrous season, 1633-34, he was identified as a gentleman, a member of Gray's Inn, and "one of the Valets of the Chamber of Queen Henrietta Maria"; he championed the court's interest in drama against William Prynne's diatribe, *Histriomastix*; he enjoyed the applause of the Master of the Revels when *The Young Admiral* was licensed and that of the king when the play was presented at the regal birthday celebration; with premier architect Inigo Jones and foremost composers William Lawes and Simon Ives he was commissioned by the inns of court to produce a lavish masque, *The Triumph of Peace*, in reconciliatory praise of and diplomatic advice to the monarch; and he based *The Gamester* on a plot supplied by the laudatory Charles I. He must have been considered a likely successor to aging laureate Ben Jonson. Instead it was William Davenant who was graced with "her majesty's servant" on title pages after *The Temple of Love* (1635), who produced the regal masques and the "state poem" *Madagascar* (1638) with its complement of commendations by courtiers, who maintained close relations with amateur courtly dramatists and was appointed theater manager by the crown, who was granted an annual pension of £100 and virtual laureateship by his royal master in December of 1638, and who was knighted. So it has been surmised that Shirley, by reflecting contemporary mores and personages in such amiably satiric plays as *The Humourous Courtier* (1631) and *The Ball* (1632) and by joining the Irish theater from 1636 until he came to the King's Men in 1640, parted ways with palace corruption and refused to seek court preferment. [2] This hypothesis fits neither some important dates nor the contour of Shirley's career. His career exhibits consistent veneration of degree and of court; it appears to have been a quest for courtly approval and support unmatched by any other Caroline professional playwright.

According to sketchy accounts, Shirley was prepared to pursue contacts among the courtly gentry and nobility. Born in 1596 to a middling London family, he was educated at the Merchant Taylors' School, perhaps a while at Oxford, and at St. Catherine's Cambridge. After his brief service as the pastor and schoolmaster at St. Alban's in Hertfordshire, in 1625 he began writing about two plays per year until the closing of the theaters in 1642. Then he served the royalist cause. Afterward he printed a volume of poetry (1646) and produced an occasional commendatory poem, preface, or school interlude; mainly, however, he resumed teaching (he wrote two elementary grammars) until he died in 1666.[3]

Many worthies to whom Shirley offered dedications or who commended him remain but tentatively identifiable beyond the status of esquire, knight, baronet, captain, barrister he assigned to them. At times initials, names, or abbreviations which duplicate those of identifiable social, poetic, or dramatic associates may conceal other people. Often those identified are barely characterized by their family heritages or their offices. Even so, enough is known to establish Shirley's pattern of esteeming and seeking preferment from those who were well placed. Indeed, in his 1652 dedication of *The Sisters* (1642) to one "MOST WORTHILY HONOURED" William Paulet, Esq., he laments that *"COMPOSITIONS of this nature have heretofore been graced by the acceptance and protection of the greatest nobility, (I may say princes;) but in this age, when the scene of dramatic poetry is changed into a wilderness, it is hard to find a patron to a legitimate muse."* "[i]n this unequal condition of the time" the fortunes of many of his nation's betters have sunk beneath even the fortunes of poets. Fortunate worthies were more plentiful during Shirley's rise through the later 1620s and early 1630s. His elegies addressed the relatives and friends bereft by the deaths of Lord Abergavenny's eldest son, Sir John Beaumont's son, and the Viscount Savage; his verses praised the second Earl of Essex's daughter, portrayed the ideal beauty of the Countess of Ormonde, and blessed the marriage of the Earl of Thenot's daughter.

Shirley found noble dedicatees for many plays. One notable addressee was the wealthy, influential privy councillor Francis, the Earl of Rutland, a great grandson of Sir Philip Sidney; his protection Shirley begged in 1630 for *The Grateful* (or *Faithful*) *Servant* (1629). Another was George Lord Berkley, known for his learning as well as for his noble birth; to him Shirley offered the 1637 printing of *The Young Admiral* (1633). Abraham Wright, an Anglican divine who kept a notebook on Caroline productions, astutely observed more than the fact that *The Grateful Servant* has a "plot well contriued and smooth" and verses typically "full of complement": "I beeleeue [it was] purposely so studied by him for to take ye court."[4] Whether or not *The Young Admiral* was also designed to woo the court, Wright considered it "A very good play, both for lines and plot, ye last beeing excellent," and a modish one.

Shirley's efforts to win recognition from the elite were exceptionally well received. On licensing *The Young Admiral* for production, on 3 July 1633 the Master of the Revels, Sir Henry Herbert, praised the tragicomedy "for the improvement of the quality, which hath received some brushings of late. When Mr. Sherley hath read this approbation, I know it will encourage him to pursue this beneficial and cleanly way of poetry, and when other poetts heare and see his good success, I am confident they will imitate the original for their own credit, and make such copies in this harmless way, as shall speak them masters in their art, at the first sight, to all judicious spectators." Helping to assure the play's success, Herbert arranged for its presentation as part of the birthday celebration for Charles I; both the king and the queen liked it.[5] Later that season, on 6 February 1634, Charles found *The Gamester* "the best play he had seen for seven years." His approbation is scarcely surprising since this comedy elaborated "a plot of the king's, given [Shirley] by mee" (Sir Henry Herbert).[6] Shirley's works were also heralded by amateur courtly poets and playwrights bonded by their pursuit of advancement. Besides earning Massinger's commendation, *The Grateful Servant* gained the praise of William Habington, the acclaimed author of the *Castara* volume and *The Queen of Aragon*, an accomplished tragedy sumptuously mounted at Whitehall; of Thomas Randolph, a son of Ben whose plays won success at his university, Cambridge, and at court; and of Robert Stapylton, a playwright later knighted for loyalty to his king. Among the many commenders of *The Wedding* (played and printed in 1629) were Habington, Ford, the "king's poet" and playwright Thomas May, and a host of lesser would-be courtiers.

The climax of Shirley's wondrous season was the lavish production of *The Triumph of Peace*. This masque was presented by all the inns of court at Whitehall Banqueting House on the Duke of York's birthday, 3 February 1634, and again on the king's command at the Merchant Taylors' Hall on 13 February.[7] Its initial presentation was virtually mandated when Charles suggested that an "outward and splendid visible testimony of a Royal Masque" would demonstrate the legal establishment's loyal "affections" despite the infamous *"Vtter-Barrester of* Lincolnes Inne" who dedicated *Histriomastix* to the "4 famous Innes of Court." William Prynne's polemic must have seemed to be directed against the offended royal couple as well as against the stage. At least the Star Chamber condemned the Puritan for defaming the queen and her ladies in waiting, who in 1632 had taken roles in Walter Montague's trend-setting *The Shepherds' Paradise*. Because of Shirley's popularity with the benchers he was a likely choice to invent the masque. And he had positioned himself well by attacking Prynne in a commendatory poem for Ford's *Love's Sacrifice* and by sarcastically dedicating *The Bird in a Cage* (1633) to the prisoner in the Tower, before the Star Chamber issued its savage sentence.

Probably because the London theaters were closed, Shirley next joined the Master of the Revels for Dublin, John Ogilby, in trying to establish an Irish stage. This post was conspicuously involved with noble patronage. The impresario and the playwright tried to place dramatic productions at the center of a court culture surrounding the Earl of Strafford and Lord Deputy of Ireland, Sir Thomas Wentworth. Shirley honored his putative elite audience with poems and offerings. In 1638, for example, he dedicated *The Royal Master* (1637) to the Earl of Kildare, the most highly esteemed lord of Ireland. A host of commenders, apparently Irish as well as English and including Ogilby, graced this play's opening pages. And Shirley's special New Year's epilogue extolled Charles, the royal master of the realm, and Charles's most powerful lord, the *"never enough Honoured"* Strafford, the patron for whom Shirley and Ogilby produced *The Royal Master.* It was Strafford whom Shirley commemorated for recovering from dysentery and gout in 1640, and it was Strafford's son whom Shirley chose for the dedication of the "Never Acted" *The Court Secret* when it was printed in 1653. Shirley courted and exhorted the Irish gentry and nobility in the prologues to eight plays by others (including Fletcher, Jonson, and Middleton) that were produced while he was there. Once again begging a larger audience of elite patrons, he vents his frustrations and proclaims his hopes in "A Prologue there to the *Irish Gent,"* addressing the gentry and nobility as well as naming the play. He opens frustrated about the failure of his hope that literature civilizes:

> We know at first, what black and generall curse
> Fell on the earth; but shall this Isle be worse?
> While others are repair'd, and grow refin'd
> By Arts, shall this onely to weeds be kinde?
> Let it not prove a storie of your time,
> And told abroad to staine this promising Clime,
> That wit, and soule-enriching Poesie,
> Transported hither must like Serpents dye.

Then he renews his hope of refining the manners of the isle through the small number of nobility who appreciate his stage:

> But truce Poetic rage, and let not what
> Concernes the Countrey, fall upon a spot
> Of it, a few here met to see a Play:
> All these are innocent; the better they
> To tell this fault abroad, that there may be,
> Some repaire done to injur'd Poesie.
>> Then we may grow, and this place by your raies,
>> Cherish'd, may turne into a Grove of Bayes.

In 1640, when Shirley returned to London as Massinger's successor with the King's Men he found theaters emptier than when he had left. Potential English audiences seemed as unappreciative as the Irish he had chastised in prologues to *The Toy* or *The Generall* for having "sickly . . . Palats" apter to pay for hobby horses than "Wits sacrifice." His puns on the dread "vacation" of the theaters and his esteem for the vanishing appreciative nobility were noted by at least two patrons, particularly after the closing of the theaters. In 1635 Shirley had dedicated *The Traitor* (1631) to William Cavendish, the Earl of Newcastle, whose *"general knowledge and excellent nature, both an ornament to your blood . . . [made him] the rare and justified example to our age."* This exemplary patron of Jonson, of Ford, and of Brome as well as of Shirley was apparently seen by these different playwrights with different eyes. For Shirley, as well perhaps as for Ford, Cavendish appeared as the nostalgic model of Elizabethan knighthood.[8] During the early 1640s Shirley served in the royal forces under the command of this "great Preserver of the King / And your owne honour." Shirley's brief ode eulogizes Newcastle for literary creation as well as for patriotism. According to Anthony à Wood, "Our author Shirley did also much assist his generous patron William duke of Newcastle in the composure of certain plays, which the duke afterwards published."[9] Shirley's patron in the mid-1640s was young Thomas Stanley, who apparently supported a coterie of budding poet/scholars around Shirley.[10] Besides the epithalamion for Stanley's wedding in 1648, Shirley contributed an appreciative verse commendation to Stanley's edition of "elegant" poems in 1647. In 1652 he dedicated *The Brothers* (1641) to Stanley in *"memory and contemplation of good offices received . . . [and] the greatness and number [of] favours"* which obliged his service. In "On a black Ribband" Shirley took the risk of commending Stanley's flaunted loyalty to the recaptured Charles; so Stanley's favors must have included uncommon moral and political as well as financial support.[11]

Through and beyond his dramatic career Shirley sought recognition and patronage from the gentry and the nobility. He did not seek them in vain, but won an elite audience. This fact has been accentuated by frequent quotation of the prologue to his public theater production in London of a play written for the private theater in Dublin under the title *Rosania, or Loves Victory* (1638?). *"A Prologue at the* Globe *to his Comedy call'd* The Doubtfull Heire, *which should have been presented at the* Black-Friers" opens,

> Gentlemen, I am onely sent to say
> Our Author did not calculate his Play,
> For this Meridian; The Bank-side he knowes
> Is far more skilful at the ebbes and flowes
> Of Water then of Wit.

It goes on to ask this public house audience o elevate their expectations above slapstick and bawdry and to conduct themselves with the decorum of the elite, "As you were now in the *Black-Friers* pit." More pointed than comments in previous years, these lines represent a late, dark mood.

Though Shirley's audience disappointed him from time to time, it had been drawn from the privileged caste ever since his first play. Before he moved to Ireland, all but one of his plays were produced at the Cock-pit or Phoenix, a "private House in Drury Lane," by Queen Henrietta's Men. Such a production was second in prestige only to the King's Men at Blackfriars. Moreover, the single exception, *The Changes, or Love in a Maze* (1632), "was presented at the Private House in Salisbury Court, by the Company of His Majesties Revels," the third among the elite theaters. In Ireland James Shirley "Gent." tried to help create a courtly theater modeled on the elite companies in London; this goal accounts for much of his didactic approach to that audience. And on his return to London he assumed the post of playwright to the King's Men. There he designed his plays, according to their title pages, exclusively for Blackfriars.

Perhaps tinged bitter, Shirley's late assessment of the genteel, noble, even royal audience he wooed and won seems accurate. He, of all the Caroline professional playwrights, most definitively severs his plays and their privileged audience from the despised crowd who came to demand the blameworthy plays which deserved the 1642 ban: *"Though the severity of the times took away those dramatic recreations, (whose language so much glorified the English scene,) and perhaps looking at some abuses of the common theatres, which were not so happily purged from scurrility and under-wit, (the only entertainment of vulgar capacities,) they have outed the more noble and ingenious actions of the eminent stages."* The *"many lovers of this exiled poesy left, who are great masters of reason, and that dare conscientiously own this musical part of human learning, when it is presented without the stains of impudence and profanation"* include the honorable Walter Moyle, esq., to whom Shirley dedicated *The Politician* (1639?) in 1655. In retirement Shirley continued to seek the elite patronage he had courted from the beginning of his dramatic career, that courtship which Abraham Wright astutely discerned. And their traditional sociopolitical values he, most like Ford among the Caroline professionals, extolled in his plays.

Degree's Prerogatives, Abuses, and Standards

Rendering tribute in his introduction of the 1647 Beaumont and Fletcher folio, Shirley identified his social ends with those of fellow playwrights who valued drama for teaching by pleasing. Primarily he shows a predilection for modeling behavior. First he commends the social perspicacity of any dramatist, *"there being required in him a* Soule miraculously *knowing, and conversing with all mankind, inabling him to expresse not onely the Phlegme and folly* of thick-skin'd men, *but the strength and maturity* of the wise, *the Aire and insinuations of the* Court, *the discipline and Resolution of the Soldier, the Vertues and passions of every noble condition, nay the councells and characters of the greatest Princes."* [12] Praising the dramatist for universal empathy, Shirley acknowledges a task of correction but emphasizes the task of exemplification. So he spotlights the model behavior of the elite who most deserve to be imitated: the prudent members of martial, courtly, noble, and regal circles. The renowned dramatic collaborators are monumental for all ages and supreme among all literatures because *"the Authentick witt that made Blackfriars an Academy, where the three howers spectacle, while* Beaumont *and* Fletcher *were presented, were usually of more advantage to the hopefull young Heire then a costly, dangerous forraigne Travell."*

Shirley concludes this paragraph by combining his two primary concerns—drama's pleasurable presentation of exemplary noble behavior and drama's didactic potency: *"it cannot be denied but that the young spirits of the Time, whose birth & quality made them impatient of the sowrer wayes of education, have from the attentive hearing these pieces, got ground in point of wit and carriage of the most severely-employed Students, while these Recreations were digested into Rules, and the very Pleasure did edifie. How many passable discoursing dining witts stand yet in good credit upon the bare stock of two or three of these single Scenes."* Drama provides an alluring conduct book for gentlemen and ladies. Its crucial task is to represent effectively and so teach the elite how to model their behavior on courtly values and roles.

Only Shirley among the Caroline professional playwrights claims to mentor his privileged audience by delightful examples. His prologue to the Irish *Rosania* promises that "Not the least rude uncivill Language shall / Approach your ear, or make one cheek look pale" (27-28), a promise of "clean wit" he reiterates before *The Doubtfull Heire*, the play's London title. The prologue to *The Imposture* (1640, printed 1653) likewise pledges that no ladies will have to "wrinckle now that fair / Smooth Alablaster of your brow, no fright / Shall strike chast eares, or dye the harmless white / Of any cheek with blushes" (24-27). In this characteristically gentle satire he abides by the promise he made before the rougher *The Duke's Mistress* (1636, printed 1638), to chasten general errors and to cure. Rarely did Shirley commit himself so explicitly as when he labeled *The Example* (1634, printed 1637), a traditional didactic drama that presents genteel social behavior; yet his prologues imply and his plays reflect just such a commitment.

Shirley's contemporary reputation indicates that his declarations reflect a career-long goal of teaching civility. When Thomas May commended *The Wedding* for exalted passions and harmless mirth, delight for the soul as well as the eye, he recognized Shirley's commitment to a drama that depicts courtly manners. Commending the same play, William Habington initiates a virtual refrain about the chasteness of Shirley's Muse; the innocence and devotion of his verse oppose the "Atheisticke Rimes" of the rude contingent of courtiers. In honoring *The Grateful Servant* John Hall sings anew about Shirley's chaste Muse on a stage and in a society abused by malicious art. Maybe the most telling, surely the most memorable, testimony is Massinger's commendation of *The Grateful Servant*. Protesting his own reasoned moderation, Massinger honors Shirley's clear verse and social responsibility. In the play can be found

> no beleeu'd defence
> To strengthen the bold atheists insolence,
> No obscene sillable, that may compell
> A blush from a chast maide, but all so well
> Exprest and orderd, as wise men must say
> It is a gratefull Poem, a good play.   [17-22]

Grace and goodness seem to describe Shirley's civic didacticism and his civil style.

Perhaps a commitment to present the exemplars of his elite society caused Shirley to set over half his comedies, and only his comedies, in England but generally to place his troubled tragicomedies and tragedies in Italy. For comedies can especially reflect models for gentry and nobility while they criticize the flawed and the fraud. Perhaps such a commitment helps explain why in his comedies Shirley is prone to present the social institutions of the English elite, *The School of Compliment*, *The Ball*, the spring races at *Hyde Park*. Surely his commitment is largely responsible for the conventional sociopolitical stances he presents. Like Ford he promotes hierarchical status empowered by ascription, but he does not display the rigid idealism that typifies Ford's characteristic tragedy. Rather Shirley's plays present felicitous adaptations of strictly defined, privileged roles within a virtually unchallengeable elite hierarchy that exalts royalism, ascribed sociopolitical status, paternalism, and male dominion. His plays further exemplify social responsibilities as well as prerogatives within that structure, so that two groups fall to his censure: upstarts incapable of meeting his standard and failures unwilling to abide by it. At their most interesting his plays present elite role models that incorporate admirable variations on strict norms of noble behavior; they thereby allow adaptations in incidental matters as they ridicule the failures of adherence to polite norms.

Shirley affirmed absolute royal will as law. His military service for the king, his steadfast loyalty to the Wentworths and Stanley, and his risk of the 1646 publication of "On a black Ribband," which proclaims royalist loyalty and exhorts support of a forlorn Charles, seem incontrovertible evidence. His assumption of monarchical absolutism so pervades his plays and diction as to be unquestionable.[13] His first monarch is a Duke of Savoy whom all the exemplary society of *The Grateful Servant* strive to please. The self-sacrificing love of the title character, who disappears so his lady can marry their prince, is gauged by the rule that a prince commands all the allegiance and all the love of all his subjects. From *Love's Cruelty* (1631) to *The Court Secret* (unacted) statements reaffirm the divine right of monarchs; monarchs command fidelity because a loyalty to hierarchy appears as the only alternative to sociopolitical disarray. The principle holds despite weak and vacillating rulers, like the yielding king in the tragicomic *The Young Admiral*, or rulers misled by machiavels, like princes in the tragedies, *The Traitor* and *The Politician*, or the tragicomedies, *The Royal Master* and *The Imposture*. Usually Shirley's corrupted monarchs get rehabilitated while their magistrates get blamed. The pattern of aberration followed by restoration is exemplified in *The Duke's Mistress*. In this tragicomedy a monarch forsakes his faithful wife to pursue an infatuation until, before its consummation, he is reconverted.[14]

While Shirley's support of the right of royal will is unimpeachable, his works can suggest a melioration of absolutism that might seem like Massinger's reforming accommodation. An instance of the questioning they invite is evident in interpretations of *The Triumph of Peace*. Charles attested to his pleasure with the masque when he made the rare command for its second performance. Yet Bulstrode Whitelocke provides a historical foundation for a different evaluation. So Orgel can judge that the masque is "diplomatically but unequivocally critical of royal policy" that elevated rex over lex, and Sharpe can decide that the entertainment is " 'a successful vehicle for critical opinion' " about court practices. Their inferences follow from the masque's setting (a peace piazza), its presentation of the king's commoners in the antimasques, and its explanation of the necessity of Eunomia (Law) for Irene (Peace). Only after the union of Eunomia and Irene does Dice (Justice) join them: since "The world shall give prerogative to neither. / We cannot flourish but together" (560-61).[15] But there remains evidence for the contrary view, that the masque concludes favorably for Charles. The peace celebrated is attributed to Charles. Moreover, allusions in the antimasques promote Charles's policies of prohibiting the gentry from residing in London and of limiting their control over local affairs; the allusions also lend support to his grants of monopolies. So Lawrence Venuti can conclude, primarily from references in the antimasques, that the masque favors rex over lex and that it approves Charles's isolation and alarmist repression of political disgruntlement among some of the elite.[16]

These opposed stances of critique and approval of Charles's policies allow the opportunity to suggest mediation. So Martin Butler can deduce, mostly from the sociopolitical context of the performance, that the masque lauds Charles's reforms and finds common ground for agreement between Charles's advisers and the disaffected elite, mainly on Charles's turf.[17] Contention over *The Triumph of Peace* forms an interpretive paradigm of Shirley's political stance: he stands steadfast, foremost and finally, in favor of the prerogatives of royal will; but in between he shuffles so as to permit limited alleviation and to warn against the abuse of power. Sometimes a critic may discover in Shirley a reminder that kingship is based on upholding justice.[18] But Shirley's monarchs rarely need reminding; generally they are just by definition. Shirley's plays often reaffirm monarchical rights, along with the prerogatives of degree, when they reveal the concealed royal and noble bloodlines of characters whose behavior has confirmed rightful, i.e. inherited or ascribed, status.

The popular Caroline motif that bloodlines, like murder, will out recurs prominently through Shirley's plays. Pervasive in his later dramatic career, this theme first appears as a central motif in *The Coronation* (1635). This tragicomedy juxtaposes a machiavellian guardian's wrongful attempt to usurp an adolescent queen's power and a born prince's inalienable right to seize absolute rule despite his apparently lower station. All the characters, honoring Sophia's rights as God's representative, are preoccupied with attending to the well-being of their queen and thus of the body politic. But the discovery of the inherent regal rights of others establishes irresistible new allegiances. Since royalty will unto royalty, when Sophia chooses a noble husband she instinctively picks one of her unrecognized brothers, Demetrius. Then Seleucus's overweening rebellion is legitimized as he turns out to be the prime prince of the realm, Leonatus. He expounds to his newfound siblings,

> there were seeds
> Scatterd upon my heart, that made it swell
> With thought of Empire, Princes, I see cannot
> Be totally eclipst, but wherefore stayes
> *Demetrius*, and *Sophia*, at whose names
> A gentle spirit walk'd upon my blood.
> . . . .
> Nature has rectifi'd in me *Demetrius*,
> The wandrings of ambition.   [V.iii/537-38]

Shirley's ascription of absolute royal prerogatives to nature, here through Seleucus/Leonatus, recurs emphatically. Years before the start of his prince-and-pauper tale, *The Gentleman of Venice*, a wetnurse to the duke of Venice exchanged her son and the prince. Her Thomazo remains a lecherous, debauched rebel by nature despite his palatial nurture whereas Roberto proves regal by making the palace garden a court and by fighting nobly. The subplot confirms the importance of blood degree; it presents an impotent noble desperately trying to compel a paragon of courtiers to beget an heir for him so he can save his family line from the polluting succession of a dissolute nephew.[19] Characters from late in Shirley's career are often revealed by their deeds as either noble or peasant by birth well before their origins are corroborated by testimony: such include the regal presence of Ferdinand in *The Doubtful Heir,* the comeuppance of the vain, boorish "older sister" in *The Sisters* (1642), and the royal match of the discernible albeit concealed prince in *The Court Secret* (unperformed).

While the assumption of absolute royal prerogatives pervades his plays and the theme of bloodlines telling recurs throughout them, Shirley's plays pay special heed to the manners that identify the elite and degrade the presumptuous. Although all the Caroline professional playwrights are noteworthy for their attentiveness to manners and social codes, the degree of Shirley's preoccupation distinguishes him. Nor can such an interest be easily dismissed as an index of shallow decadence. Martin Butler has recently pressed the minority opinion advanced by such earlier scholars as Douglas Sedge and Richard Morton: significant political comments are embedded in social codes.[20] Moreover, social scientists have increasingly set forth the ways by which political and moral principles are created, enforced, and modified by social behavior. The roles played by Shirley's characters create their personalities, social types praiseworthy and blameworthy on the basis of moral and political principles that sustain and are sustained by types and society.

Shirley's plays exhibit a particular preoccupation with interactions between members of different estates, a preoccupation bracketed by a brief morality he wrote early in his dramatic career and expanded much later, perhaps after his dramatic career was over. *A Contention for Honour and Riches* was published in 1633; the augmented *Mammon and Honoria* appeared in 1658. In *A Contention* two pairs of suitors, representing estates and professions, vie for two ladies, Honour and Riches. Clod, a country gentleman whose native resources and bluff loyalty lay a foundation for the body politic, and Gettings, a citizen merchant whose business builds on that foundation, pursue Lady Riches; meanwhile a Courtier and a Soldier court Lady Honour. After self-promotions that eulogize the ideals and scoffs that satirize the failings of society's strata, Gettings wins Riches; but Ingenuity, a scholar, gains Lady Honour because she believes that he unites martial valor and courtly polish. In this interlude the betrothals seem to reconcile the strife between rival estates.

Mammon and Honoria expands *A Contention* by presenting a vision of what the commonweal might become if members of the estates played their given roles to perfection. Shirley's revisions emphasize citizen and country cowardice, isolate and banish other destructive elements in the society, and idealize the potential of the courtier, the officer, and the scholar. The didact's fantasy still grants Lady Honoria to the scholar, Alworth. But the merchant, Fulbank, surrenders Lady Mammon to Colonel Conquest. The problems Citizen Fulbank stores for the nation appear as well in his country counterpart, Maslin. The word *maslin*, a medley of grains, suggests the country gentleman's push toward strife over differences as well as his pull toward generous community. Martial braggadochio and waste are now laid to a Captain Squanderbag. Two other new characters show how a commonwealth can be damaged by selfishness. Phantasm, Lady Mammon's gentleman usher, creates false expectations for the representative of each estate, disabuses him, then vanishes. Traverse, a lawyer, exacerbates and manages others' contentions for his own ends before he repents at having caused strife and promotes justice. In contrast, Lady Honoria praises Alamode's potential as a statesman who considers only the nation's prosperity, Conquest's promise as a guardian who defends the nation's achievements, and Alworth's achievement as a self-sacrificing if affected visionary who proclaims an ideal body politic in which each estate plays its part dutifully. Shirley's second version follows his typical resolution whereby military valor and courtly manner put upstarts in their proper places. In the comic plot of *The Doubtful Heir,* for example, a captain abuses and disciplines citizens as a courtier explains their rightful roles.

Shirley's principle—that the hierarchy's stratified roles, prerogatives, and duties deserve reverence—can be misconstrued as Massinger's accommodation. For it allows some variation, criticizes abuses, and sounds genial. But Shirley permits scant individuality within a rigid structure; characters who counter the system get marked as climbers. *The Ball* (1632) provides an instructive example, since it is cited to support claims that Shirley became critical of the Caroline court.[21] At one time this social satire identified some courtiers recognizably enough to earn Henry Herbert's censorship: "In the play of *The Ball*, written by Sherley, and acted by the Queens players, ther were divers personated so naturally, both of lords and others of the court, that I took it ill, and would have forbidden the play, but that Biston promiste many things which I found faulte withall should be left out."[22] *The Ball* roused enough interest that in *The Lady of Pleasure* Sir Thomas Bornwell can chastise his wife for so indulging in this faddish, reputedly promiscuous "subscription dance" that its playwright had to be "brib'd to a modest / Expression of your Anticke gambolls in't, / [lest] Some darkes had beene discover'd, and the deeds too" (I.i.124-26).[23]

This comedy defends the innocence of balls. It portrays a coterie who enjoy the pleasures of chaste love as celebrated in a final masque in honor of Diana with Venus. Moreover, this comedy explains away the ill repute of balls as envious slander-mongering, represented by the play's principal satirist. The aptly named Barker, masqued as a Satyr, decides to "traduce / Your Ball" when he gets rejected by Lady Honoria for thinking that she is loose-hilted instead of "loose-witted" (flirtatious). The play satirizes, in interlinked sets of fortune hunters, common stage butts adapted to the aspiring gentry who swirled round the Caroline court. One set, knights and relatives of nobility, quest after the fortune of the brilliant widow Lady Lucina; once rejected, they next seek acclaim and worldly goods, Ladies Honoria and Rosamond. The venturers: Sir Ambrose Lamount, who tries to mount any prize, Sir Marmaduke Travers, who traverses all terrain, and Colonel Winfield, who wins the battle of the sexes. All seem kin to the last suitor, Bostock, who lives up to his name by bragging about his noble lineage, excusing his palpable cowardice as guaranteeing future generation, and dropping names. The second set, Honoria and Rosamond, compete for a pot of gold, Lord Rainbow, who supports Bostock and sponsors subscription balls. The scene is filled out by two affectations. A French dancing master, Monsieur Le Frisk, caricatures shallow, bawdy mimicry of the entourage, fashions, and demeanor imported by Queen Henrietta Maria. And an English traveler whose peregrinations are limited to his moniker, Freshwater, displays a motley of national stereotypes and mangled references to continental commonplaces. Typically, he sells his family estate to invest in capital markets, ineptly sharks exorbitant loans to the play's pretenders to privilege, then ends bankrupt at Gravesend.

The Ball ridicules the failings of social and economic climbers whose success might verify their pretensions to ascribed privilege. In a private conference with each of her suitors Lucina appears to have elected him; but she jeers when he reveals his complicity in some practice that drew contemporary complaints about marginal gentry. Her criticism is most relevant when she asks Travers about alleged projects to drain fens, construct iron mills, establish a foundry for brass buttons, or get a patent for vinegar during this "age / For men to look about them" (II.iii/28). Puzzled over how to respond, Travers follows a hunch about her "appetite" for commercial wealth and declares such ventures. Likely she has caught Travers managing business affairs a nobleman would despise; perhaps, though, she points to his decay resulting from neglect of the increasingly dominant cash commerce that a prudent nobleman would eye to improve his estate.[24] Lucina attacks Lamount for displaying his dancing legs and giving locks of his hair as love tokens, two lures when fishing for a marriage to an estate and increased status. She makes Bostock confess the spuriousness of his claim to the bloodlines he trades on. And she sneers at Winfield for campaigning for a petticoat fortune instead of waging war for maintenance.

At the same time that *The Ball* exposes social climbers, it presents an imitable privileged style. Shirley thereby admits the ease with which master impersonators could mime the manners of their betters while he disallows the legitimacy of their claims to higher rank. His critique holds true for cits, like the Barnacles who trade on the cycle of merchants aspiring to land and landholders seeking cash, and it holds for wits, like the Will Hazards who hunt rich widows and heiresses, through such plays as *The Gamester* (1633). It holds true for the greater gentry who come to town seeking entry into courtly circles, like Lady Aretina Bornwell, and it holds for the gallants who surround her in *The Lady of Pleasure* (1635). It holds for such lesser courtiers as the trio in *The Bird in a Cage* (1633) who aver that all anyone needs for success at court is wit plentiful enough to invent mischief and memory scant enough to forget debts, and for the greater councillors whom the Duchess of Mantua tests for the foolish and knavish ambition of trying to ascend to monarchy by way of her bed in *The Humorous Courtier* (1631). It holds just as truly for upwardly mobile gentlemen, like Aurelio Andreozzi, granted *The Opportunity* (1634), by a mistake, to marry into monarchy, as it does for servants, like his Pimponio who mistakes himself for a bully "natural prince." As Lucow observes, Shirley insists "that individual identity is best determined by birth and status. Individual fulfillment arises not from seizing opportunities to advance oneself beyond one's station, but from working faithfully and steadily within the limitations of one's class." Yet Lucow admits that Shirley shows how the imitation of elite styles can be effective for short periods.[25] Shirley seems aware of the problems that can be created by master mimics of privileged role models, but he keeps faith with the safeguards presumably transmitted by blood.

Shirley's awareness of such problems has led some critics to point to his dissatisfaction with individual Caroline courtiers and incidents.[26] They quote the familiar designs of the steward Jacomo in *The Grateful Servant* (1629): "Mee thinkes I talke, like a peremptorie Statesman already, I shall quickly learne to forget my selfe when I am in great office, I will oppresse the Subiect, flatter the Prince, take bribes a both sides, doe right to neyther, serue Heauen as farre as my profit will giue mee leaue, and tremble, only at the Summons of a Parliament" (II.i/25). And they describe the play's satire on sleazy, sycophantic climbers when Grimundo imitates them to cure the Duke of Savoy's wild brother. But critics are wrong to conclude from Shirley's satire of isolated instances of unworthy representatives of the caste system that he was inclined, like Massinger, to be disaffected with an absolute hierarchy based on heredity. Rather, like Ford, he supported it. His presentations are generally reassuring about the failure of threats by the ambitious machiavellian favorites who mislead or supplant princes: Lorenzo and his fidgety accomplice Depazzi in *The Traitor* (1631), Valerio in *The Duke's Mistress* (1636), Montalto in *The Royal Master* (1637), Gotharus in *The Politician* (1639?), Flaviano in *The Imposture* (1640), and Columbo's churchman brother in *The Cardinal* (1641). While the increasing incidence of such villains might indicate a growing uneasiness about heredity or alarm at the power of impersonation, Shirley's target is the perversion of posts not held by the right of bloodlines. The very failure of his villains to gain their unworthy ambitions signals the ultimate insufficiency of the subversive imitation of forms. It signals, too, Shirley's courtly stance.

Another way to rescue Shirley from absolute royalism and reverence for degree is ventured by Butler: "I shall later argue . . . that an upholding of 'place' and decorum was characteristic of 'gentry' attitudes to politics and was a very effective form of criticism when directed from those lower down in the hierarchy against those exceeding their 'place' above them (for example, in Shirley's own city comedies)." The thesis that some inter-related gentry and city families were poised as mediators between "court" and "country" is important. "But clearly," Butler acknowledges a problem, "this idea is not the same when advanced from above, in a court context, against critics from below, when it becomes merely a justification of the freedom of action of the constituted powers."[27] *The Lady of Pleasure*, *The Example*, and *Hyde Park* do not likely speak for mediation. These plays can, like *The Triumph of Peace*, be interpreted as critical of the court, but in the context of all of Shirley's works they seem finally to support it. Furthermore, to satirize those who abuse a system is one thing, to attack the inadequacies of a system is something altogether different. Shirley's corpus shows that, willing to allow some adaptation, he represented a hierarchy which permitted only a few eccentricities.

Much more than the tenet of a hierarchy based on degree, even more than the tenet of absolute monarchy, Shirley's tenet of patriarchy appears to form a fundamental assumption. The moderation suggested by a chastened and thus concerned father in his earliest known comedy, *Love Tricks*, and by a disastrously rigid father in his earliest known tragedy, *The Maid's Revenge*, disappears with *The Wedding* (1626-29). This comedy first presents his pattern in which patriarchs rightly employ their powers in seemingly obstructive but truly provident ways in such plays as *The Brothers* (a misnomer for the late *The Politic Father?*); such powers are also exercised by an occasional "lady mother," as in *The Constant Maid*.[28] More typically, when Shirley's fathers impede their children, the children, as in *The Witty Fair One* (1628), seek paternal blessings. Shirley honors filial piety from the gratified Gratiana of *The Wedding* to the martyred Haraldas in *The Politician*. Demands on children are often made so that interlocking authorities reinforce each other. The Duke of Mantua, for example, incarcerates princess Eugenia; thus *The Bird in a Cage* applies to her as well as to her disguised suitor. And the patriotism of the hero's father in *The Young Admiral* fosters his son's loyalty in spite of the wrongs done him by his prince. Shirley's portrayal of fathers virtually prohibits anything more than nonessential variations of his culture's patriarchal hierarchies.

Beyond that, Shirley's presentation of male superiority consistently reinforces and interlocks with his other hierarchical views. In *The Sisters* Angellina proves her nobility when her quiet manner, humility, and obedience win a prince; meanwhile her changeling sister, Paulina, reveals her commonness as her display, vanity, and social climbing earn her misalliance with a bandit. Shirley, less often and less forcefully than Massinger, criticizes the double standard, limits male prodigality, and allows women to speak up. So his presentation of traditional male dominion could be seen as melioration. But Shirley's women, more like Ford's, must acquiesce. As a wealthy widow, *The Ball*'s Lucina begins in the most independent status available to a Caroline woman. Falling for Winfield's ploy of inciting rival suitors to chastise her so he can make a chivalrous rescue, she ambushes the veteran campaigner by her condition for marriage: he must have been "honest of [his] body." Yet he, his stage society, and presumably his audience agree that no one could reasonably expect a gentleman of his breeding, parts, and profession to be so constrained. Since, then, she must pardon anything beyond his oath of freedom from infection, he cavalierly reciprocates. But his gesture is so empty that she lies transparently about a dozen dependent children; a *lady* is, of course, wealthy, landed, degreed, heirless—and chaste. His offer of equivalent sexual forgiveness is predicated on the inconceivability of her needing it. Shirley does not permit equivalent sexual activity to any lady other than the critically infamous Aretina Bornwell. And she repents mightily and is disciplined to traditional feminine virtue. "Tis a false glass," she moans while facing her mirror, "sure I am more deformed. / What have I done? My soule is miserable" (V.i. 287-88). Filled with self-loathing, she submits her higher station to her husband. For receiving a gigolo anonymously one time Lady Aretina suffers far greater remorse than Shirley's whole crowd of lecherous male prodigals who are forgiven—some scarcely repentant, few reformed.[29]

There has been conjecture that Charles and Henrietta Maria's celebrated fidelity promoted more equitable marital relations than heretofore. But Charles gave Shirley the plot for a blatantly male chauvinist play, *The Gamester*.[30] If the play is representative, Charles's and Shirley's interest in reforming social behavior is limited to curbing the double standard—after marriage—just as the prodigally lustful husband, aptly named Wilding, is tamed by his obediently faithful wife and her chaste ward, notably named Penelope. Motivated more by ego than by lust, Wilding arranges to bed Penelope and marry her off so as to conceal their liaison: he can be titillated by adultery; he can bully his obedient wife into abetting it; he can enjoy clever villainy; "mainly" he can revel in making a cuckold, "The only pleasure o' the world" "Which sweetens the rest" (III.i/225). But he is horrified to hear afterward that the night he, wanting to go on gambling, hired Hazard as his substitute at the assignation, his wife replaced Penelope. Imagining his humiliation popping out in a pair of horns, desperately covering his shame, and accusing his wife of being a whore, the cuckold maker suffers the anguish of being cuckolded until he arranges a wedding settlement profitable for Hazard and Penelope. Then the women and Hazard convert the situation, Wilding, and the audience; they reveal that they recognized the bed trick in time to save everyone's virtue. Chastely faithful, obediently loving feminine virtue forgives the contrite transgressor so that the play reaffirms an old marriage and promises a new one. Charles and Shirley's plot remains strictly inside convention.[31] Wilding and virtue depend on women, yet he retains dominion. Early in the play he describes the lines of his power to Penelope: "my wife, I allow / Your kinswoman far off, to whom, a widow, / Your father left you, with a handsome fortune, / Which, by marriage, I have in possession, / And you too" (I.i/187). Late in the play he still controls Penelope's dowry and he presides over her marriage pact. Never mind his likely reversion or Hazard's occupation, gigolo.

In *The Example* (1634) Shirley, without royal prompting, proffered another version of his paradigm that features the conversion of a prodigal man by a chaste subordinate woman. While Shirley, as Nathan Cogan has recognized, was concerned about libertinage,[32] his solution depends on a premarital double standard and on the woman's responsibility for chastity despite enticement and duress. The rapacious Lord Fitzavarice seduces women for his "credit": "The world takes notice I have courted her, / And if I mount her not, I lose my honour" (I.i/297). Driven by ego, "honour," he lusts to "mould" each "wench" "into a wanton shape, / And quicken her to air by my own art . . . till she become / A glorified spirit, and acknowledge / She took her exaltation from me." The transformational techniques of the sexual alchemical master are scarcely mysteries: he offers a woman the honor of his station, bribes her with jewels, pledges his love to her, discounts her allegiance to a husband who is absent, accepts the blame (and the credit). Since Peregrine, the officer husband, wanders abroad to pay off his debts, Fitzavarice promises to cancel these on the sweetly lovable Bellamia's first surrender and to pay exorbitantly for each subsequent compliance. Spurned, he starts to force Bellamia until, recognizing her virtue, he converts. Or does he, realizing that force confesses failure, avoid shame? Whatever, the redeemed prodigal is granted Bellamia's younger sister, who has saved her chastity for a match that affords wealth, status, and honor (issuing in part from Fitzavarice's sexual repute). Shirley habitually retains this hierarchical gender status. Typically, the imitation of male sexual prerogatives by a Clariana leads to the tragic outcome of *Love's Cruelty* (1631). Habitually, maiden Penelopes, beginning with the heroine of *The Witty Fair One*, live up to her name by way of fabrications that save their Fowlers; and wives remain redeemingly loyal to actual philanderers (Astella to Lodwick in *The Grateful Servant*) or to would-be ones (the Duchess Euphemia to Farnese in *The Duke's Mistress*). Often, as in these instances, wives are abetted by their husbands' supposedly loose but actually chaste prey.

Finally, though the independent wit of many of Shirley's heroines might suggest their enhanced status, that inference is delusive because women's free speech is restricted to minor adaptations of rigid role norms. The illusion of frankness by a Lucina in *The Ball* or a Violetta in *The Witty Fair One* can be seen in Shirley's most popular heroine, the heavenly, loveworthy Celestina, Lady Bellamour of *The Lady of Pleasure*. Butler argues that this rich, independent widow makes a sociopolitical contrast to Lady Aretina Bornwell, who is a caricature of the debasement, extravagance, and promiscuity among citified "country" gentry who imitate the corrupted pretensions, opulence, and license at court. In her assured behavior, liberal expenditures, and free talk Celestina exemplifies a "town" magnanimity proportioned from country, city, and court. She holds privileges that she inherited, but she must maintain them.[33] From this perspective she teaches two novices the "becomming fortitude" of virtuous acts and satiric wit aimed so as to "not lose my priviledge" of independence (II.ii.11, 21). But from another vantage she tutors them in every unattached woman's dependence on a marriage mart wherein birth and rich widowhood virtally supplant her personal attributes. This market Celestina plays by maintaining "thrift" in her "reward" to keep men devoted and to "preserve / Our selves in stocke" (II.ii.72-73), whereas less calculating ladies waste "prodigal" favors. By this barter economy she converts the lord of the play from two prominent love fashions: early, from an old-fashioned abstinent neoplatonic devotion to his dead lady and later from a libertine "now court Platonic way." The lord's courtship is doubly flawed. Celestina's economic exemplum confirms that the honor he would have her sacrifice is as precious to a lady and her family as a coat of arms is to him and his. And the lord's need for the gigolo "Scentlove" corroborates Littleworth's description of a debasement that depends on two ever-present attendants: a fool on a ship of fools and a pimp on a ladder descending from monarch through gentlemen. So Celestina, with shrewd wit, conforms to his "fair opinion" as he serves her. She plays another of Shirley's converting Penelopes. Moreover, she does not ques-

tion but wholeheartedly trusts the court position and the vacillating lord
on whom her worth now depends. *The Lady of Pleasure*'s resolution
typifies Shirley's allegiance to courtly attitudes about manners and prerogatives.

Shirley's show of adaptability in political rights, in meritorious advancement, and in more independence for women and children might
seem to resemble Massinger's accommodation. But Shirley, like Ford,
restricts the viable options to rigid monarchical absolutism, position by
blood degree, and the maintenance of traditional patriarchal status and
family norms. His criticisms, which might seem to resemble Massinger's
reforms, attack the debasement and abuse of traditional standards; so,
like Ford's, they support a courtly value system. Shirley's works appeal,
like his women, by using clever language to shape roles in slightly
asymmetrical conformity to dominant social patterns. Celestina proves
attractive when she one-ups Aretina's court French and puts down the
gallants' sneers, when she exemplifies courtly conceits and employs
"linsey-woolsey" against fatuous, licentious conceits. Likewise, Shirley
makes a winning appeal through a witty style that mainly displays role-
constituting language, manners, and social occasions in support of the
privileges, powers, and customs of the Caroline court as it apparently
liked to be considered.

The Clean Wit of Playful Conformity

In his prefatory praise of the 1647 Beaumont and Fletcher folio, Shirley
esteems dramatic craft in superlatives: "POETRY *is the Child of* Nature, *which
regulated and made beautifull by* Art, *presenteth the most Harmonious of all other
compositions; among which (if we rightly consider) the* Dramaticall *is the most
absolute, in regard of those transcendent* Abilities, *which should waite upon the*
Composer; *who must have more then the instruction of Libraries (which of it selfe
is but a cold contemplative knowledge) there being required in him a* Soule
miraculously *knowing.*" The focus here on genius and intuitive empathy
makes it all too easy to ignore the value that Shirley, with the other
Caroline professional playwrights, attributed to art. Shirley's esteem of
the nurture of nature favors his own accomplishments, for he was a
playwright who not only honored but also obviously learned from earlier
masters. Like Massinger, he primarily imitated Fletcher, though not as
Fletcher's apprentice and collaborator. In prologues to two Fletcher comedies presented in Ireland, Shirley claims Fletcher to be the laureate who
tests the wit of an audience. Like most Caroline playwrights, he also
imitated Jonson, though not, like Brome, as Jonson's apprentice. In his
dedication of *The Grateful Servant* he acknowledges Jonson as his learned
master, and in a prologue introducing *The Alchemist* to Ireland he pro-

nounces Jonson the monarch of poets and Jonson's play the comic master-
piece of all climes and times.

To honor, allude to, and borrow from his predecessors Shirley studied them early and often. In the prologue to *Love Tricks, or The School of
Compliment* he declares that "He first kist bayes, that wore them on his
brow." And throughout his writings, as in the prologue to *The Example*
and the dedication to *The Politician*, he joins his fellow professionals in
decrying the assessments of criticotasters and the plays of poetasters,
both of which fail because the perpetrators are ignorant of dramatic craft.
His prologue to *The Cardinal* deplores the general abandonment of Shakespeare's, Fletcher's, and Jonson's art. From Harvey's commendation of
The Wedding, admirers of Shirley's art associate him with Beaumont; from
Habington's commendation of *The Grateful Servant* they declare him Jonson's heir; and from Mervyn's commendation of *The Royal Master* they
endow him with the attributes of Beaumont and Fletcher and Shakespeare. Scholars ever since have recognized Shirley's learned craft, especially since Robert Stanley Forsythe, after cataloguing sources and
analogs from more than 500 earlier Tudor/Stuart plays, concluded that
*"Most often his source is not a single play but the various groups of plays which
employ in common with his dramas certain situations, incidents, devices, and
characters."*[34]

Richard Levin and Nathan Cogan have updated Forsythe's and
Nason's demonstration that Shirley's intricate and surprising Fletcherian
plots, like those of his fellow Caroline professionals, are so entwined that
his main and subordinate plots can scarcely be separated. Shirley's characteristic plotting can be seen in the ways he incorporates plays within
plays and masques in his plays.[35] Some of his plays conclude with revelatory and celebratory masques. *The Ball* achieves a climax in a masque
wherein Cupid chooses Diana over Venus; *Love Tricks* ends with a shepherds' masque that reveals the reunion of lovers once segregated by their
families but now blessed by them; *The Changes, or Love in a Maze* concludes
with a masque that sorts out the play's quartet of changeable lovers. Other
masques and playlets within Shirley's plays set up parallels and turns. In
The Bird in a Cage Eugenia and her ladies act out the *New Prison*, a Danae
and Jupiter analog of her incarceration that suggests her suitor's imminent
success; in *The Maid's Revenge* a soldiers' masque signals a retributive
bloodletting; in *The Cardinal* Columbo enters with masquers to kill his
rival and trigger further revenge; and in *The Traitor* a prophetic masque
by a righteous brother warns the corrupted duke against lusting after
the sister. Shirley's characters often design masques and other performances to manipulate and transform other characters. In *The Constant Maid*
masquers fool a usurer with a dreamlike subterfuge of his court preferment, including a masque presentation of the judgment of Paris, to cover

the escape of the usurer's niece and ward. A presentation of lapsed Love's reconciliation with Honor in *The Coronation* reminds Arcadius to choose love over kingdom; a staging of a near-seduction by a ravishing "devil" who is attended by threatening satyrs and nymphs cures a terrified libertine in *The Grateful Servant;* and Penelope's mock funeral for Fowler converts the prodigal in *The Witty Fair One.*

Shirley's plays teem with characters who play roles so as to out-maneuver each other. So Winfield spies on and then manipulates Lucina in *The Ball* and Wilding's family vary a bed trick in *The Gamester.* Forsythe's catalog of "stock incidents" indicates Shirley's extraordinary reliance, even among his peers, on manipulative playacting. His plays depend on amatory and political proxies and emissaries, pretenses and disguises (Forsythe's categories 2, 3, 6, 7, 8, 32-35, 41), on testings (15, 16, 17), on misleading ambigities and imaginings (25, 27, 28), and on the highest incidence of eavesdroppings in the period (30). Shirley forged a full repertoire of situations in which characters play on each other into a cor-pus of elaborately intricate, surprising, and revelatory Fletcherian plots.

Staging their own elaborate plots in Shirley's world are the "stock characters" who populate it. They are also tabulated by Forsythe: male and female machiavels, lustful misled princes, avaricious old men, blunt soldiers, foolish suitors with gullible accomplices, witty gallants and ladies attended by clever servants (often pages), clowns. While Lucow notes that stereotypes are kin to masque abstractions, they may suggest even more characters playing assigned parts, adapting to roles shaped by their society.[36]

The kaleidoscopic *The Changes, or Love in a Maze*(ment?) shows Shir-ley's characters as adolescents searching for appropriate role adaptations, accomplishments, and consorts. It features the improbable situation that identical twin marital prizes named Chrysolina and Aurelia Goldsworth love the same gentleman. But since Gerard, as blind love, is unable to choose between the two, he contracts with Thornay to woo either one. After a series of jealousies, slights, subterfuges, and changes Gerard plans a misogynistic monastery while Chrysolina becomes enamored of one Yongrave. This wooer of Chrysolina's friend Eugenia serves as Eu-genia's messenger, advocate, and champion in converting, challenging, and testing her prodigal betrothed, none other than Thornay; finally he diverts her avaricious guardian Woodhamore so this couple can be joined. Since Eugenia bestows the pliably dedicated Yongrave on Chrysolina and since Aurelia recovers Gerard, all the characters manage to meander onto suitable partners, duplicitously fooling each other sometimes, themselves somewhat, and their parents often. All, that is, keep trying on apt roles and searching for meet mates until they find comfortable matches. Often Shirley's characters self-consciously seek and create identities and matches through playfully adapting and varying roles that fit inside the norms accepted by the privileged, court-imitating audience he bonded with.

Two other typical suitors lost in *The Change*'s maze illustrate the failure to adapt language that signals a failure to make a role one's own. Sir Gervase Simple has sold his country estate to buy a new knighthood and an education in town compliment so he can set up as a gallant. But he lapses into homey formulas, bawdy malaprops, and inappropriate tags from *The Spanish Tragedy*; and he falls for the chirping of Lady Bird, a witty page in disguise. Caperwit falls to become a poetaster; his Aganippe spring flows with the outworn devices of courtly poetry and compliment, inept references to poetic muses and loci, futile attempts to associate with Sidney, needless allusions to classical myths, and tedious catalogs of ladies' attractions until he floods the stage with contrary fashions. His discourses on the preeminence of adjectives (he needs to consider substantives) or on blank verse and numbers (his lines are too weak to hang himself in), along with his less than successful courtship of tropes and figures, mark him as an affectation mated by rather than to poetry. The fatuous language as well as the empty characters in Shirley's plays often result from role experiments and adaptations that fail. Only when one of his characters discovers the normative role for which she or he has the aptitude and lineage can the role or the language fit.

Thus Shirley's "Prologue" to *The Changes* invokes the muse "whose ear / Is able to distinguish strains that are / Clear and *Phoebean*, from the popular / And sinfull dregs of the adulterate brain"; and it segregates his "fresh *Thalia*" from the sewage on the stage. His prologues often repeat the claim that introduces *The Brothers:* "He would have you beleeve no language good, / And artfull, but what's clearly understood." Consistently, Shirley's commenders admire his "clear," "sweet," "smooth" diction, syntax, and metrics, and his "fancy," his "conceited" "metaphorical" language. Both the commendations of his early *The Wedding* and *The Grateful Servant* by playwrights such as May, Ford, Habington, Randolph, and Massinger, and also the reminiscence by George Blakeston before the late grammar suggest an interpretation different from the one Juliet McGrath proposes in "James Shirley's Uses of *Language*."[37] Shirley produced a polished style that does not seem to derive from a distrust of language's inadequacy and deceptiveness, but instead from an understanding of language's potential for signaling and reinforcing courtliness. He offered to his privileged audience a limited number of variations on admirable models of interlinked talk and behavior. He created a "conceited" style that celebrates language play, and comic protagonists who try on sometimes misleading roles and make beginners' mistakes as they develop personalities through talk. Shirley further employed small but notable deviations in language decorum to attack significant violations of behavioral norms. Much that might be seen as evidence of language's inadequacy actually reveals incorrigible fools who are as inept at using language as they are at imitating and adapting roles. And much that might be seen as evidence of language's deceptions actually reveals machiavels who are as adept at manipulating language as they are at perpetrating duplicitous roles. Satiric butts and villains exhibit Shirley's awareness of language abuse.

The early *Love Tricks* makes a significant example of Shirley's presentation of linguistic norms of wit and behavioral norms of courtliness that reinforce each other. It rewards consideration under its better known title, *The School of Compliment,* because even though the centerpiece scene has little to do with the plot it has everything to do with the play. Most of the play's characters, not just the pretentious, gullible boors at the academy of modish manners and discourse, are discovering, adopting, and adapting roles and voices. Moreover, the centerpiece scene has everything to do with a critical perspective on Shirley from the social sciences that I have used to look at Massinger and Ford. Though academies of behavior appear prominently in plays by all the Caroline professionals, they are particularly presented by Shirley. These institutions for social modeling earned their profits by teaching the same kinds of social skills that are described in Renaissance manuals of conduct, rhetoric, and poetics. Both focus on self-presentation for the promotion of courtly maintenance and advancement; both are based on the humanist and courtly assumption that style in language most presents a man or woman; and both indicate extraordinary awareness of the interdependence of language and behavior. Yet thus far only the printed rhetorics of behavior and language have drawn the important scrutiny of scholars such as Daniel Javitch and especially Frank Whigham.[38]

In sociohistorical analyses of George Puttenham's *The Arte of English Poesie* and other comprehensive books on conduct and rhetoric, Javitch and Whigham depend on some of the same central assumptions that sociologist Harold Garfinkel makes for his pragmatic ethnomethodology.[39] Garfinkel's program can be summed up by the proposition that "the activities whereby members produce and manage settings of organized everyday affairs are identical with members' procedures for making those settings 'account-able.' The 'reflexive,' or 'incarnate' character of accounting practices makes up the crux of that recommendation."[40] This proposition posits that people rely on a host of presuppositions about mutual, "commonsense" understandings of complex everyday events; members of a society take these for granted as they maintain, try out, adjust, and recreate norms and deviations in dealing daily with their circumstances. It further posits that people account their understandings resources as much as determinants when they observe, describe, and interpret so as to act. And it especially considers the language of their accounts. The late Tudor and early Stuart observers who created that era's manuals and academies of the rhetoric of conduct, speech, and poetry, along with the students who bought these accounts and lessons, relied on the same set of assumptions and foci of attention as ethnomethodologists. For they hoped to profit from accounts of how to ingratiate themselves with, gain the rewards of, and produce valuable affects from a discriminating society that lived by nuances of courtliness.

The masters and disciples of *The School of Compliment* become Shirley's targets of inaptitude because they claim that courtliness is teachable to those who do not inherit degree. The school's cony-catching faculty consists of a "most ingenious and noble Criticotaster," the disguised gallant Gasparo; his "*Hypodidascall*, in English, his Vsher," one guise of the sly servant Gorgon; and their "disciple," a chambermaid named Delia who, as Diana's associate, will bestow horns on a husband because the goddess of chastity placed them on Actaeon (III.v). These fantastic characterizations indicate satire born of the recognition that naming, or accounting in language, can have great efficacy in creating roles.

The school's students are gulls lured by handbills that promise instruction in whatever language is appropriate to the role anyone aspires to. Bubulcus, "a Gentleman in *folio*," "desires to suck the hony of [Criticotaster's] eloquence" so as to become "practis'd" in the "verbosity" of "amorous complement" and "mouth-gun" challenge. As he reduces love and war to mannerisms of speech, so he mingles silly battle of the sexes metaphors and meiotic love conceits with absurd hyperbolic challenges. He thereby proves his born incapacity for the role he desires. A new justice of the peace, Sir Valentine Wantbrain, sends for a latinate, periphrastic inaugural address. The country widow Medulla seeks a tongue of cunning courtship that is capable of expressing mourning for her late husband in a manner that can attract a knight to elevate her. Orlando Furioso perfects mavorsian bombast in a "deuillish good speech" threatening a hell of destruction. The yeoman's son and JP's clerk Ingeniolo rehearses "his passion in blanke Verse." A Welshman who admits to "no pleasures and delectations in vrds and phrases of Rhetricks" and who claims to abhor "oratories" tries courtly pastoralism. And a countryman brings his son, the "Oaf," to be "edoctrinated," "taught to speake" as befits a courtier. The assumption that people's abilities with language demark their achievements in society is built into the curriculum, since students get "advanced to a higher Classe" after they learn "postures of [the] body." Thus Shirley's burlesque of their aspirations to high status and accomplished roles becomes all the more obvious when even they recognize their classmates as being "great children" who lack any inbred capacity for elevated speech.

The thematic contribution made by the school of compliment becomes clear when the cacophany of lessons modulates into a set of satiric prose characters. These are the responses to a question by Infortunio, a mad, disdained lover who mistakes the school for hell in a sexual game called barley break. In answering why they are damned, the tutors and especially the students break character and present crafted satires. The teachers indict themselves: Gasparo as the "conscience of an Vsurer," Gorgon as the complicitous "soule of a Watchman," and Delia as a chaste "Chamber-maid." The gulls present roles analogous to their own, contributing acute observations through punning wordplay and repartee: the widow becomes a "Iustices wife ith' the countrie," Ingeniolo describes a compassionate and hence cashiered "under-sheriff," the Oaf embodies a "younger brother," and Bubulcus represents a "Horse-courser" in a triple sense that plays off proverbial lore, multiple puns, and wordgames from various domains of speech. When the Welshman gets condemned for the dialect of his tribe, the play's principals follow him to the Elysian fields of courtly pastoralism where *Love Tricks* ends.

The conclusion of *The School of Compliment*, since it is made up of a set of satirical prose characters, recalls the opening of *Love Tricks*, where Gasparo employs this same minor genre to describe one kind of rhetorician, a "newes-maker": a cynical younger brother who invents dispatches about imaginary military campaigns on the Continent. Both the satiric closing of the inset and the satiric opening of the play signal Shirley's abiding interest in how language creates roles and sometimes fraud. For the same roles that are discovered, adopted, and adapted by the privileged audience Shirley honors also provide norms whereby he can measure pretenders and find them wanting. In *Love Tricks* both sorts of role-players are represented in two sets of characters who are clustered around two blocking fathers. The pretentious, who need satiric cure, appear with a pantaloon, Rufaldo; he believes he is growing youthful by courting the young Selina and prohibiting her brother, Antonio, from marrying his daughter. In a transvestite disguise Antonio physically and psychologically abuses the pantaloon until he cures him. The seekers, who need to find suitable roles, appear with Selina's compassionate father, Cornelio; he is an erstwhile patriarch whose elder daughter, Felice, has disappeared because he thwarted her marriage to Gasparo. For a time Cornelio loses his son, the spoiled Selina, and her rejected suitor, Infortunio, as well. These characters, whose talk represents pretenses, disguises, and searches, get matched appropriately when they arrive in a curative setting of courtly pastoral otium, where Felice and carefree innocents sing lilting lyrics about commonplace rural virtues. Here all discover the lines (the language and the roles they can adopt comfortably) that guide them out of the twisting, surprising plot. Here, for instance, an

Infortunio, who spouted the oxymora and conceits of a puling courtly lover, and Selina, who played a disdainful witty lady until she drove this melancholy suitor mad, can renew their love.

Since Forsythe's compilation and extension of nineteenth-century source studies, critics have recognized that through an increasingly sophisticated emulation of the traditions of dramatic poetry Shirley surpassed the stilted and overladen *Love Tricks*.[41] But critics have not seemed cognizant of Shirley's sophisticated presentation of characters who find, try, learn, and adapt stereotypical privileged roles by experimenting with model speech. Nor have critics seemed aware of Shirley's correction of pretenders who prove their innate lack of degree by their lack of facility with language which distinguishes the elite. By tabulating the interlocking games of language and role playing in Shirley's plays, Forsythe corroborates the notion that while Massinger examines reflexive and reciprocal social behavior and Ford considers ceremonial creation and reinforcement of social behavior, Shirley presents language accounting for and molding social behavior.

Shirley frequently presents long accounts of subgroup role norms (Forsythe's category 21), such as the initial characterizations in *The Witty Fair One* and *The Wedding*, Lucina's evaluations of suitors in *The Ball*, or Hazard's analyses of gamblers in *The Gamester*. In jeerings by a Lucina, a Celestina in *The Lady of Pleasure*, or many in *The Bird in a Cage* he often displays satiric accounts of types (20). He regularly lets stylistic burlesques dominate characters and plays (22): Caperwit's poetic fineness in *Love in a Maze* represents a fatuous extreme and Sir Confident Rapture's courtly sexual advances in *The Example* exhibit a debased one. And he offers set speeches as self-conscious artifices in the service of role playing. His paragons produce long avowals of chastity and long rejections of seduction speeches (9), then his reformed seducers and remorseful villains often respond with long repentances (10), as in *The Gamester* and *The Example*. Shirley links most of the socially acute accountings and adept employments of role-forming language to recurring word games, which define his characters' status by testing their sensitivity to ambiguous implications and ambivalent inferences (27, 28). It scarcely seems coincidental that far more often than any of his colleagues' characters Shirley's characters refer to the names of his plays (31), especially to those that label social roles, such as *The Grateful Servant, The Humorous Courtier, The Politician, The Cardinal*, and social occasions, such as *The Wedding, The Coronation, The Ball*. For Shirley's characters define themselves by way of sociolinguistic roles and contexts.

Shirley's clear, witty lines provide a linguistic frame of behavioral norms within which his characters can discover, play, adapt, and become the language roles his privileged society sanctioned. His frame makes still more sophisticated one of Fletcher's refinements of English dramatic tradition: when their plays track stereotypical characters through intricate plots set in familiar situations, they model a privileged social network. Shirley's exemplary style thus enforces limited variations on the received roles of the courtly elite he honored and it embeds veneration of absolute monarchy, hierarchies of inherited status, absolute patriarchy, and male dominion, including double sexual and social standards. His satiric style castigates deviations from courtly sociolinguistic norms. More than those of any other Caroline professional playwright, Shirley's presentations reflect, reinforce, and honor the specially privileged patrons who dominated the private theaters that supported him. To these the elite could resort to watch representations that confirmed the mutually reinforcing talk and mores of their caste and that provided the flatteringly proper, wittily urbane role and language models of achieved ascription. Then they could practice these models at other social events, such as the opening of the racing season at Hyde Park.

Adapting Roles in HYDE PARK

At the end of *Hyde Park* (1632, printed 1637) Master Bonavent makes his final entrance wearing a mask and carrying four willow garlands, then a typical witty page sings the last of the play's several ditties:

> *Roome for the melancholy wight,*
> *Some doe call him willow Knight,*
> *Who this paines hath undertaken,*
> *To finde out lovers are forsaken,*
> *Whose heads, because but little witted,*
> *Shall with Garlands straight be fitted.*   [V.ii/538]

While others urge the gentlemen being fitted to "obey the Ceremony," Bonavent garlands the heads of four who have lost marital competitions: the racers and gamblers, Rider and Venture, had vied for Mistress Carol; a gentleman, Trier, had presumed to claim Mistress Julietta Fairfield; another, Lacy, had this very day married Mistress Bonavent, wife of the doubly vizored missing husband who presides over the masque. Remarkably, instead of challenging the winners, delivering bitter denunciations, or showing petulance, the "brotherhood" or "Messe of willowgentlemen," claim "to see a providence" and obey, since "In such good company twould never grieve / A man to weare the willow." Their participation in a ceremony which ridicules them is especially noteworthy because it is general, not dependent on their particular situations: the latter two seemed favorites to win their ladies whereas the former pair seemed part of a pack of suitors destined to be also-rans. Their uniform politeness is significant because it represents the pervasive urbanity of the competitions that swirl through their fashionable privileged pastimes and particularly through a season and a place set aside for games and gambling.

Expanding on Levin's plot analogies, Albert Wertheim has shown that *Hyde Park* presents the pleasures and gains of games and gambling as a genteel way of life.[42] Not only do the play's primary actions appear against the backdrop of a footrace and a horserace on which the gentlemen wager money and the ladies accessories, but often characters talk in terms of betting and card playing, as when Bonavent questions Carol about his wife's fidelity in his absence (III.i/498-99). The concluding festivities of victory, defeat, and good sportsmanship are celebrated with another song after dancing songs, courting songs, and a horse racing ballad, *"if I be just all praises must / Be giuen to wellbreathed Iilian Thrust"* (IV.iii/512-13). And a wedding dance, a morris for spring rites, and a revenge dance depend on and reinforce the central pastime of gaming. Drinking the park's famous syllabub accompanies gaming. Preparations for and reflections on wooing get considered as gambling. Finally, Wertheim proves that beating the odds forms a paradigm for both the races and the three interlocked plots of *Hyde Park:* every time a dark horse wins. A local favorite is ahead until an Irishman pulls out the footrace; Venture is leading comfortably when his horse throws him into a slough; both reversals come when the odds have peaked. Just so, when favorites for the ladies feel assured of victory, the surprising denouement grants their ladies' hands to darkhorses and garlands the favorites with willow. Curiously, the higher the stakes in these competitive pastimes, the greater the civility: none of the several challenges goes beyond drawing a sword for show; and vengeance is won by jeering, compelling dances, and enforcing ceremonies. The (mainly language) games take place in bounds.

The civility of these competitive pastimes of the leisured elite is mirrored in the play's setting. And to the Keeper of the Crown Land of Hyde Park, Henry the Earl of Holland, Chancellor of Cambridge, Knight of the Garter, and member of Charles's Privy Council, Shirley dedicated his play. Perhaps he did so because the lord made the park a privileged, urbane site for games, with a racecourse and a dairy bar, walks for private strolls, bowers for intimate meetings, and natural life so domesticated as to forecast the results of various games. When in the midst of the play and the park Fairfield, Carol's destined husband, seems to have been rejected, the couple hear that herald of good fortune, the nightingale; so does Lord Bonvile while Julietta is rejecting his lascivious proposition. But Trier, all but betrothed to Julietta, and Lacy, just married to Mistress Bonavent, are warned by the foreboding cuckoo. So are Rider, who discounts it, and Venture, who knows better; he loses the horserace, both lose their wagers and Carol.

The civilized natural setting, which caters to the games of courtship and polite conversation these privileged characters live for and by, the polite gaming festivities with accompanying urbane recreations in song, dance, and drink they enjoy, and the intricate plotting, which arranges that dark horses surprise favorites, together support the general critical agreement that *Hyde Park* presents an imitation of the apparent self-conception of Shirley's privileged Caroline audience. Critics see represented a complacent, cultured hierarchical society that viewed itself in the poised manners and status of its members as being a perfectly integrated, witty elite who model dignified roles. At the same time there is general critical applause for a *Hyde Park* that presents a vision of self-reliant women and in which Shirley gently criticizes the values of the elite.[43] The golden mirror of idealization thus represents the virtues of a privileged caste and presents as well an occasional steely challenge to those virtues. Perhaps the two views are reconcilable in a comic accommodation similar to Massinger's tragicomic one; in it playful ceremonies would reinforce heightened courtly norms more happily than do Ford's tragic ceremonies. But another interpretation emerges from a focus on the parallel stereotyped roles and especially on the urbane language that in several senses models these roles. *Hyde Park* provides a linguistic demonstration of Shirley's aesthetics and sociopolitics. These celebrate variations on appropriate behavior and speech, adaptations of acceptable roles, and diversities within established practices—as norm-enforcing games of role decorum played within the boundaries of a regally sanctioned hierarchy of monarch, patriarch, degree, and male. The model language, a fluent, witty, idealized courtly style, is the central instrument for creating the privileged roles and actions and for delineating and reinforcing the system in place; it accounts for the social system.

The paramount importance of language in defining, exemplifying, and accounting for social norms becomes evident in *Hyde Park*'s first scene: a polite conversation between Trier and Lacy, two complacently unsure favorites, gives way to a marginal flyting between two cocky pretenders, Venture and Rider. Trier and Lacy set a normative privileged mode as they discuss the prospects of the latter's prolonged wooing of Mistress Bonavent during her seven-year wait for her husband. Uncertain of the measure of her respect and unable to wait longer, Lacy indicates more concern at losing face than a bride. His exemplary pedigreed talk seems casually elaborate. In hopes of her wandering husband's return Mistress Bonavent may, he opines, have conjured up some extravagantly improbable salvation like Arion's deliverance by a dolphin, Jonah's redemption from the great fish, or a traveler's fantastic hibernation with mice under Alpine snows. In a pun that honors both Lacy's fanciful assessment of Bonaventure's erring journey (showing off his knowledge

of classical, biblical, and popular lore) and also the speaker's own knowing appreciation, Trier remarks, "This were a Vagary" (I.i/462). Clever
allusions and linguistic elaborations so worked as to appear effortless
create the witty repartee this privileged class employs to display a courtier's *sprezzatura*, his gracefully facile manner of displaying accomplishments as being inbred rather than learned. This quality of language,
presumed to set degree apart from climbing or to conceal the practice
anatomized in Whigham's explanation of social tropes, distinguishes the
polite characters in *Hyde Park* and defines the margins of their acceptance
of others.

Venture and Rider, labeled buffoonish gamesters, exhibit marginal
near deviations from model privileged discourse. Venture introduces
leering bawdry when, entering, he wonders if Lacy is being summoned
"To give [Mistress Bonavent] a heate." Later, after a brief appearance by
the lecherous Lord Bonvile, he brags that he used to enjoy "ladies of
pleasure" and calls attention to his jockey's legs. Like Lacy, Venture is
complacently concerned that "I have a Mistresse. . . . And yet I have her
not." As he brags he becomes ever more certain of victory in a courtship
game: if Carol wavered, this compass needle now points steadily to him as
her "true North." Rider, entering, declares himself the game's victor in a
river metaphor: he has channeled all Carol's flow of emotions toward
himself. Unbeknownst to the suitors, Carol has exchanged love tokens
with both. Venture received a diamond ring and gave her a pearl necklace;
Rider gave her the ring and received the necklace. Her joke comes out
when each vaunts his victory and taunts his rival. But it was foreshad-
owed when Trier kidded Venture that Carol gave him the diamond "Cause
she saw you a Sparke. . . . Youle see [the necklace] hang'd." And she
recalls it when, discrediting their sexual climbing, she jeers both Rider,
"Because I tooke your Diamond, must you presently / Bound like a ston'd
horse?" and Venture, if he believes that because he can "make a better
legge, then you were borne to . . . that I must / Strait fall in love w'e yee?"
(II.iv/486).

Obviousness and strain segregate Venture's and Rider's parallelisms,
sexual punning, and imagistic analogies from Carol's casual, forceful
elaborations. While she represents the apparently effortless modishness
of the privileged caste, the gamesters get obnoxious. Each competitor
sees her as a trophy. Each enters the arena expressly to taunt his rival
under the sham of offering friendly advice. Each is quick to feel insulted
and to suggest assuaging his honor by the swords they wear to display
caste superiority. Both have to be admonished to keep the "nakednesse of
[their] tooles" "covered" and to be "discreet" about their phallic combativeness (I.i/465-66). The thrust and parry in the vaunts and taunts of
the rival suitors serve for dueling when each one (egged on by Trier) turns

his opponent's claims and clauses back on him in repetitive parallel antitheses. In the wrangle over the "trophies / Of vanquisht love," clauses—such as Rider's warning that "There wil be lesse affront then to expect / Till the last minute, and behold the victory / Anothers" and Venture's "A Ladies love is mortall, I know that, / And if a thousand men should love a woman, / The dice must carry her, but one of all / Can weare the Garland"—rebound to mock the speaker. Trier's verdict that Carol has "fitted [the rivals] / With a paire of fooles Coates, as hansomely / As any Taylor, that had taken measure" returns to the norm of casually introduced and varied figures related to playing.

As it initiates role definition through language, the opening scene also initiates onstage appreciation of sophisticated talk, one signal of accounting. The rivals have Trier "observe" them "make you a little sport." So he does, exhorting them, until they, humiliated, resolve to team up on the woman who has mocked them: "Lets walke, and thinke how to behave our selves." They too then make accounts. All of *Hyde Park*'s characters appreciate the urbane linguistic performance that verifies as it creates their privileged roles. Even in disguise Bonavent makes easy sexual puns on "servant" and converses in ways that demark his gentility (II.i). And Lacy's invitation for him to join the betrothal dance, "Your tongue does walke our language, and your feete / Shall do as we do" (II.ii/478), recognizes his sociopolitical status as much as his nationality. When Lord Bonvile welcomes Julietta to springtime and the park with the elaborate manners and discourse of courtly pastoral, she demurs that while "You expresse / A Master of all Complement, I have / Nothing but plaine humilitie, my Lord, / To answere you." Simultaneously she observes the decorum of their unequal social status and suggests that they share a privileged linguistic precinct. Likewise, Bonvile gallantly and perceptively confesses linguistic artifice at the same time that he honors it, and their facility: "But ile speake our owne English, / Hang these affected straines, which we sometimes / Practise, to please the curiosity / Of talking Ladyes" (III.i/492). After his extended salacious verbal play on the "honor" that names his title and Julietta's virginity, he appreciates the class of her rebuff in his own terms, which create double references to betting the horses and sexual gaming: "That was a witty one" (III.i/494). In contrast, Venture's vanity over his poetic abilities sets up Carol's use and abuse of him. She can encourage him to compose a poem on "how much you dare suffer for me" and then ridicule his doggerel travesty; moreover, by attributing it to Fairfield she can signal her receptiveness to his overtures. She thereby proves Venture's marginality and her superior caste.

These three named instances—Bonavent's good arrival, Bonvile's potential virtue in venality, and Carol's choice of the Fair(est)field offered by her suitors—indicate the privileged linguistic behavior created through the three plots of *Hyde Park*. Each plot presents a variation on personality formation within the hierarchical bounds of monarchy, ascribed degree, and male dominion promoted by Charles's court. A counter hypothesis, by Butler, argues Julietta's reform of the prodigal Lord Bonvile: Representing a "town" elite for whom property and propriety merge, Julietta maintains traditional humility and reverent distance from the lord who would seduce her; at the same time she implies her superior merit by admonishing him that his status obliges him to guard morality.[44] Bonvile's change, however, is no reformation but a reconversion to a set of standards already in place; Julietta takes for granted his reclamation for the courtly status quo. Moreover, Julietta, no less than Mistress Bonavent and Carol, remains subordinate, dependent for any leverage on marital brokerage. However independent-minded or free-spirited any may seem, no character trespasses the limits of talk and action observed by privileged followers of the court. The case is conspicuously implicit in the martial or gaming figures that most critics (Levin for example) borrow from the play when they write about the final marriage plans: men win, women succumb.[45]

One limitation of Butler's hypothesis is the exclusion of Carol, and probably Julietta, from the game playing and role manipulation that occupy the privileged characters in *Hyde Park*. Each is intent on trying on roles, adapting roles, and especially testing others for matching roles. Their general preoccupation with testing is named in Julietta's Trier. He introduces his fiancée to his patron, Lord Bonvile, as a "lady of pleasure" in order (following venerable dramatic tradition) to "try" her "honor": "If shee resist his siege, she is a brave one, / I know hee'le put her too't, he that doth love / Wisely, will see the triall of his Mistris" (II.iii/482). By making a phony excuse to leave he cues Bonvile to pursue his customary designs. When the bothered Julietta demurs, "You wonot use me well, and shew no care / Of me, nor of my honour, I pray stay!" Trier affirms her fidelity:

> Thou hast vertue to secure all, I am confident,
> Temptations will shake thy innocence,
> Not more then waves, that clime a Rocke, which soone
> Betray their weakenesse, and discover thee,
> More cleare and more impregnable.

While he accurately estimates her honor, his suspicious motive startles her into exclaiming, "How is this?" She has been personally stung by the distrust of the chastity of ladies on the part of gentlemen generally.

Julietta's rejection of Trier is instructive. He shadows Bonvile and Julietta's meeting at Hyde Park, then initiates a lovers' tiff. When she refuses to estimate the odds of converting the promiscuous Bonvile until she meets him again, Trier gets upset. When she interrogates whether he suspects her or the lord, Trier politely and evasively "dare[s] not conclude that but from the matter / Of his discourse, on which there may depend / A circumstance that may not prove so happy." But she presses the case of distrust, warning him that his very trial of her indicates his projection of his own potential infidelities: "Now I must tell you, Sir, I see your heart / Is not so just as I deserve, you have / Engag'd me to his conversation, / Provok'd by jealous thoughts, and now your feare / Betrayes your want of goodnes, for he never / Was right at home, that dare suspect his Mistris" (III.i/496). However Trier may want to call off his test of her honor, she determines to undergo it. His jealous observation becomes ever more annoying until at the beginning of the final scene he brags on the successful trial to Bonvile and Julietta: "Know Lady, I ha tryed you. . . . And I have found thee right / And perfect gold, nor will I change thee for / A Crowne imperiall" (V.ii). But he is shocked out of presumption into echoing her "How is this?" when she accuses him:

> And I have tryed you,
> And found you drosse, nor doe I love my heart
> So ill, to change it with you.
>
> . . . .
>
> Vnworthily you have suspected me,
> And cherish'd that bad humor, for which know
> You never must have hope to gaine my love,
> He that shall doubt my vertue, out of fancy,
> Merits my just suspition and disdaine.   [V.ii/536]

Since Julietta resists Bonvile's seduction without any resentment that might indicate her balking at privileged mores, Bonvile discovers in her "a wife for him, / Whose thoughts were nere corrupted." Both ladies and gentlemen in this society assume that gentlemen require their own reassuring trials of ladies.

A need to test his wife's fidelity must move Bonavent's otherwise unmotivated decision to disguise his return on the seventh anniversary of his departure. When he questions what kind of longterm "servant" Mistress Bonavent's new husband Lacy has been, he disregards the obvious answer of a suitor to suggest a gigolo or a gentleman usher. And when he comes to the races he proves that he is a gentleman by questioning Carol about his wife's fidelity in witty gaming diction: "In English has he plaid the forward gamester / And turnd up trump?" (III.i/498). Only after he is satisfied does he reveal himself.

The most telling trial in *Hyde Park* is that of Fairfield by Carol. By initiating the trial she highlights the importance, in a society governed by the double standard, for women to test the fidelity of men. Like Julietta, Carol several times, particularly in her second scene with Fairfield, mentions how much she needs friends she can trust. Then mid-play and mid-park, in a brief confession of love that she masks in an immediate trick and taunt, Carol explains to Fairfield her motives for testing his love by thwarting him: "Pardon me sir, if I have seem'd too light, / It was not rudeness from my heart, but a / Disguise to save my honour if I found / You still incredulous" (III.ii/503). Carol does not merely play the conventional role of disdainful lady in the courtship game. Since in her society the seduction of ladies by gentlemen dominates the game, she adapts the role to prove a suitor's loyalty before she takes him seriously. She thereby guards her chastity, her gaming chip, and tests a potential husband's propensity for philandering before she makes a commitment.

Privileged roles, with the language that molds as well as models them, are explicitly accounted for in the three principal plots of *Hyde Park*. Just as the Bonavents' actions frame *Hyde Park*, so their behavior sets a court-espoused norm for roles. Then Julietta, Bonvile, and Trier, and Carol, Fairfield, Venture, and Rider conform to it. The way these characters discover, test, adapt, and account for roles disproves two arguments about Julietta's conversion of Bonvile: that a somewhat mobile social status determined by merit is at work and that those born to higher station have to respect the rights of those born subordinate. It also disproves two interpretations by critics who are influenced by Shakespeare's Beatrice when they consider Carol: that her treatment of Rider and Venture exhibits her vivacious independence and that her bouts with Fairfield demonstrate the settlement of a balanced amorous partnership. Instead, Julietta's conversion of Bonvile amounts to a reversion to the prerogatives of privilege that are embedded in the Bonavent plot; and Carol's satiric wit amounts to a socially sanctioned, somewhat livelier mode of feminine subservience that is bounded by the Bonavent plot.

Two Bonavent scenes define *Hyde Park*'s norms: Carol's morning argument against Mistress Bonavent's remarriage and Bonavent's afternoon retaliation against Lacy for forcing him to dance in honor of the wedding. In the morning Mistress Bonavent tells Carol her intentions:

> I have
> Bin carefull of my vow; and were there hope
> Yet to embrace [my husband], I would thinke another
> Seven years [of waiting] no penance, but I should thus
> Be held a cruell woman, in his certaine
> Losse, to despise the love of all mankinde.
> And therefore I resolve, upon so large

A triall of [Lacy's] Constancy, at last
To give him the reward of his respects
To me, and—
    Ca. Marry him.   [I.ii/469]

Mistress Bonavent affirms fidelity to the institution of marriage more than to her husband. As marriage is the only state she conceives for a woman, she questions only to whom she will be married. If the possibility exists that her husband still lives after seven years, then she is obliged to him; if it does not, then she is obliged to reward her long-term suitor. She owes herself to some man, as Carol puts it out of "charity," more accurately out of custom. After Mistress Bonavent agrees to marry Lacy posthaste and Carol rebuffs Fairfield, Carol emphasizes the subservience involved. She cannot fathom why a widow, who has gained the most independent female status available in the era, would give up her liberties: owning property and purchasing whatever clothing she wants, choosing and ruling household servants and pets without worrying about a jealous husband's spies, picking her own tailors and doctors and priests, maintaining her own company, and being answerable to no one for her behavior. "Will you lose all this? For 'I *Sisley* take thee, *Iohn*, / To be my husband'?" Though Carol advises keeping love servants instead, Mistress Bonavent feels comfortable with and honors socially sanctioned feminine subordination in marriage.

That afternoon Bonavent demonstrates an equivalent adherence to his privileged society's norm of masculine games of aggressive dominance. He draws on and forces Lacy to jig, pursuing the quarrel almost to a duel. Then he explicitly accounts for his standard when Mistress Bonavent admonishes her two men not to break the peace on her marriage day. First, he justifies his zealous quarreling and dueling as a requirement of his status. His honor as an unarmed guest and gentleman has been affronted: "I had bin / Lesse than a man, to thinke of no return, / And had he beene the onely of my blood, / I would not be so much the shame of soldier / To have beene tam'd and suffered." Second, he declares the requisites of a gentleman beyond the ken of a lady, who needs only to obey her guardian male: "you are / Too hasty in your judgement, I could say / More, but tis dishonour to expostulate / These causes with a woman." Third, for now Bonavent conceals his test of his wife because his ultimate honor depends on proving her fidelity: "I had reason / To call him to account, you know not all / My provocation, things are not with me / As with another man." When, despite his seven years' absence, she puts a divorce from him in question, she passes the covert test that remains a mystery she is supposedly disqualified by sex to understand. Bonavent proves overanxious for his mistress to prove her faithful, obedient subservience to his memory. The instant she acknowledges that she is a sign of the masculine prerogatives and pride of whoever is her husband and doubts that Bonavent is in fact dead and she freed—"'Las, I am part of [Lacy] now, and betweene / A Widdow and his wife, if I be thus / Divorc'd"—Bonavent interrupts her: "Ile be his servant" (IV.iii/522-23).

Julietta and Lord Bonvile's relationship is also epitomized by a climactic scene. When she insists that he maintain his honor by preserving hers she reconverts him to a renewed sense of obligation from a prodigality licensed doubly, for many, by his manhood and degree. And she accomplishes this reconversion by accounting for nobility. The defining of nobility begins when Trier takes into account a masculine gentility that has molded Bonvile into "A gentleman that loves cleane Napery":

> A Lady of pleasure, tis no shame for Men
> Of his high birth to love a Wench, his honour
> May priviledge more sinnes, next to a Woman
> He loves a running-horse, setting a side these recreations,
> He has a Noble Nature, valiant, bountifull.   [I.i/464]

Thereafter the couple's verbal games create a context for defining any license permitted and the responsibilities obliged by masculine nobility. From Trier's introduction of Julietta (as a lady of pleasure) to Lord Bonvile, through the couple's two encounters, to the conversion scene, the pair play with dual social and gender connotations. The designations *lord* and *noble* for him, *humble* and *gentle* for her, and *honor* for both mark their model language and come to account for their roles. Trier's commendation of his patron as the "Perfection of honour," Julietta's nomination of herself as her patron's "humble" servant, and Bonvile's description of the statements as formal "complement" (indicating his desire to close the sexual if not social distance), establish the linguistic and behavioral roles that undergo mutual definition. Bonvile, courtly when courting a courtesan, employs a series of double entendres to press his sexual desires. Julietta, diplomatic in defense, maintains social and sexual distance by employing a decorum of knowing innocence to express multiple aspects of honor. Their first scene builds to her putting him off by calling "merry" his declaration that "theres no hansome woman / Complaines that she has lost her maidenhead, / But I wish mine had bin lost with it" (II.iii/481). Such an aware, privileged discourse of facile, witty repartee can encourage, without incriminating laboriousness or stifling earnestness, the discovery and adaptation of roles within the bounds of a game. Moreover, the playfulness of the discourse is emphasized in its imitation. A cleverly lecherous approach by Bonvile's witty page burlesques his lord's good breeding, and its repulse by Julietta's honest but simple waiting woman sets off her mistress's born gentility.

In the park Bonvile shows two aspects of his status: he provides worthy leadership by promoting good humored festivity while inhibiting clashes over gaming; and he displays licensed lechery by pursuing Julietta through the alleys. Because of his polished, versatile language and accomplishments he attracts Julietta in both aspects. Likewise, her polite evasions of his importunate pursuit, which maintain her social and gender inferiority, attract him. After he opens the third act with a facile salute to her as the mistress of spring festivities, they jockey over their roles. When she declares him to be the "Master of all Complement" in contrast to her "plaine humilitie," he drops the "affected straines." When he asks her to serve his honor with hers, she pretends to understand him only in part, then she redefines the honor of lordship and the obligations of subservience. And when he pretends that she means license and "Vpon [his] honour" asks her to "lend [him] then / But a nights lodging," she declines to take his "knowledge" as other than "mirth."

For the conversion Julietta, having adapted her role and language as close to Bonvile's as she can while preserving her honor in their elite society, demands that he adopt the honor his king promulgates. Having pledged to perform any "Noble worke" for a lord "born to't," she is pressed by his insistence that a "gentlewoman" must increase a "lord"'s "pleasure" by "serving [his] turn." So she boldly takes her "first libertie" to delineate the heretofore diplomatically blurred differences between their respective definitions of lordship: licensed prerogative versus obliged responsibility. After denying that she owes her superiors sexual duties, she begins her account of his obligations: "T'were better not to have beene borne to honours, / Than forfeit em so poorely, he is truely / Noble, and best justifies his blood, / When he can number the descents of virtue" (V.i/529). When Bonvile demands to know if Julietta wants to "degrade" him, she declares that since his "high blood" keeps him "separate and distinct," since he is mystified beyond her comprehension, and since she dutifully worships his genuine prerogatives, she possesses neither the power nor the desire to do so: "It is my duty, where the king has seal'd / His favours, I should shew humility / My best obedience, to his act."

At the same time that on her monarch's authority she obeys the Caroline court's hierarchy by degree, she redefines that inheritance: a title remains good when its holder maintains the virtues on which it was founded. Having in her exordium established an ethos of loyalty and proposed her topic, Julietta continues her speech, interrupted intermittently by Bonvile's licentious interpretations. At her most daring she challenges him. "In such a vitious age" he will deserve the reverence due his status and he may command "any noble tryall" only when he sets an "example too of goodnesse,"

> but I must
> Be bold to tell you sir, unlesse you prove
> A friend to vertue were your honour centupled,
> Could you pile titles till you reach the Clouds,
> Were every petty Mannor you possesse
> A Kingdome, and the bloud of many Princes
> Vnited in your veynes, with these had you
> A person that had more attraction
> Than Poesie can furnish, love withall,
> Yet I, I in such infinite distance am
> As much above you in my innocence.

Taken aback, Bonvile demurs that her speech "becomes not," that she has exceeded her social and gender status, that her harangue is tedious. Recalled to the duty of his station, his promise of an eventual conversion after their liaison allows Julietta a *contemptus mundi* peroration. Whereas he could maintain a "seat among the grave nobility" by playing the role that models his "Countries honour," for a lifelong dishonor of wives and virgins she foresees his old age burdened with impotence and remorse. Throughout this speech Julietta has reminded Bonvile of the old definition of nobility that he has been repressing and she defining all along. Thus she reconverts him. He contritely acknowledges the moral that goes without saying: "If this be true? what a wretched thing should I / Appeare now, if I were anything but a Lord, I do not like my selfe." Since he promises to preserve his honor by preserving hers, Julietta is honored to serve as his handmaid; so she honors and obeys her husband "in Noble waies."

If Julietta has to remind Lord Bonvile of the professed norms of his caste, Carol constantly considers them, particularly when she appears to be violating the gender conventions of her privileged society. Beyond responding sensitively to the conventions necessary for roles, she accounts precisely for various roles. Playing the incredulous misogamist against Mistress Bonavent's embrace of marriage, she opens by belittling her friend's eager surrender to male dominion, lamenting feminine frailty in love, and projecting a world of Amazons. More importantly, she points out her own dependence on the society's marriage mart when she advises Mistress Bonavent on how to play the wooing game to her advantage:

> Keepe [Lacy] still to be your servant,
> Imitate me, a hundred suiters cannot
> Be halfe the trouble of one husband. I

Dispose my frownes, and favours like a Princesse
Deject, advance, undo, create again
It keepes the Subjects in obedience,
And teaches em to looke at me with distance.   [I.ii/475]

Since Carol recognizes that without social conventions she would have to
play a very different way from the earlier disdainful lady, her progress
with Fairfield entails adapting the received role to her needs. Once
Fairfield has employed reverse psychology, extracting her oath "for no
reason to affect" him, the audience entertains no doubts (whatever his
fears) that Carol is choosing a role within privileged social constraints to
match his:

              An oath that for the present,
    I had no affection to him, had beene reasonable,
    But for the time to come, never to love,
    For any cause or reason, that may move me
    Hereafter, very strange, I know not what to thinke on't,
    Although I never meant, to thinke well on him,
    Yet to be limitted, and be prescrib'd,
    I must not doe it? twas a poore tricke in him.   [II.iv/491]

She reconfirms her interest in private. When she sees Fairfield with a
decoy, his sister Julietta, she gets jealous in an aside: "Keepe in great
heart" (III.i/498). When she mistreats him, apart from the others she
berates herself. In a stereotypical feminine act, she hides in her coach to
cry because she has perhaps lost him. Now Carol plays for Fairfield more
deviously than he played for her, by keeping up the manbaiting role she
has adapted from the repertoire of roles her privileged society allows.

    Carol and Fairfield develop their roles by repeatedly playing a restric-
tive scenario that defines roles by discarding alternatives. In opening, one
of Carol's suitors, generally Fairfield, overplays the wooing role and turns
it into a travesty; mid-game Carol satirizes the absurd burlesque; in the
endgame Fairfield falls back to a moderate portrayal of a mutually acceptable variation on the role, which Carol accepts as a role different in kind.
The couple's first meeting (I.ii) initiates play when Fairfield, sensing a
pose, approaches her as a disdainful lady. But she perversely miscontrues
the approach so as to oppose "your Courtship . . . [of] Cupids devices . . .
whirligiggs . . . [and] a mad packet." Next, he overreacts to her advice to
leave off imitating servile suitors who flatter with stale similes and wornout poesies, and instead to assume traditional "priviledge / Your Masculine property." But she teases him for scolding like a gamester. Finally
he tries to hold her hand and win her for procreation. But she discounts as
brainless anyone who serves a blind boy. Although Fairfield leaves in

frustration, his last part approaches an acceptable mean between silly suitor and blustering railer. Carol has turned him away from absurd stereotypes and toward a role he might reasonably perform: a gentleman with the self-respect to engage a lady. And she has signalled how she can be wooed, to any gentleman sensitive enough to match her witty, versatile employment of her set's condoned roles.

At the beginning of their second scene (II.iv), when Fairfield sets up the reverse wooing and the central love declarations, Venture and Rider substitute as butts for Carol's ridicule of witless role-players. When Fairfield offers to depart in exchange for her oath to keep some promise he will not yet reveal, her provisos further define roles she finds acceptable for her self and any wooers. Her refusal to give up any traditional feminine fancies indicates that she values conventional roles. But her refusal to submit to the desires of a set of burlesque suitors—whatever a young wooer would pursue, a disgruntled reject compel, or a tyrant command—indicates that she does not find all conventional roles acceptable. When she finally states the unbargainable issue implicit in her rejection of the extreme feminine roles demanded by possessive suitors, she sets her role: she "must have [her] humor" to continue appearing as a misogamist and satirist of stereotypes. While content to choose from among her society's roles, then, she insists on her right to make a choice. Since Fairfield promises not to be possessive, Carol swears by a kiss to the entrapping pact.

In their last scene, which closes the brackets around their defining scene, Carol and Fairfield negotiate marital roles that will satisfy her needs, his needs, and their society's constraints. Carol sets up a travesty of a self-sacrificing lover for him to play and her to pity by forging Fairfield's signature to Venture's rime, "how much [he] dare[s] suffer for" her. She offers to accept him out of fear for his safety and dread of public censure if he goes berserk. But she has him read the burlesque vows to endure tartarean punishments for her love, to help her "frame [her] selfe to love [him]. . . . to save [his] life" (V.i/532ff). In reaction to Carol's condescension Fairfield overplays a misogynist. Far in excess of ordinary claims that he will "never dote again; / Nor marry nor endure the imaginations / Of your fraile sex, this very night I will / Be fitted for you all, Ile geld my selfe." Having tried extreme roles, the couple settle on a middle variant: committed but skittish lovers who add diversion inside the bounds permitted by their privileged society.

Though their roles get resolved in the last act, Carol and Fairfield settle their relationship earlier. Fairfield answers Carol's summons in the park by hiding Trier to witness how he has "miraculously" "brought things about" to "humble her" (III.i/500, ii/501). But Carol is not about to simply surrender her independence. "He has gone a strange way to worke with me" suggests that she will choose him. But "I am asham'd to thinke what I must say now" implies a problem. She may refer to the love vow she is ready to make after she tests him or she may mean any outrageous lie she is prepared to perpetrate later, as when she embarrasses him in front of Trier. It is clear that she will be testing roles as the scene and the relationship progress. By denying that she has gone against her oath by sending for him, she at once puts off his triumph. Then she imagines another burlesque role for him:

> Be you no prompter to insinuate
> The first word of your studied Oration,
> He's out ons part, come, come Ile imagine it,
> Was it not something to this purpose—Lady,
> Or Mistresse, or what you will, although
> I must confesse; you may with justice laugh at
> My most ridiculous suite, and you will say
> I am a fool. . . . .
> To come agen, whom you have so tormented,
> For nere was simple Camomile so trod on,
> Yet still I grow in love . . . .

And so on through the euphuistic absurdity of committing suicide over her. "Am not I a witch?" (III.ii/502-3) Unfooled, Fairfield seeks capitulation:

> Oh woman!
> How farre thy tongue and heart doe live asunder.
> Come; I ha found you out, off with this vayle,
> It hides not your complexion I doe tell thee,
> I see thy heart, and every thought within it
> A little peevishnesse to save your credit
> Had not beene much amisse, but this over
> Over doing the business it appeares
> Ridiculous.

Fairfield reverses their parts, advising Carol against extravagant self-portrayal. At the same time he lets her know that some coyness is becoming. "I love thee better / For thy Vagaries," he responds when she begs pardon for testing his sincerity. Encouraged, she overplays to his desire, hyperbolically confessing her love for him:

> I must confesse y'ave caught me, had you still
> Pursued the common path, I had fled from you,
> You found the constitution of women
> In me, whose will, not reason is their law,

> Most apt to doe what most they are forbidden,
> Impatient of curbes in their desires.
>   *Fa.* Thou sayest right.
>   *Ca.* Oh love I am thy Captive.

Having agreed on a basis for their relationship, Carol continues to jockey for mutually agreeable, face-saving adaptations of received roles. When she recalls her oath not to affect him, Fairfield gallantly rationalizes that since her previous oath was to have her humor or be sick, she can void her subsequent oath by designating that her humor is to break the oath. As Fairfield becomes more conciliatory Carol surrenders: "You have releev'd me! / But do not triumph in your conquest sir, / Be modest in your victory." In her surrender, however, she warns as she requests. While in private she accepts the feminine subordination exemplified by Mistress Bonavent and honored by Julietta, she is not going to play the role of subservient wife in public. So, when Fairfield calls Trier as a witness of their match and his triumph, she tosses off the meeting as a request for her to cosign a loan; then she joins Trier's laughter at him. Fairfield has to learn that if he approaches her in public "by strategem and Ambuscado," she will retaliate. She confesses to her privileged audience her qualms that "I am an infidell to use him thus" and her fears that "I shall foole too much." But she will not broadcast her submission. Still, as he stomps away she lets him know that in private she will play her society's assignment of submissive woman; for hearkening to the nightingale's song, she notes that it brings lovers good luck. Thus are set the rules of this couple's game.

Through formative and enforcing language and role games Shirley reaffirmed the ground rules and bounds of courtly values: of absolute monarchy, ascribed hierarchy, patriarchy, and male dominion. He varied a tradition of poetic drama that he lauded as witty and involved, sophisticated and didactic, both for the way it models parts and for the way it sentences the violations of strict courtly norms. His elite audience could resort to *Hyde Park* and his other plays to find models for re-creative games, just as they could resort to Hyde Park to enjoy recreative gaming. At his plays his audience could observe an exemplary mirror that governed the situations and language roles of their social gaming, their personal development, and their relations to the norms of privilege that maintained their mutually reinforcing identities and caste, just as the park enclosed a setting for their gambling.

At a glance Shirley's social game playing might seem not unlike Massinger's interest in passing on traditions reformed through accommodation. But Shirley's recreative game is enclosed in the same social preserve of intact traditional hierarchies that is enforced by Ford's ceremonial. Still, Shirley is not as concerned as Ford is with the integrity of an essential self that seems directed into tragedy by a noble society. Instead, like Brome, he foregrounds roles; the difference is that his characters and games are rule bound. Shirley's repertoire of roles amounts to a set of assignments that permit slight variations and adaptations within straitened models sanctioned by a courtly heritage whereas Brome's array of roles encourages experiments and challenges which can try new possibilities that counter tradition.

5

Brome's Comedy of Types and Inversions

The Revisionary Potential of Brome's Backgrounds

There is even less information about Richard Brome and his acquaintances than there is about his colleagues and theirs. Apart from evidence about his theatrical associates, few traces of his background remain. Compared to that loyal son of the adviser and agent of noble patrons, Massinger, that genteel son placed at the inns of court by his well connected family, Ford, or that ambitious son of a moderately prosperous merchant, Shirley, we have scant knowledge of Brome's family, schooling, or friendships. So his attitudes remain even more open to conjecture than theirs. The hints left for us indicate that he came from common origins and worked his way up. One pattern among overachievers is to turn on their heritages, try to ignore their pasts, and take on their patrons' values. Most critics, such as McLuskie in The Revels History of English Drama, have accepted Kaufmann's description of a morally, socially, and politically normative as well as artistically traditional Brome.[1] But another pattern is also familiar: overachievers can cultivate their origins, develop critiques of current sociopolitical and artistic givens, and suggest revisions. This view, which has been recommended by Sedge, intimated by Shaw, and argued by Butler, seems to offer an increasingly attractive hypothesis about Brome's attitudes and plays.[2]

No biography has been verified before the famous reference to Jonson's "man, Master Brome," in the induction to Bartholomew Fair (1614). Because Brome had a penchant and an ear for dialects it does not seem unlikely that he came to London from the outlands. And because a Richard Brome is listed among the Queen of Bohemia's Players, it seems likely that he was once an itinerant player in a troupe traveling the provinces.[3] He was thoroughly professional, and many of his friends were theater professionals. Jonson proclaimed and Brome took pride in his rare master's professional paternity; Dekker made the same claim; and Heywood collaborated with Brome twice. Ford and Shirley wrote commendatory verses for his plays, and he returned the compliment to Shirley. John Tatham, who succeeded Heywood both as the Poet Laureate of London for the Lord Mayor's pageants and as the principal writer for the Red Bull theater, traded commendatory verses with Brome. Other lesser literary figures, too, wrote to honor him: Robert Chamberlain, an apothegmatist; John Hall, a friend of Shirley as well as a pamphleteer commended by Cromwell. And Brome wrote to honor many of them: Shakerley Marmion, a boon companion of Suckling and the author of *Cupid and Psyche;* Thomas Nabbes, another playwright who was associated with the Salisbury Court theater; Humphrey Mills, a hack. Other friends apart from Stephen(?) Brome, his brother, and Alexander Brome, his unrelated editor, seem to stem from stage associations. His closest known friends, Christopher and especially William Beeston, father and son, were theatrical impresarios; the son risked, and got, censorship and reprimand with Brome. A double commender, C.G., if Christopher Goad, was a member of the King's Revels at Salisbury Court; he also praised Tatham. Most of these theater professionals were closer to the city than to the court.

After his initial success with the King's Men at the private Blackfriars as well as at the public Globe, Brome concentrated on less prestigious theaters and so on privileged audiences less likely to have been ranked with courtiers. After producing *The Northern Lass* (1629) and perhaps *The Queen's Exchange* (1629-31?), certainly *The Novella* and probably *The Covent-Garden Weeded* (both 1632) for the King's Men, Brome seems to have written primarily for a succession of companies at the Salisbury Court theater. Brome did his last plays, beginning with *A Mad Couple Well Match'd* (1639), for Beeston's Boys at the Cockpit in Drury Lane. While Salisbury Court and the Cockpit in Drury Lane were private theaters, neither proved as courtly or as prestigious as Blackfriars. And only the Cockpit presumed so high.

The final meager evidence about Brome's projected audience comes with two of his three dedicatees. To William Seymour, Earl of Hertford, Brome presented a manuscript of *The English Moor* (1637) and dedicated *The Antipodes* (1638). Hertford was appointed governor of the Prince of Wales in 1641 and he did ultimately support the king. But through the 1630s he was, as Butler shows, one of the nobles who criticized many of Charles's actions. Brome's most significant dedication was to William Cavendish, the Earl of Newcastle, that notable patron especially associated with Brome's mentor, Jonson, and with Shirley. To Newcastle, Brome dedicated *The Sparagus Garden* (1635) when he published it in 1640; and for Newcastle's comedy, *The Variety* (1641?), he wrote a commendatory poem. Butler recounts Newcastle's nostalgia for the Elizabethan court and his desire for reforms in the Stuart court. Similar sentiments compelled a number of privileged Carolines to express the need for changes in view of the future, not merely in retrospect on the past.[4] There are indications, then, that Brome shared with much of his known audience a nostalgia for tradition combined with some dismay over the current court scrambling that thrived on absolutism and favoritism; moreover, such feelings could take the form of proposed changes. A similar tendency appears in Brome's revisionary adoption of dramatic traditions. Both inclinations are revealed in the ways Brome's plays repeatedly present problems requiring personal and sociopolitical change.

Political and Social Questioning

Situating Brome's political and social views, like characterizing his associations, is more difficult than for the other Caroline professional playwrights. Evaluations from Kaufmann's in the 1950s through Shaw's and Butler's in the 1980s have made clearer for Brome than for Massinger—much clearer than for Ford or for Shirley—that here was neither an evasion of the present nor a mirror of decadence. Brome presented pressing issues in a pressing time. His persistent concern with Caroline sociopolitics, like Shirley's, is indicated by the settings and subjects of his plays. All those extant present contemporary London or its environs, except for a few tragicomedies. *The Queen's Exchange* is set in British antiquity, *The Novella* in contemporary Venice, and *The Love-sick Court* (1633-38?) in a burlesque domain of current plays; *The Queen and Concubine* (1635-36) is set in Sicily but it comments on favoritism in sociopolitics and on adherence to hierarchy. Like Shirley and a few other Caroline dramatists, Brome employed local sites such as Ram Alley for *A Mad Couple Well-Match'd;* some of these are mentioned in his titles, as in *The Covent-Garden Weeded* and *The Sparagus Garden.*[5] More often than Shirley's, Brome's plays target celebrities, such as Inigo Jones in *The Covent-Garden Weeded*, who is joined by Sir John Suckling and Sir William Davenant in *The Court Beggar* (1640).[6] Brome serves social historians better than the other Caroline professionals do because he perpetually mentions new fads such as balconies, litters, men's pocket combs, and women's black bags. And he rivals Shirley's record for presenting contemporary institutions, such as *The New Academy, or The New Exchange* (1635?), *The Damoiselle, or The New Ordinary* (1638?), and the blackface masque in *The English Moor, or The Mock-Marriage,* as vehicles for themes.

Brome's contemporary allusions do not seem casual. His pointed albeit intermittent references to courts and legalities provide more than evidence of irritations that culminated in the well-known lawsuit over his contract with the Salisbury Court company. They indicate ire at authorities who abuse their positions and subjects who scramble for status to abuse. From *The Northern Lass's* aptly named blustering Bulfinch and overbearing, lecherous Squelch, who are attended by the larcenous Constable Vexhem, to *A Jovial Crew's* verbosely abusive Justice Clack, his portraits of justices show a Brome disturbed by peremptory, tyrannous authority. His recurring stories about victims of malicious and predatory lawsuits reveal a Brome anguished by the misuse of the courts. Yet legal suits in Brome can be atoned for. For instance, Meanwell and Rashley entangle *The English Moor* in their repentance for an unjust suit against decayed Winloss. And often in Brome the law's victims have counterbalances. Ruined Brookall, who rails against the law's inequities and refuses to perjure himself as a paid witness, contrasts in *The Damoiselle* with Justice Bumpsey, who maintains his family by shrewd generosity.

If there is plenty of evidence for what Brome took to be political and social problems in his era, there is little agreement in ours as to what attitudes he held. Kaufmann portrays a nostalgic conservative concerned to preserve Elizabethan values, Butler a radical political critic. Though contradictory, these views are not necessarily contrary. Recent historians corroborate that few of the political or social inclinations held by privileged Carolines as yet constituted oppositions. And visions of the past provided a primary source and motive for most of the era's calls for reform as well as for reaction. Peter Burke represents many students of the era: then "popular political consciousness was negative rather than positive."[7] Just so, Brome's predominant social and political targets are obvious, yet no consistent Brome platform is discernible. Apparently he saw no solutions apart from recognizing individual merit and granting mutual forgiveness. But he did come to suggest a way to try out change.

Brome's commitment to facing sociopolitical problems and his difficulty with offering solutions can be exemplified by what is often considered escapist, his last play before the closing of the theaters, *A Jovial Crew: or The Merry Beggars* (1641). Kaufmann was the first to reject a frothy *Jovial Crew*. He saw a "profoundly escapist" play that provided a dual moral: When the members of society become disenchanted they surrender to social dissolution. And only a few segments of society, probably particular extended households, can preserve Elizabethan values—by withdrawing into gentrified small gardens where each individual contributes to a tiny hierarchy.[8] So the opening of Brome's prologue offers forthright melancholia:

> The title of our play, *A Jovial Crew,*
> May seem to promise mirth, which were a new
> And forc'd thing in these sad and tragic days
> For you to find, or we express in plays.
> We wish you then would change that expectation,
> Since jovial mirth is now grown out of fashion.[9]

There comes to be no question that vagabondage fails to provide any escape. From the time that two sisters propose to become vagrants with their suitors, idyllic retreat gets undercut. Meriel may rhapsodize about

"Couchant and passant, guardant, rampant beggars" as "th'only happy people in a nation,"

> The only free men of a commonwealth;
> Free above scot-free; that observe no law,
> Obey no governor, use no religion,
> But what they draw from their own ancient custom,
> Or constitute themselves, yet are no rebels.   [II.i.172-76]

But as she fantasizes, the young men discern a far different heraldry for beggarage: "current and vagrant . . . Stockant, whippant." The runaways' public affirmations get confuted by their asides begging out. An oft quoted encomium extolls vagabondage as a conventionally utopian "wealth for public benefit" where "no grievance or perplexity; / No fear of war, or state disturbances. / No alteration in a commonwealth, / Or innovation, shakes a thought of theirs" (IV.ii.90-93, 98). But the interrupting "Of ours, you should say" corrects the Freudian slip, accentuating that each wishes the status on anybody else. This paean functions like the songs and dances that the beggars use to hide the anguished cries of a mother giving birth.

For beggars, freedom from responsibilities does not mean freedom from want, or from the struggle to survive by begging, prostitution, and theft, or from powerlessness before arbitrary threats, beatings, rapes, and imprisonments, or from the dread that drives many of them to bravado revelry and drunkenness. Economically it means they have nothing left to lose. Politically it means subjection to the arbitrary exercise of police power or ordinary force, to the wills of the physically and verbally domineering Justice Clack and his venal and vicious son Oliver. Butler recognizes here a reflection of the difficulties of gaining freedom without creating license, which confronted England during the short parliament of 1640.[10] For if beggarage fails, so does Kaufmann's nostalgic escape into small preserves of idyllic Elizabethan gentility. The gentry get undercut by their patent self-indulgence: Tallboy's moping over the flight of his enforced bride, Oliver Clack's leering and lecherous threats of force, Justice Clack's capricious and willful misuses of prerogative, Hearty's irresponsible retreat in vinous revelry. More important, the play's agents of resolution get undercut: the runaways' father, Oldrents, whose name indicates his station, and the good steward of Oldrents's estate, Springlove, who returns each year to the beggars' commonwealth.

Springlove is one director in *A Jovial Crew*. Another is a vagabond poet. As the beggars celebrate the wedding of an impotent old man and a drunken old woman, this master of the revels proposes to "present a commonwealth: Utopia, / With all her branches and consistencies," "The

country, the city, the court, and the camp, epitomiz'd and personated by a
gentleman, a merchant, a courtier, and a soldier," plus three professions,
"Divinity and Law" and learning (IV.ii.179-91). The roles in this induction
are filled by beggars who have fallen from the estates they represent, with
Springlove standing for a citizen merchant and a runaway lover for a
country gentleman. The poet proposes for his plot civil strife concluding
in a revolution: "I would have the country, the city, and the court, be at
great variance for superiority. Then would I have Divinity and Law stretch
their wide throats to appease and reconcile them; then would I have the
soldier cudgel them all together and overtop them all. Stay . . . . A beggar
. . . must at last overcome the soldier, and bring them all to Beggars' Hall"
(IV.ii.207-17). This apocalyptic fantasy of the victory of disenfranchised
beggars and disenchanted poets, Sidney's *vates*, may mirror the radical
social prophecies promulgated among the increasing number of "master-
less men" portrayed in Christopher Hill's *The World Turned Upside Down*.[11]
But in *A Jovial Crew* the fantasy never gets produced since the magistrates
ride in, cut off the presentation, break up the assembly, then threaten,
arrest, and impound the beggars.

What finally gets presented is an induction for Oldrents at Justice
Clack's. Instead of projecting revolution Springlove's production recalls
the inexplicable melancholy of the old country gentleman who typifies
the malaise and the nostalgia of his caste. Oldrents balks at the original,
empathetic titles for the inset, *The Two Lost Daughters* and *The Vagrant
Steward*. Instead he consents to see *The Merry Beggars*, a prescription for
escaping melancholy and a choice that implicitly indicts him for indulging
in revelry so as to evade his responsibilities. The hedge-priest, Patrico,
presents actors who play their own roles in Oldrents's life. So the performance dissolves the distinctions between the lives of the inset's characters
and those of its onstage audience. Oldrents's masked runaway daughters
and steward reveal their attempt to revive him by temporarily joining the
merry beggars and thereby fulfilling without harm the fortune teller's sad
prophecy. Springlove has directed a restorative comedy during which
loyal daughters renew their patriarch's mirth and through which the
good steward fulfills his perpetual promise: "this is your birthnight into
a new world. And we all know (or have been told) that all come crying
into the world, when the whole world of pleasures is before us. The
world itself had ne'er been glorious, had it not first been a confused
chaos" (III.i.34-38).

But recovery from unease may not seem reassuring. After the inset
dissolves into the play Patrico reveals a family disease: he is the beggared
grandson of one Wrought-on, whom Oldrents's grandfather "craftily
wrought out / Of his estate" by unjust lawsuits (V.i.412-13, 320-26).
Oldrents's estates are not so ancient nor so sound nor so secure as might

be inferred from his name and status. As degree comes by lineal descent, so do sins. Moreover, Wrought-on reveals, descendants commit new sins: Oldrents sired a bastard on Wrought-on's sister, who died in childbirth. Following romance tradition, the lost child is recovered in the good steward, Springlove, and miraculously reconciled to the father he never knew. But despite reparation of this estate, Brome's play does not suggest any easy restoration of society. For that would require the incredibly charitable forgiveness of a Wrought-on, who for a tiny competence agrees to finish his days as Oldrents's "faithful beadsman," and of a Springlove, who proves to be a saint.

The dissolving of distinctions between the inset, *The Merry Beggars*, and the play for a Caroline audience, *A Jovial Crew*, suggests that Brome's presentation reflected his society and warned it of its need to meet sociopolitical responsibilities. *A Jovial Crew* sketches a matrix of problems Brome attacked in domains political, social, and familial, including pervasive interests economical. In Brome's plays all three arenas of human interaction exhibit complementary problems: abusing and hustling power. In politics some people exercise arbitrary authority while others scramble for preferment. In society some take advantage of status while others assault the hierarchy. In families fathers compel their children's occupational and marital decisions while children use and deny their fathers. Brome's families further implicate interlocking sexual questions: a double standard of philandering lovers and husbands versus faithful maids and wives threatens gender relations; and the exploitation and dread of cuckoldry undermine families. But while Brome finds plenty of problems he also discredits potential programs for recovery. So no specific political or social responses, other than charitable forgiveness, ever get defined in *A Jovial Crew*. Too much here depends on Hearty's idea of human action and reaction for "the whim of it" and on the conclusion's impractical reliance on "great providence."

Brome's plays are pervaded with precisely this same combination of an exhortation to face sociopolitical problems with an absence of principles on which change might be based or goals to which it could conform. His later plays became progressively more irresolute as Caroline dilemmas became more defined, and less avoidable. In sum, he consistently castigates oppressive authority and authoritarian abuses, thereby seeming subversive; yet he also adheres uneasily to inequitable received sexual norms and demonstrates inevitable human failures, thereby seeming traditional. Not atypical of the era, Brome is a subversive traditionalist whose plays, reflecting and satirizing human folly, damn no one. Had the aborted apocalyptic induction by the beggars' poet been performed, it might have suggested means of resolution. For elsewhere Brome proffers a process and a mood whereby tradition might be reformed.

Agreeing with Massinger's stance and opposing Ford's and Shirley's, Brome criticizes a monarch's use of authority for being tyrannical in two tragicomedies: his uneven variation of *King Lear*'s ancient setting, state, and family in *The Queen's Exchange* (presumably early) and his unusual hagiographic *The Queen and Concubine* (apparently mid-career). In both Brome also features a target for all the Caroline professionals, the sycophantic scramble for unmerited preferment to royal favoritism. And in both he joins Massinger in presenting sociopolitical climbing as sustaining and being fostered by absolutism. Willful tyranny appears at the opening of *The Queen's Exchange*. The queen of the West Saxons, Bertha, imposes on her council her choice of a husband, Osriick of Northumbria, who is alien to her citizens by his absolutism as well as by his birth. Invoking divine sovereignty, Bertha demands that her advisers "rectify" their "scrupulous judgement" to her commandment. But Kentlike Segebert, pleading his oath to the late king, pledges loyalty to nationalist commonweal traditions. After Segebert is banished, the sycophancy of Northumbrians vacillating before the passionate, despotic Osriick is mirrored by one Jeffrey. Jeffrey's destructive zeal when celebrating the king's forthcoming marriage initially earns him promotion from village to court fool; reflecting court madness he mounts "the hobby horse of preferment" and gallops away from country virtues (II.ii).[12] Thereafter he points up the advancements for folly and the penalties for merit. He describes the bribery, purchase, backbiting, dealings, and wheelings of court fortune whereby the desertless rise by each others' falls (especially III/500-504). After miraculous tragicomic reversals, *The Queen's Exchange* concludes with a political homily: Osriick, who has been reawakened to responsible monarchy, praises the allegiance and care of his country's lords who counteracted his commands; and Bertha begs the loyal Segebert's pardon.

The Queen and Concubine presents a spectacle of mutually reinforcing tyrannical authority and sycophantic competition. Gonzago, an absolute, capricious ruler who envies recognition for anyone else, banishes his patient Griselda queen, Eulalia, and orders the execution of his victorious general, Sforza, on false charges of adultery; meanwhile he elevates the queen's protégé and Sforza's daughter, Alinda, to royal mistress, then queen, and he recalls Sforza's rival to be his commander-in-chief. Alinda, who has learned at court to seek preferment regardless of the price to others, leads a set of treacherous climbers. In one of several damning scenes she concludes instructions to her machiavellian accomplice with a stairway of ambition metaphor: she might pity her former protectress and her father "For being hew'd out and squar'd thus to my use, / But that they make those necessary steps / By which I must ascend to my Ambition. / They that will rise unto a supream Head / Should not regard upon whose Necks they tread" (I.ix/19-20). The banished queen, who remains faithful despite provocation and temptation, leads a loyally obedient citizenry. Attended by her fool and her councillor, she heals, teaches, and wins all the countryside of her plagued Palermo. Another opposition pits the chief sycophant Horatio, who labels himself with variations on the formulaic "old courtiers . . . still true to the Crown" and with his ludicrous imitations of his monarch's vacillations, against the rival generals, who make a pact to save the king from his own order to execute the crown prince. Alinda's and Gonzago's overweening conniving becomes so disgusting that they have to retire to separate religious retreats, leaving the body politic to the fit leadership of others.

Though other plays by Brome rarely focus on arbitrary rule as a specific problem, they criticize it implicitly for sponsoring, perhaps requiring, destructive preferment-seeking. Brome's ploy is aligned with the popular conservative subversion best known through Robin Hood: attack your king's agents as you declare your loyalty to and common cause with him.[13] Brome's trenchant attack on the system of preferment, *The Court Beggar*, is potent because of the play's obvious parallels to current sociopolitics and its readily recognized butts. Scholars since Kaufmann have recognized that the play attacks the system of dissolute, rapacious patronage represented by Sir John Suckling—the personal vanity, lechery, gambling, and mad abuse of status, along with the public military ineptitude if not cowardice.[14] Butler has specified and amplified the play's implications beyond its condemnation of the personal and social bankruptcy when courtiers beg the unmerited monopolies that buy them clout. The play pinpoints those political failures of the Caroline court that led to the double debacle of the Royal Expedition to the North during the First Bishops' War and of the Short Parliament of 1640. With Civil War looming, no wonder the Master of the Revels, presumably reflecting the king's fury, prohibited this play or any like it by Beeston's Boys and threatened the Cockpit players and their manager.[15] Brome is hard on the complementary political evils of tyrannical abuses of authority and greedy, ambitious scrambling for preferment. He is even more antagonistic in his frequent satires of related manifestations in social domains that overlap with these.

Like many other Caroline plays, *The Queen's Exchange* and *The Queen and Concubine* highlight the contrast between a virtuous communal country and an arrogant absolutist court. In *The Queen and Concubine* the country's moral superiority appears in Alinda's transformation at court from "simple Countrey Innocence" to "comely Ambition." The philandering king's arousal by Alinda's prostitution for advancement epitomizes his court's system of preferment: underlings get status, wealth, and power by offering themselves for use by their superiors. Poised against this violation of traditional ideals of social bonding is the loyalty of Eulalia's exiles and provincials. Though comic characters, their shrewd hospitality maintains a roughhewn country of honest thrift, prudent labor, and service to the hierarchical community. Brome's wittiest attack on courtly morals and sensibilities appears in *The Love-sick Court* (1633-34, 1638?). Since Kaufmann's analysis this tragicomedy has been recognized as a travesty on the extravagant platonic love and political courtship fostered by Henrietta Maria.[16] Brome's hostile representation of court abuses and his occasional representations of country virtues, however, do not signify the embrace of country inferred by Butler. Brome's gentry, as in *A Jovial Crew,* cause significant problems. A more difficult problem is posed by the third major sociopolitical sphere. The commercial city, which is foregrounded by Brome as well as by Shirley, appears briefly in *A Jovial Crew* and often in Citwit's skirmishes with Courtwit and Swaynwit in *The Court Beggar.* Most of Brome's plays continue to display the ambivalence notable in the early *Northern Lass*'s portrayal of the circle of Lady Fitchow, the ambitious and successful city widow. Against the country innocence of the title heroine, Constance, most members of Fitchow's circle seem grasping; but against the other Constance, the mercenary whore Holdup, they come off well. And Master Tridewell makes an appealing concerned citizen.

Brome's sociopolitical sets can be summed up in *The Court Beggar's* Courtwit, Swaynwit, and Citwit. These hangers-on, who earn their support by amusing the "humorous" widow, Lady Strangelove, are notable for both distinctive folly and individual potential. The fulsome Courtwit greases the social wheel. The cowardly backbiting Citwit evolves into a blustering reformer. The punitive enforcer Swaynwit makes a forthright traditional critic. Though their flaws must be taken into account, each is capable of contibuting to society. And though none is granted approval, their final mutual acceptance and dealings may intimate possible social consensus.

Although the potential for community among Courtwit, Swaynwit, and Citwit indicates that Brome represents London's spectrum of social types with more ambivalence than does Shirley, Brome's city particularly breeds sharpers. Especially in his topographical comedies and in *The City Wit, The English Moor,* and *A Mad Couple Well Match'd,* the prevalent upward striving and greedy grasping of London's citizens, combined with their endemic failure of courage, seem to be fostered by the city's environs. Brome's arraignment of the city appears in his early, then revised, genial satire *The City Wit.* An "honest" merchant has to turn to disguises and deceits to recoup his losses to lying, defaulting debtors. Scorned by his ambitious mother-in-law and rebuffed by his debtors, Crasy adopts their scams to earn "more in a weeks Cosenage, then in all

[his] daies of Honesty" (V/357). He takes advantage of the ambition, greed, larceny, and lechery of representative estates: a driving mother-in-law, a compliant wife, and "a thrifty Citizen"; a witless court-aspiring brother-in-law and two other courtiers; and a pedant. Proving that knavery is as easy as it is profitable, he resents human ingratitude and feels disgust at the role he must play to gain respect (note V/357-58). Yet Crasy is typical of Brome's ambivalent presentations, for he proves both that gulls are not necessarily witless but perhaps generous, and he demonstrates that citizens can be selflessly forgiving.

In sum, through estates represented in London society Brome focuses on social abuses that are related to the political ones he attacked: the tyrannous use of power and the scramble for empowering status. The former appears most identifiably in his familiar satire on usurers.[17] Quicksands, the aptly named, rapacious usurer in *The English Moor*, represents the unrepentant destroyer. He deserves the condemnatory humiliation arranged by his former victims when they try to cuckold him and when they publicize his idiot bastard. But Vermin in *The Damoiselle* is finally restored after initially refusing to help the decayed gentry he has cheated. His victims, including his prodigal son and his pawned daughter, who rebel against his parsimony and profiteering, generate so much social pressure that he is converted to giving them approval and aid; so they in turn accept him again. Thus, depending on a repentant reaction on the part of an offender, Brome presents an alternative ending to destructive socioeconomic tyranny. While the recalcitrant deserve ostracism, the reformed gain reconciliation.

The scramble for status is featured in Brome's frequent satire of academies for the aspiring. Typical is his presentation of the new ordinary, which caters to the "fashion sick"ness for new "French frippery" and new French "court carriage" that are taught by the new instructor for whom *The Damoiselle* is named. Academies provide the Caroline professionals with easy targets because they claim they can teach climbers how to parade the manners and styles affected by those who hold a coveted status. Just so, in *The New Academy* Strigood advertises "professors of court discipline" who are prepared to teach the French manners, posturings, and fashions, Platonic love and vacuous politeness, and musical and dancing accomplishments esteemed around Henrietta Maria's court.

More distinctively, Brome takes as particular butts the gulls who enroll in academies for strivers. Strigood draws in plenty of pupils to learn absurdly elaborate, stylized conventions: the presumptuous Lady Nestlecock and her overprotected imbecile son, her melancholy suitor and his daughter, and Maudlin, her new sister-in-law and former maid to her half-brother. Often Brome targets country aspirants who are getting cheated by city slickers and court dependents. *The Sparagus Garden* spotlights the leeching of Tim Hoyden by a gang of London conmen led by the shifty knight Mony-lacks. Hoyden's blood has to be drawn out and replaced by reputedly noble, aphrodisiac asparagus, while his country yeoman's manners need to be supplanted by the rudiments of "the severall carriages and deportments by garbe, by congy, complement, &c" (IV.ix/194) practiced by gentlemen. Mainly his purse needs to be drained of £400 until he becomes dimly aware that he is imitating forms as empty as it is. Similarly, in *The Covent-Garden Weeded* Captain Driblow employs forms of compliment and elevation to bilk ignorantly aspiring Mun Clotpoll. Clotpoll, notebook perpetually at hand for recording imitable acts and witticisms, seeks initiation into the Philoblathici and Philobattici, the Brotherhood of the Blade and Battoune, with its auxiliary Sisterhood of the Scabbard. These roarers' French balls (an adaptation of Jonson's "vapors") and whores so parody court styles and ends that critics see Brome demonstrating that a society based on abusive authoritarianism and sycophantic favoritism brings forth cheating and whoring.[18]

Whereas other Caroline professional playwrights mainly relate politics to the family, Brome more often shows interactions between society and the family. Social and personal abuses reflect and inextricably reinforce each other as they parallel state abuses. Brome repeatedly features the clash of fathers forcing marital decisions on their children, thereby compelling these children into dilemmas and evasions. This pattern extends from *The Novella*, where two city and family fathers arrange a sociopolitical and economic match that would block both of their children's love choices, through *A Jovial Crew*, where Justice Clack propels his niece into running away from an enforced marriage he has proposed. Typically, patriarchal compulsion issues from greed, as when Justice Testy marries off his niece and ward, Millicent, to the usurer Quicksands in *The English Moor*, the usurer Vermin schemes about his daughter in *The Damoiselle*, or Sir Andrew Mendicant proffers his daughter in *The Court Beggar*. Usually the guardian's choice is a miser, a madman, or a booby unsuitable from any perspective other than the guardian's gain. Other familiar paternal tyrannies also appear through Brome: a father in *The Sparagus Garden* causes his son consternation by prohibiting his marriage, out of spite for the woman's family; and a father in *The New Academy* drives away his daughter, out of wrath against the family of his foster daughter. The frequency with which Brome's guardians take advantage of their rank suggests mutually supporting abuses of authority in all social domains.

The mutual support of abusive parental and social authorities compounds severe problems for children: in *The Novella* Pantaloni and Guadagni harry their children from quandaries and equivocations to subterfuges, and in *The Sparagus Garden* Sam Touchwood is driven from anguished guilt into deception. While Brome's plays generate great sympathy for adolescents, they also depict rebellion by the afflicted offspring as an unacceptable violation of traditional family norms. Brome's vilest villain appears in *The Queen's Exchange;* the ingrate son Ossa plays a betraying Edmund to Segebert's Gloucester and to his brother's Edgar. In *The Queen and Concubine* Alinda's ambition is condemned for the double perfidy against her father and against her queen and protectress, whereas the prince is honored for his loyalty in spite of his father's capricious sentence of execution. Yet the children in Brome's plays are often conditioned by repressions harsh enough and psyches burdened enough to sanction trickery as a means of gaining their fathers' sympathies and blessings. The plays allow such children the ruse of rebellion in order to evade their patriarchs' unfair use of power. When Joyce and Gabriella flee their furious patriarch in *The New Academy* or Wat and Alice flee their usurious father Vermin in *The Damoiselle,* they find new protectors who help them reform their fathers. Though the majority of offspring in Brome's plays remain obedient, some of their tricks threaten Caroline society. In *The English Moor* the ward Millicent and a host of Quicksands's victims suggest adultery as a response to her enforced marriage to the old usurer. But while her bawdy turnoff songs and her suitors' hymeneal cuckolding masque produce satisfying satiric discomfort for two old connivers, the means risk Millicent's integrity and threaten an audience left out of the con until late in the play. Brome's plays often emit an uneasy tone of subversion by children, which does not come to rest in received family practices nor to resolution in reform.

This complex of family relationships is summed up in *The Covent-Garden Weeded,* inside a complex set of multiple parallels in arbitrary royal sociopolitical regulations and arbitrary Puritan moral restrictions.[19] Crossewill so enjoys opposing everyone, particularly his children, that he alters his goals when others concur with him. Since he requires that his children achieve his ends in his way, his daughter tries to box him into blessing either her beloved or her perpetual maidenhood, his distraught elder son flees to Puritan rather than patriarchal oppression, and his younger son escapes to London to practice gallantry under the pretense of learning the law. And since he delights in thwarting their widely praised inclinations, they manipulate him by reverse psychology, pretending interest in the opposite of what they want until they get him to recognize and reform his arbitrary willfulness. In the end all turn their inversions to their society's sense of rightside up. While this presents an odd notion of filial duty, the children's ultimate allegiance to social norms amounts to their ultimate obedience to their father's best instincts. Such inversions are typical of Brome's satiric attacks on the abuses of arrogant authority and ungrateful ambition. Such irresolute endings, both affirming and criticizing his society, leave no definite basis for ethical judgments.

The most vivid examples of Brome's (and satire's) propensity to attack abuses without providing consistent grounds for resolution appear in his presentation of two sexual relations that preoccupied the Carolines and their plays: the double standard and cuckoldry. From a masculine view he depicts almost all of his characters, both male and female, as accepting without question the double standard. But though he does not suggest Massinger's general reforms or Shirley's postmarital ones, neither does he mirror Ford's tacit approval. Instead, he often establishes a bivalent perspective that sets him apart from the other Caroline professionals and that alienates many critics because of its alleged "disgusting moral decadence." [20] In Brome's plays a woman who commits adultery for socio-economic advancement comes off badly. Often, however, a woman who commits adultery, or more likely perpetrates the ruse of committing adultery, is presented as understandably countering men's waywardness; so her case gains sympathy if not approval. While cuckoldry causes psychological stress for husbands, women might justly claim equal access to reciprocal or corrective adultery, and especially to the pretense of adultery. This position Ford never entertained, Shirley abhorred, and Massinger presented only one time, briefly, in *The Picture*.

Brome's sympathetic presentation of Sir Philip Lucklesse, the prize sought and won by Constance, the popular, innocent heroine of *The Northern Lass*, sets a double standard. Only tactics are considered during the extrication of this first of Brome's many prodigals from two misogynist nightmares: an entanglement with a "cunning whore," his former mistress Constance, and an entrapment in a lucrative marital contract with a domineering widow, Mistress Fitchow. Sir Philip is the least objectionable of an ever wilder, more destructive line of familiar prodigals redeemed by some pure or "spoiled but loyal" lass. In *The Covent-Garden Weeded* roistering whoremaster Nick is married to Crossewill's niece. In *The New Academy* the braggadochio squire of city wives, Valentine Askal, is protected by his unrecognized half-sister, Hannah, whom he slanders. In *The English Moor* Nathaniel Banelass is saved by a bed trick arranged by the self-sacrificing Phillis Winlose, another maiden he has tried to train in whoredom. The ancient widower Striker in *The Sparagus Garden* is preserved by his housekeeper, Friswood, who has served him in bed for years. A marked increase in prodigal rascality shows up in *A Mad Couple Well Match'd* in the person of Carelesse. The dissolute heir is condemned not so much for his insulting attempt to seduce his virtuous young aunt, Lady Thrivewell, as for his ungrateful damage of her adulterous old husband, his benefactor. Carelesse's perversities win him the fortune of another type, the lecherous widow, Mrs. Crostill. Finally, the society of

The Damoiselle disregard the whoremongering of Wat, the prodigal son of the usurer; but they castigate him for trying to pander his prospective bride and they convert him. This last case, of the one philanderer Brome's other characters condemn, also exposes the interlocking crux of cuckoldry.

From the early *The City Wit* Brome's plays, like many a Caroline's, are preoccupied with the anxieties husbands have about cuckoldry. Torn by his jealous love of his compliant wife, Josina, Crasy decides that his least anxious course lies in disguising himself so as to appear to pander for her and to cuckold himself. He thereby regains the debts owed him by two would-be courtiers and wins revenge as they beat each other; then he says he believes Josina recognized his disguise. Unsettling, *The City Wit* nevertheless comes the closest of Brome's plays to easing the fears roused by cuckoldry. The most bothersome cases, judged by the critical response, involve tradesmen and their wives. Contrary to critical assertions, such cases do not *primarily* condemn mercenary commercial greed and ridicule imitations of some licentious female freedom practiced as Platonism, as in *The Love-sick Court*. Kaufmann and Shaw consider Rebecca Brittleware of *The Sparagus Garden* a nag who reduces her husband to subservience.[21] But she is hardly blameworthy. She desperately wants a child; so new man litters and St. Paul's steeple become as sexually laden as *The Knight of the Burning Pestle* she wants to see and the elite gardens of promiscuity she wants to visit. Moreover, Brittleware is so jealously possessive and terrified of cuckoldry that he confines her. Therefore, she tells her aunt, rather than getting revenge by acting out his suspicions she abuses his illusions in hopes of wearing out his cuckoldry "in conceit." He comes to trust rather than own her. According to some critics, the problem of Rafe Camelion in *The New Academy* is timorous uxoriousness in imitation of Platonic court fashions; he supposedly allows his wife Hannah so much unscrutinized freedom that it destroys the "natural relationship" of a superior husband's protectiveness of his wife.[22] Rather, Hannah, seeing her Camelion's neglect of her and his attraction to public amusements, needs assurance of his love. She seeks not protection (she capably guards her fidelity) but loving concern in front of a sexually cynical society eager to foul their reputations with intimations of wittolry.

The critical disapproval of the mores and art registered about these plays scarcely approaches the moral and critical wrath roused by *A Mad Couple Well Match'd*. Shaw approvingly quotes Sedge's, and presumably Kaufmann's, evaluation: "Brome's play clearly exposes the dangerous excess in feminism that can result from the Platonic non-jealousy ethic."[23] Brome's attack on the cynical manipulation of Platonic courtliness seems obvious; the so-called "dangerous excess in feminism" seems mistaken. Lady Thrivewell is generally appreciated for saving her husband from a mercenary predator on his infidelity, but she is not so loudly applauded for fooling him into believing briefly that she has cuckolded him. As Shaw notes, he needs to recognize that "what is sauce for the gander *can* be sauce for the goose"[24]; and he needs momentarily at least to suffer the anguish he apparently feels a wife is obliged to endure in silence. But Shaw's *"can"* signals the play's moral inconsistency. While reciprocity is remarkably presented as possible, understandable, and affecting, it is not approved. The Lady remains responsible for fidelity. Moreover, the parallel plots fail to show reciprocity. Saleware profits from the adultery of his wife Alice ([Ram] Ally), just as the Lady recoups her husband's payment by shrewd dealing. But rather than being commended for economic gains or for understanding his spouse's adultery, as Lady Thrivewell is, Saleware is predictably condemned for complacent cuckoldry. And this despite his wretchedness when Ally exploits his professed courtly trust and denies him the access others purchase. Likewise, Ally is utterly condemned for sexual profiteering whereas philandering and fortune hunting are amicably forgiven Carelesse, who is granted the guardian angel, Saveall, and who is rewarded by marriage to a rich widow—precisely for abusing her the way he does his whore Phoebe. The best deal for any woman in the play is the award earned by the ironically named Phoebe for her employment in Lady Thrivewell's bed trick on Carelesse: she gets married off to his man, with good riddance to Carelesse's past. In sum, Brome's radical suggestion about sexual equity is inconsistent. But the hint of women's equivalent sexual freedom sets Brome apart from his peers. And it rouses critical consternation from ours.

Brome's suggestions about family and sexual relations, like his suggestions about politics and society, combine a radical aversion to tyrannical authority with a strong disapproval of ambitious insurrection. His stance, then, is the hardest to characterize among the Caroline professional playwrights: he is similar to Massinger on the need for social and family reform but less sanguine than is Massinger's accommodation of tradition; he is like Ford in his support of traditions but more probing than is Ford's espousal of ideal absolutism; he is favorable to Shirley's role playing but averse to Shirley's embrace of court norms. Brome's radical tendencies were disallowed by critics, who annexed his increasing questions to normative positions; but Butler has resituated Brome's politics within a revisionist history that recognizes a negative sociopolitics of subversive traditionalism. Brome complicated the problems of his ambivalent perspective by his inconsistent applications, which morally uncomfortable critics compound into condemnation or frustrated defensiveness. Brome's inconsistency might be interpreted more usefully as an indication of his increasingly profound questioning and of his exploitation of satire's freedom from the need for a platform. My uneasy conclusion about Brome's values melds with an appraisal of his development of the techniques of parody and inversion into a process that taps a potential for fundamental reform.

Satiric Parodies and Inversions

Brome's parodic style presents his variation on the imitation of craft characteristic of the Caroline professional playwrights. Neither a regular collaborator with Fletcher and others like Massinger nor with Dekker and others like Ford, not an eclectic autodidact like Shirley, Brome devoted his apprenticeship to Ben Jonson. Jonson's commendation of this son on his first publication, *The Northern Lass*, in 1632, is so important that it was reprinted in 1659 at the head of the second posthumous collection of Brome, *Five New Plays* by "An Ingenious Servant, and Imitator of his Master, that famously Renowned Poet *Ben. Johnson.*" At first Jonson vented his envy of the success of his apprentice's "sweepings," malicious wordplay that some of Ben's tribe perpetuated. Then he commended Brome's play, "often Acted with good Applause, at the *Globe*, and *Black-Fryers.*" Introducing "my Old Faithful Seruant, and (by his continu'd Vertue) my loving Friend: the Author of this Work, M. RICH. BROME" with his peculiar blend of sensitive consideration and perceptive arrogance, Jonson provides a broadly applicable principle:

> I Had you for a Servant, once, *Dick Brome;*
>   And you perform'd a Servants faithful parts:
> Now, you are got into a nearer roome,
>   *Of Fellowship,* professing my old Arts.
> And you doe doe them well, with good applause,
>   Which you have justly gained from the *Stage,*
> By observation of those Comick Lawes
>   Which I, your *Master,* first did teach the Age.
> You learn'd it well; and for it, serv'd your time
>   A Prentise-ship: which few doe now a dayes.
> Now each Court-Hobby-horse will wince in rime;
>   Both learned, and unlearned, all write *Playes.*
> It was not so of old: Men tooke up trades
>   That knew the Crafts they had bin bred in, right:

Jonson applauds the technique and aesthetics achieved by apprenticeship to a master; and he sneers at poets and dramatists who never learn the mystery. He also defines one base and suggests another for Brome's creation of new art by imitation. Brome the traditionalist practiced and extended the craft he inherited by creating variations on its ideas and techniques. Brome the opponent of ignorant courtly amateurs parodied, burlesqued, and inverted their very ruptures of old techniques, thereby creating new variations.[25]

Despite recording their agreement that Brome did embody Jonson's principle of nurturing wit by imitating his master, critics have been less than specific about the nature of his imitation. All recognize that Brome often and obviously alluded to Jonson. *The City Wit* announces that it bears the "seal of Ben" before the apprentice's disguise as a conwoman recalls *Epicoene*, and his mention of an "Indenture Tripartite, and't please you, like *Subtle*, *Doll*, and *Face*" refers to *The Alchemist* (III.i/318). In emulation of "my Reverend Ancestor *Justice Adam Overdoe*" of *Bartholomew Fair*, *The Covent-Garden Weeded*'s Justice Cockbrain proposes to uproot local enormities while wearing a series of disguises in which he gets duped and beaten. *The Sparagus Garden* brings in *The Alchemist* when Monylacks agrees to shift funds from a gull to himself and his partner, just like Subtle and Lungs; and old Striker's subterfuge through feigned diseases of exaggerated age recalls *Volpone*. Similar references reappear prominently: *Epicoene*'s transvestism shows up in *The New Academy* and in *The Damoiselle*; so do a Cokes-influenced Nehemiah Nestlecock and the Overdone Bumpseys. Scholars have, however, neglected the middle ground of design between their annotations of specific echoes and inspirations and their assumptions that Brome reproduced Jonson's moral concerns in a flawed medium.[26] Brome's designs are supplied in part through his adherence to Jonson's principle of imitating from the best exempla available.

This principle is suggested by other poems that usher in *The Northern Lass*. One claim of paternity, "To my Sonne Broom and his LASSE," is made by Dekker; his London settings and Middleton irony proved important to *The City Wit*, *A Mad Couple*, and Brome's various topographical satires, and his romantic comedies about the city's citizens are reflected in this play and others. Another commendation is made by Ford; his promotion of curative drama became a central principle for Brome. In a poem before *A Jovial Crew* fellow playwright John Tatham added Beaumont and Fletcher and Shakespeare as Brome's antecedents. These statements are confirmed by Brome's edition and reintroduction of Fletcher's *Monsieur Thomas* in 1639 and his employment of Fletcherian intrigue comedy in *The Novella* and tragicomedy in *The Queen and Concubine*. They are also confirmed by his early variation on Shakespeare's Gloucester plot in *The Queen's Exchange*.[27] In addition Brome later collaborated with Heywood (extant is *The Late Lancashire Witches* [1634]) and perhaps with Chapman. From the prologue to *The Sparagus Garden* to the epilogue of *The English Moor* Brome modestly affirmed his debt to English dramatic traditions and claimed never to trespass against the old "laws of comedy." These facts corroborate both his outrage over the violations committed by unprofessional Sucklings and his ability to burlesque and invert the violations. Neither the commendations nor the acknowledgments indicate the freedom Brome expanded from a frequent imitation of folk game and song motifs, as in his *Lass*. The commendations do, however, consistently praise his ingenuity and ability to imitate "souls language," apparently in appreciation of his playful prose of dialect and jargon, idiolect and character tag, quip and saw. And they universally praise his moral point, apparently in admiration of his satire.

One quality contemporaries regularly acclaimed in Brome is typical of the Caroline professionals: he manipulated complex multiple plots in the manner of the old masters. In a 1640 commendation prefacing *The Sparagus Garden* C.G. delights in the mazelike "designment" that encompasses plentiful variety within "proportion." And in "To the Readers" of the 1659 *Five New Plays* the collector opens by praising the playwright's understanding of the *"Proportions* and *Beauties* of a *Scene."* Brome developed this skill through imitation of the plotting conventions of traditional genres. By the revived, and likely early, version of *The City Wit*, he was mastering Jonsonian adaptations of the estates morality play. His city and topographical satires depend on reviews of stereotyped sociopolitical estates, from courtiers to citizen merchants, and of the professions of teacher, doctor, soldier, and lawyer to indict failures to contribute to the commonweal. The traditional morality play remains visible in *The Queen and Concubine;* the antithesis between the queen's saintliness and the whore's ambitions is augmented by parallel antithetical types—good councillor versus evil usher, country magistrates versus court politicians, and country clowns versus court knaves. The most characteristic of Brome's plot designs, as Shaw repeatedly demonstrates, links multiple plots around triangles of characters; usually these feature the intrigues and counter-intrigues of an antagonist with his cronies who block a sympathetic pair with their associates. While such exemplary plots as *The Northern Lass, The Novella,* and *The Court Beggar* do not maintain the restrictive social and moral hierarchies posited by Levin, Brome creates unity through the mutual personal associations and common locations, interdependently effecting events, and social and moral thematics of his plots.[28]

In addition, Brome's mature craft was affected considerably by innovations in drama that repelled him and his fellow professionals. The prologue and epilogue to *The Court Beggar* express blunt antipathy toward those new "wits o' Court" who, by subsidizing performances of faddish, ghostwritten fluff and by bribing audiences, were destroying the professional dramatic heritage. He refuses to create *"gaudy Sceane(s),"* outline plots, or deploy facile sentiment even though his audience has *"grown, / Deeply in love with a new Strayne of wit / Which he condemns, at least disliketh it.*" So in the play he satirizes the courtly pseudo-dramatist/producers, Suckling and Davenant, who threaten his art as much as his livelihood.[29] Moreover, he burlesques their tragicomic mode, thereby clarifying his own characteristics. Kaufmann first identified Brome's *The Love-sick Court* as a burlesque of voguish courtly romantic productions.[30] The title puns on the maladies of two courts, the dramatic presentations that inflated courts and the histrionics and social predilections of the Caroline court. The play's typically twisting and surprising tragicomic plot turns on the friendship of two apparent brothers who compete for a princess enamored of both. This narrative provides a frame on which are woven ragtag clichés of courtly love and manners drama: self-sacrifice, the insidious plotting and miraculous conversion of a throne-seeking villain, an attempted rape, a quest for an ambiguous oracle, a mistaken identity arising from the ancient concealment of a baby, the insinuation of incest, the resurrection of a possum-playing protagonist. Types include righteous councillors and ambitious machiavels, a fickle populace, a possessive mother with a blackmailing old nurse, and a set of comic servants who travesty the royal plot. The characters ingratiate themselves in inflated courtly compliments and agonize over their choices in high-flown soliloquies. If emblems such as the duel (when the protagonists hurl themselves at each other in a feigned pass before each whirls round spreading his arms and baring his breast for his "brother's" deadly thrust) just slash, other burlesques prove fatal. Especially mordant moments include the old nurse Garula's interrupting leers over a titillating double identity, the pointlessness of its concealment, and her use of it to aid the pretensions of her idiotic son. *The Love-sick Court* exhibits the talent in adaptive imitation that Brome employed to create his own, freer style.

Brome's innovative, liberating forms evolved out of his imitation of traditions, particularly out of his extension of interpolated songs and masques, plays within plays, characters playing deceptive roles, native folk performances, and improvisations, all of which can point beyond any immediate scene. Prominent in the final *A Jovial Crew*, such devices constituted a repertoire that Brome developed from *The Northern Lass*, whose country heroine is characterized by lyrics about her innocent love-longing. These do as much to further her cause as the deceptive roles played by the city sharpers; and they appear the purer against Constance Holdup's bawdy songs.[31] Her cause and the play's resolution are fostered by a marriage masque that thwarts one impropitious marriage and encourages two auspicious ones (II.vi/41–42). Brome's interest in dissolving a play in its climactic masque comes with *The City Wit*. Its late hymeneal offering evolves into bawdy songs, revelations of the multiple disguises and counterplots perpetrated by Crasy's crew, and a celebration of human venality's absolution in a general amnesty and communion of the erring—in the play and in the world.

The English Moor further expands masquings: a scoffing "Horn-masque" is presented by gallants ruined by the old usurer Quicksands so as to threaten him with cuckoldry, one of the "miseries of inforced marriage"; a later queen of "Ethiop" masque is mounted by Quicksands to disclose his chaste wife's protective disguise. These masques within the play give way to play acting as they provide opportunities for characters to manipulate roles so as to effect the heroine's escape, perpetrate a reclaiming bed trick, and reveal Quicksands's idiot bastard. Disguises and deceptions aid these and other character manipulations; they include the apparent mutually fatal duel of supposedly rival fathers, several transvestite appearances, and the racial masking of the title character. The practical ends of the masquers and the dissolution of the insets' boundaries inside the play's world are possible in part because Brome imitates another dramatic tradition—improvisation. The characters' manipulative play is warranted by a tradition of free play within specified dramatic situations. Cope makes a forceful case for Brome's adaptation of *commedia dell'arte* because the pedant introduces the masque in *The City Wit* as following "the fashion of *Italy*" in employing "extempore" speeches and because *The Novella,* which is set in Venice, uses names and roles transmitted by that tradition.[32]

All these metadramatic devices—song and implied folk fest, masque and revel, role manipulation and extemporaneous acting—do more than blur if not obliterate boundaries between plays and life, inside Brome's plays. They help bring about Brome's well-known use of comedy as a moral and psychological curative. Besides alluding to extempore acting, Brome's prologue to *The Novella* requires his auditors to judge the play by laws, since understanding precedes an appreciation of his mirth. In *"To the* Stationer, *on the publishing* Mr. Bromes *Comedies"* Alexander Brome specifies that Brome's style "Makes us at once both serious, and smile. / Wraps serious truths in fab'lous mysteries, / And thereby makes us merry, and yet wise" (vii). His commendation praises Brome's "Instructive Recreations" (viii), which satirize vice and vanity while they praise virtue, so that they satisfy poetry's traditional goal of mixing profit with pleasure. This praise is duly repeated in the stationers' introduction to the 1659 edition. T.S.'s commendatory poem to the same edition uses a traditional trope to declare that Brome lances not men but manners; like a surgeon he binds people's wounds, concealing the patient's identity while he treats the sore. And C.G.'s commendation of the earlier *The Sparagus Garden* suggests that Brome's representations that purge humors or moderate neuroses are more effective than others that remove vices by surgery.

Critics have noted that Brome developed Ford's dreamlike metadramatic cures in *The Lover's Melancholy* into a central technique that Cope calls the "psychiatric manipulation of reality" for the good of characters.[33]

Cope maps the technique from the entranced role playing and identity trade that relieve the king in *The Queen's Exchange* through a prelude in *The English Moor,* a center in *The Antipodes,* and a postlude in *A Jovial Crew.* To these should be added plays during which role playing in itself effects some cure. For instance, *The Court Beggar*'s concluding masque unmasks the rapacious fraud of Sir Ferdinand. As Butler points out, when the representative court beggar Mendicant breaks in with his projectors, the scene turns into a masque that emblemizes a problem beyond the play: madness in England's court and society. It implies a national malady's desperate need of the kind of cure prescribed for many of the play's characters.[34] Though perhaps it reveals evidence of an epidemic, the intrigue play-acting in Brome usually treats onstage patients and effects a theater audience's pleasurable profit more than it prescribes to the nation. In *The Covent-Garden Weeded,* for example, Mihil produces an elaborate scene wherein whores and swaggerers act out complementary Puritan roles in a drunken party to disabuse, then revive, his brother from an extended stupor; and in *The Damoiselle* Drygrounds arranges an elaborate staging to heal relations in several families.

Although Brome's prologue to *The Sparagus Garden* reminds his audience "that to expect high Language, or much Cost, / Were a sure way, now, to make all be lost," audiences have long recognized his linguistic ingenuity. Dekker called attention to it in commending *The Northern Lass,* his brother and F.T. made reference to it, Alexander Brome observed it before the 1653 plays and T.S. before the 1659 plays. Like the rest of his craft, Brome's style issues from imitation, particularly burlesque. Shaw has observed that while Brome's wooing verse is often couched in a stiff, dated Petrarchism, his frequent songs can achieve a lyric, if bawdy, grace. And his presentation of comic repartee and retorts, extended clichés, dialects, foreign accents, occupational jargons and social registers, stock character tags, and occasional series of balanced passages of account or abuse—that is, his parody—can be very effective.[35] Frequently he underscores mimicry by stacking absurd, heavily alliterated parallel gradations. Often he manages comic bawdry through the double sexual meanings inadvertently produced by innocents, like those by Rebecca in *The Sparagus Garden.* More often he creates caricatures like those in *The City Wit,* where the pedant Sarpego pours forth from his cornucopia inkhornisms, transmogrified translations, fragments of Erasmian adages, inept and inaccurate allusions, fractured etymologies, and corrupted conjugations, and Crasy as a doctor offers dubious prognoses and suspicious prescriptions. Brome produces clever imitations of regionalisms, as in *The Northern Lass* or in *The Sparagus Garden*'s buffoonery of the traditional clown of Taunton Dean, Tom Hoyden.[36] And he mimics foreign accents, as in the pageant of suitors in *The Novella.*

Characterization through parodies of social registers is particularly significant in Brome. In *A Jovial Crew* he marks off the beggars' cant by the failure of the gentrified begging of the four disguised runaways; they know not how to "duly and truly pray for you." Brome exploits social register in his satire on usage by the upwardly mobile court apes who try out the "single rapier complement" and the "Back-sword complement" or "swipe" taught in *The Sparagus Garden*. And social register is given particular heed in the epilogue after Citwit's absurd challenges in imitation of Swaynwit in *The Court Beggar*. Brome's telling burlesque style is perhaps most effective in the many character tags that reinforce his social themes. Illustrative are the false nonchalance in the tag of the disturbed wittol, Saleware, "*Sapientia mea mihi, stultitia tua tibi,*" and his groveling punctuation, "ant like your Lordship," during a conference with his wife's master, Lord Lovely, in *A Mad Couple Well Match'd* (V.i/84-85). An early tag, the pedant Sarpego's empty-headed if well-meaning salutation "salvete salvetote," and the last, Justice Clack's overbearing interruption "if we both speak together, how shall we hear one another," reverse the order of Brome's stylistic development. His linguistic parody becomes more potent as it escapes from oppressive authority into blessed release.

As in his stylistic burlesque, which dissolves as it designates social boundaries, Brome more than any other Caroline professional playwright expanded rigorous imitation of traditional masters and genres. He notably expanded Jonsonian estates morality and citizen intrigue comedy through multilevel plots to extemporaneous play, generic parody through travesty to topsyturvydom, interpolated songs through drama-dissolving masques and plays within plays to folk carnival, manipulative role performance to curative audience participation. Brome's craft developed from traditional discipleship to independent inventiveness, from imitation to discovery in *The Antipodes*.

Generating Experimental Reform in THE ANTIPODES

As much as any other Caroline professional play, from prefatory commendations through concluding antimasque and masque, Brome's *The Antipodes* (composed 1636, played 1637, printed 1640) proclaims its heritage. C.G. tells censorious critics that poets need not elegize Jonson since his mode "sojourns" in Brome's traditional comedy. "The Prologue" says that this servant, then journeyman, and now master "cannot court" new writing fads but instead emulates old mentors:

> The poets late sublimed from our age,
> Who best could understand and best devise
> Works that must ever live upon the stage,

> Did well approve and lead this humble way,
> Which we are bound to travail in tonight.[37]

The puns on traveling and toiling, enduring agony and birth pangs signal a play that stages a fantasy voyage to the Antipodes, topsyturvy anti-London, to cure mad Peregrine Joyless, a young gentleman so taken with *The Travels of Sir John Mandeville* that he has not yet bedded his wife of three years, and to cure the troubles of the rest of his family, the lord who presents the inset play, and perhaps all of society. Typically, in concluding the prologue Brome claims that his old-fashioned play and its "low and homebred subjects have their use" beyond any amateur high-flown, pastoral, tragicomic theatrical in vogue at court; moreover, he offers his audience delight, perhaps renewal.

Critics have investigated the implications of this prefatory matter to discover how Jonson's comic traditions work in *The Antipodes*. Its inversions of tropes and of types from estates moralities, for example, have been mentioned by Ian Donaldson and developed by Martin Butler.[38] The most influential critics have focused on Brome's use of Jonsonian enhanced metatheatrics in inset plays, role-playing, antimasque and masque for satire and Fordian cure. In his part of the epilogue Doctor Hughball, the psychiatrist who helps direct such devices, signals the importance of metadramatic extension. He begins a traditional plea for applause by confessing, "Whether my cure be perfect yet or no, / It lies not in my doctorship to know." Thus, however fully he has explained the traditional attempt to cure through play-acting, he leaves the results open to question. This opening Joe Lee Davis has exploited in a seminal essay describing Brome's curative drama. Davis demonstrates that the play's satire does much more than expose vices to correction. Through the play within the play and the concluding masque, satire provides therapeutic psychological catharsis and realignment by "engrossing [characters] in a world more incongruously out of balance than they" are.[39] Modified in Haaker's introduction and Shaw's discussion, Davis's insights have been focused on the multiple neurotic audiences of *The Antipodes*, for the circles of sickness expand around Peregrine to take in his family, the disturbed couple Blaze and Barbara, Hughball and his patron, the impresario Lord Letoy, and the Salisbury Court audience. Then they have been extended in opposed directions by Donaldson and Cope.

Donaldson employs some traditions of topsyturvydom, a functional explanation of holiday by anthropologist Max Gluckman, and a related dramatic hypothesis by C.L. Barber. He sees sharp contrasts between virtue and iniquity, normality and absurdity. For him, then, the exposure of audiences to extremes during holiday release reinforces conformity to the normative hierarchy during work days, since it facilitates the restoration of controls or grants new clarification.[40] The most convincing emblem for Donaldson's interpretation is Letoy's concluding presentation of a Jonsonian antimasque and masque. To *"A most untunable flourish"* Discord ushers in a retinue she presents in a "SONG IN UNTUNABLE NOTES":

> *Come forth my darlings, you that breed*
> *The common strifes that discord feed:*
>   *Come in the first place, my dear Folly;*
>   *Jealousy next, then Melancholy.*
>   *And last come Madness; thou art he*
>   *That bear'st th' effects of all those three.*   [V.xi.12-17]

After their dance another flourish announces an encompassing song and dance by Harmony and her train. Letoy explains their actions:

> See Harmony approaches, leading on
> 'Gainst Discord's factions four great deities:
> Mercury, Cupid, Bacchus, and Apollo.
> Wit against Folly, Love against Jealousy,
> Wine against Melancholy, and 'gainst Madness, Health.
> Observe the matter and the method.
> And how upon the approach of Harmony,
> Discord and her disorders are confounded.   [V.xii.1-8]

Letoy thus claims that the discord and antipodal world his players presented to Peregrine and the other audiences were temporary; they revert to control. But the condition of restoration may not be reversion. Since Hughball questions the suitability of this presentation in the first place and since Letoy disclaims any insight into what form of good the presentation will effect in Peregrine, restoration may include change. Hence Cope's emphasis.

Cope engages a tradition where dreams and play(s), particularly metadramatic improvisations, release participants and observers from maladies. He focuses on the tradition of freeplay represented by the leading actor in Letoy's troupe, Byplay or Extempore.[41] Byplay's very name evokes both the theme of sexuality and the potential for change despite the governance of directors or social norms. Cope's idea of technique is especially appropriate to an Elizabethan theater Steven Mullaney has since emphasized in *The Place of the Stage: License, Play, and Power in Renaissance England*. Elizabethan theaters were situated on physical and sociopolitical boundaries that dramatists and players could exploit as liberties, undefinable or variably defined margins freed for vicarious experiment.

Even many critics who are fixed on setting a more constrained situation and a stricter definition than Cope and Mullaney propose practically concede that the normative function theory of metadrama is not able to define, to delimit, *The Antipodes*. Davis cannot discover any stable satiric target; Kaufmann perceives "a loss of proper proportion"; and Haaker finds affinities with Rabelais's disorienting *Gargantua and Pantagruel*.[42] *The Antipodes'* characters themselves note the inset play's remarkable likenesses as well as contrasts to their society. When a gentleman in the inset tells his servingman how to wear his cloak so as to display its showy lining, Peregrine remarks that he has seen this fashion and so Letoy claims that the custom "was deriv'd from the Antipodes" (IV.ii.15); later, antipodal projectors appear favored and antipodal lawyers ultimately accept fees, like their London counterparts. Butler uses such parallels to show Brome's indictment of current politics. From passages such as Diana's naively shrewd estimate of anti-London, which implicates that in London too "Courtiers are the best beggars" and churchmen are usurers, Butler draws a convincing conclusion: "Anti-London is not always an inversion of normality but a revelation of what normality ordinarily hides; inversion—sickness—is part of 'normal' life," at least under Charles I. His serendipitous Cokayne seems less a saturnalian safety valve than a "radical critique."[43] Butler further describes Brome's dedicatee, William Seymour, the Earl of Hertford, to whom Brome also dedicated his only extant manuscript. Seymour was reputedly a plain lord who was disaffected despite his royal posts—like Letoy. Finally Butler implies connections between *The Antipodes* and popular broadside and likely dramatic traditions of satiric emblems, which were aimed at practices associated with Charles's court.[44] He could have extended his context to include antipodal and festival emblems in popular culture that differ from Donaldson's. Furthermore, he could have taken comfort in a revisionary anthropological hypothesis about liminal and antipodal revelry that counters Gluckman's and also in a revisionary thesis about festive folk drama that modifies Barber's.

In "World Upside Down: The Iconography of a European Broadsheet Type," David Kunzle catalogs popular printed images of inversion from the early Renaissance through the eighteenth century.[45] Just as many of these depictions invert predator and prey, human and animal, so Hughball prepares Peregrine for his dream voyage: "Our hawks become their game, our game their hawks. / And so the like in hunting: there the deer Pursue/ the hounds . . . one sheep worr[ies] a dozen foxes . . . . their parrots teach / Their mistresses to talk" (I.vi.152-54, 159-60). But the predominant broadside scenes, like *The Antipodes*, invert social and gender roles. In the broadsides maids and servants rule mistresses and masters, children teach their elders, and the old seek childish amusements; just so Hughball describes "here (heaven be prais'd) the magistrates / Govern the people; there the people rule / The magistrates. . . . As parents here, and masters / Command, there they obey the child and servant" (I.vi.118-27).

Particularly pertinent to *The Antipodes*, women in these broadsides rule men and hunt combat, playing duelists and roarers, whereas men obey and prove physically passive, playing sempsters and man-scolds. Hughball's introduction to such role reversals is tellingly confused. He claims that feminine-masculine gender roles are natural, but his testimony demonstrates that they are social:

> DOCTOR.   Nay, lady, 'tis by nature.
> Here generally men govern the women—
>
> . . . .
>
> But there the women overrule the men.
> DIANA.
> But pray, sir, is't by nature or by art
> That wives o'ersway their husbands there?
> DOCTOR.   By nature.
> DIANA.
> Then art's above nature, as they are under us.
> DOCTOR.
> In brief, sir, all
> Degrees of people, both in sex and quality,
> Deport themselves in life and conversation
> Quite contrary to us.
> DIANA.   Why then, the women
> Do get the men with child, and put the poor fools
> To grievous pain, I warrant you, in bearing.
>
> . . . .
>
> DOCTOR.
> No, lady, no; that were to make men women,
> And women men. But there the maids do woo
> The bachelors, and 'tis most probable,
> The wives lie uppermost.   [I.vi.121-42]

Despite Hughball's denial and Joyless's ineffectual interruptions to control his wife by invoking traditional prerogatives of authority (omitted here), Diana perceives more through topsyturvydom than the men concede, perhaps more than they conceive. Traditional popular inversions in revelry can offer satiric critique and illuminating vicarious trial of subversion just as well as they can provide temporary release, clarification, and reversion to repression.

More evidence and interpretation is supplied by Natalie Zemon Davis

and other social historians. "The Reasons of Misrule," on customs of festive carnival, masking, and misrule, primarily concerns French charivari,
but "Women on Top" draws on extensive English materials.[46] Davis
concludes that fests, particularly those associated with adolescents, not
only reinforce traditional norms, they also offer alternative mores and
social structures. Comic and festive inversions of women's roles can
particularly be seen to provide a mode of protest and to suggest political
and social innovation: "Play with various images of woman-on-top, then,
kept open an alternate way of conceiving family structure." Historians of
popular English culture have documented that revelry considered amusing diversion by authorities did at times erupt into rebellion, particularly
on the traditional carnival days, Shrove Tuesday, Ascension Day, Mayday,
Midsummer, and Saint Bartholomew's Day.[47]

Looking for support from social theorists, Davis considers revisions
of Gluckman's hypothesis that holidays serve as instruments of repression. In "Betwixt and Between: The Liminal Period of *Rites de Pasage*,"
Victor Turner taps some of the revolutionary potential latent in Arnold
van Gennep's middle stage of ritual passage between separation and
incorporation.[48] And in *Carnival and Theater; Plebeian Culture and the Structure of Authority in Renaissance England* Michael D. Bristol combines this
modified hypothesis with Mikhail Bakhtin's influential study of the radical popular backgrounds of festivity, *Rabelais and His World*. He thereby
puts Elizabethan, primarily Shakespearean, drama in a frame very different from the conservative setting of folk carnival promulgated by E.K.
Chambers and C.L. Barber. He concludes that traditions of disrespect,
which represent spiritualized sociopolitical and moral norms as bodily,
bawdily material ones, supply a plebeian counter to official consolidations
of authority and tendencies to tyrannize; they provide a "second culture's" resistance to absolutism. In sum, instead of a normative theory of
how festival functions in society, these scholars focus on how festival can
produce unpredictable outcomes.

The aptness of considering *The Antipodes* as resistance and vicarious
experiment with the unpredictable can be seen in various ways—from the
play's language of physical bawdry to its antipodal extemporaneous
forms. There is only one memorable scatological reference, when Barbara
misunderstands Blaze doing "two mutes" (V.v.24-27). But Brome's customary sexual bawdry pervades the play from its opening, particularly in
references to cuckoldry: Blaze plays nothing; Martha makes naively telling remarks, even unwittingly suggesting lesbianism (I.iv.55-58); the
man-scold is forbidden the "use" of his chiefest "natural members . . .
that man takes pleasure in, / The tongue!" (IV.v.19-22); gentlemen and
schoolboys get mad about the license masters take with the "behinds" of
their students, suggesting homosexuality (IV.vi, vii); Joyless mistakes
Barbara's euphemistic references to Letoy's "daughters" (V.ii, iii).

Characters also turn specifically to popular culture for relief and sanction. A threatened Joyless whistles the common "Fortune My Foe" (III.v.61); when Peregrine attacks Letoy's tiring house he follows the apprentices' traditional Shrove Tuesday demolition of whore houses (III.vi); Byplay and Letoy find precedents for extemporaneous play in Tarlton's and Kemp's jigs (II.ii.43ff). Charivari's treatment of apprehensions about May-December weddings (a normative practice in anti-London [I.vi.179-83]) provides a setting for the cure of old Joyless's insane jealousy of his young wife. Topsyturvy festivity provides a new clime for the passage beyond the prolonged adolescence of Peregrine's mad exploration to escape parental controls and beyond Martha's married maidenhood and withheld motherhood. Topsyturvy festivity also provides the opportunity to restore Diana to her biological father after his years of paranoia over her legitimacy.

The Antipodes shows the necessity of a healing reform beyond the necessity of some release from tyranny. Moreover, it shows that necessity in three arenas: an oppressive social hierarchy that requires self-destructive climbing, an unjust political tyranny that compels sycophancy and leads to frustrated rebellion, and a family patriarchy that drives both the authoritarian father and the subject children and wife mad. But *The Antipodes* refuses to specify reforms, presumably because that would institute new oppressions. Instead it exemplifies a process of extemporaneous free play, of improvisation, of vicarious trial of potential reforms whereby tradition suggests and initiates change.

The first act and the beginning of the second act set the terms of *The Antipodes*. Blaze welcomes Joyless to London after the "time's calamity," the eighteen-month plague of 1636-37, which oppressed the population and led to the prohibition of vicarious release at theaters. But now the restrictions, "Thanks to high Providence," have been removed and a doctor approaches who can cure the "sorrow" "In the sad number of [Joyless's] family." Hughball performs miraculous psychological cures in a desperately stricken society. Blaze's litany of recoveries and chant of variations on "I name no man; but this / Was pretty well, you'll say" outlines major social and political plagues that parallel major family and personal ills. The doctor has cured a bankrupt country gentleman so that he plays the profligate gallant with the best. He has cured confused magistrates so that they "can now distinguish / And know both when and how to take of both" bribes and fees so as to increase their security and wealth (I.i.68-70). He has cured a woman mad from studying how to love her husband till "now she lies as lovingly on a flockbed / With her own knight as she had done on down / With many others" (I.i.61-63). The impressive result in terms of numbers, desperate need, and efficacy is his cure of "horn-mad" husbands, authoritarian guardians of their families, "by the dozens." Blaze even lets slip that he credits Hughball with his own recovery. Hughball depends for his cures on a popular tradition: a festive performance that "begets both wonder and delight / In his observers, while the stupid patient / Finds health at unawares" (I.i.26-28). Everything indicates that the time that plagued has come to foster health and that progress in Hughball's cure of the Joylesses would promise a mode of curing authorities who abuse a stricken society.

Joyless's authoritarianism suppresses play. He has deprived his son of travel; so Peregrine has been mad the five years since he turned twenty:

> His mother and
> Myself oppos'd him still in all and, strongly
> Against his will, still held him in and won
> Him into marriage, hoping that would call
> In his extravagant thoughts; but all prevail'd not,
> Nor stay'd him, though at home, from traveling
> So far beyond himself that now, too late,
> I wish he had gone abroad to meet his fate.   [I.ii.46-53]

The density of restrictive signifiers, "oppos'd," the repeated "still," "hold," "would call in," "stay'd," forbidding the son's "will" to wander in "extravagant" "traveling," parodies paternal repression. Thus confined, the son named for a roving hawk can escape only through madness. His madness includes sexual abstinence, which has left his deprived wife Martha "full of passion." Joyless's fear of cuckoldry threatens his new wife's sanity and his own. From her first appearance he keeps threatening to banish her to isolation and imprisonment:

> And let no looser words, or wand'ring look,
> Bewray an intimation of the slight
> Regard you bear your husband, lest I send you
> Upon a further pilgrimage than [Hughball]
> Feigns to convey my son.   [I.vi.19-23]

Masculine husbandry, oppression of the wife, threatens the same madness that paternalism has visited upon the son. Joyless indeed.

The Joylesses are not an isolated case. Blaze is often disturbed and Barbara can be stung by bawdry, which is innocently introduced by Martha. To Barbara's guilt-stricken conscience Martha's incredulity about husbands procreating hints at a slur about adultery. So when this "poor piece of innocence three years married" wonders "what a man does in child-getting" her request unwittingly accuses: "Pray take me for a night or two, or take / My husband and instruct him but one night. / Our country folks will say you London wives/ Do not lie every night with your own husbands" (I.iv.67-70). Brome's bawdry is most telling among *The*

Antipodes' women. Martha, who like Rebecca in *The Sparagus Garden* is preoccupied with having a baby, makes unwitting bawdry. But Diana, also like Rebecca, employs bawdry to purge her husband's jealousy; following Hughball's prescription, she tries to "spur [Joyless's] jealousy off o'the legs" (II.i.38). And Barbara uses bawdry to express revelry and to maintain her sexual independence.

Their bawdry confirms the central preoccupation of *The Antipodes*. Barbara states the problem succinctly in response to Martha's funnily pathetic query about whether Barbara really has two children or her husband lied: "I am sure / I groan'd for mine and bore 'em, when at best / He but believes he got 'em" (I.iv.26-28). The play's central issue is precisely the male's anguish and insecure tyranny, which rise from his pride in the power of patrilineage despite the fact that he can possess only uncertain faith that he perpetuates and governs his own family's traditionally continuous identity. This predicament Hughball undertakes to cure through participatory role playing among Letoy's troupe: "[These] Shall all be your guests tonight, and not alone / Spectators, but (as we will carry it) actors / To fill your comic scenes with double mirth" (II.i.42-44). Just earlier the healer assured Letoy of Diana's entry wearing Letoy's ring, a taunting emblem of the men's predicament in its sexual connotations of foreplay and consummation, marriage and free play. When Letoy sent it to Diana by Blaze it disturbed Blaze's memories: "Tell [Hughball] it wants a finger? My small wit / Already finds what finger it must fit" (I.vi.91-92). Ironically, perhaps inevitably, although Letoy's ring harasses Joyless throughout the play and even though Letoy serves as an agent for the cure, Letoy also proves to have been the sickest patriarch.

His first appearance is marked by anxiety over the issues of genus. For he recognizes in his tribe or family, his *gens*, the root or origin that identifies stock or generations and their continuity in begetting or generating by genitalia. As he enters he is questioning Blaze, the emblazoner of his coat of arms:

> LETOY.
>   Why, broughtst thou not mine arms and pedigree
>   Home with thee, Blaze, mine honest herald's painter?
> BLAZE.
>   I have not yet, my lord, but all's in readiness
>   According to the herald's full directions.
> LETOY.
>   But has he gone to the root; has he deriv'd me
>   *Ex origine, ab antiquo?*   [I.v.1-6]

Letoy's fixation on genus becomes increasingly obvious when he cites family precedents and insists on untrammeled prerogatives as he "toys" with Joyless's fear of cuckoldry. Near the end, after he has fulfilled literary tradition by testing Diana's virtue, he reveals that at one time his obsession with his family's past plus his concern for his current ego and his family's future purity intensified into mania. Out of a groundless suspicion of cuckoldry he madly denied his daughter, who was rightly christened Diana:

> Now shall you know what mov'd me, sir, I was
> A thing beyond a madman, like yourself
> Jealous; and had that strong distrust, and fancied
> Such proofs unto myself against my wife
> That I conceiv'd the child was not mine own,
> And scorn'd to father it; yet I gave to breed her
> And marry her as the daughter of this gentleman
> (Two thousand pound I guess you had with her);
> But since your match, my wife upon her death bed
> So clear'd herself of all my foul suspicions
> (Blest be her memory) that I then resolv'd
> By some quaint way (for I am still Letoy)
> To see and try her throughly; and so much
> To make her mine, as I should find her worthy.
> And now thou art my daughter and mine heir,
> Provided still (for I am still Letoy)
> You honorably love her, and defy
> The cuckold-making fiend, foul jealousy.   [V.vii.30-47]

Letoy's success in facing his angst over genus is limited and retrospective. Thus his mixed motives in trying to cure Joyless's malady.

Joyless's terrified oppression of himself and his family is repeatedly revealed to be destructive rather than generative. The disastrous outcome for both his wife and his son is perhaps most graphic when Diana, trying to cure her husband by participating in the play for his son's benefit, identifies the symptoms of Joyless's madness:

> JOYLESS.
>   Diana, yet be wise; bear not the name
>   Of sober chastity to play the beast in.
> DIANA.
>   Think not yourself, nor make yourself a beast
>   Before you are one; and when you appear so,
>   Then thank yourself. Your Jealousy durst not trust me.
>   . . . .
>
> JOYLESS.
>   I now could wish my son had been as far

> In the Antipodes as he thinks himself,
> Ere I had run this hazard.
>
> . . . .
>
> DIANA.
>
> Why should you wish so? Had you rather lose
> Your son than please your wife? You show your love both
> ways.   [III.vi.50-63]

Joyless's jealous possessiveness and paranoid ego do worse than bar love; they threaten to end his family. His oppressiveness seems to prohibit enjoyment with his new wife, thereby cutting off more progeny; at the same time it continues to render his heir impotent to continue the line. Hughball's and Letoy's cure of horn madness, the phobia of cuckoldry, compels the patient to accept the threat.

Apparently the physician and the layman practice the radical method of confirming the jealous husband's worst fears. Blaze and Barbara, Hughball and Letoy hint at the cure. Barbara describes it when she loquaciously agrees with Letoy's vaunt of having "wrought" more than twenty cures: "You [Letoy] were the means to make me an honest woman, / Or (at the least) [Blaze] a contented man. . . . I know what was done first, if my lord took / That course with you as me . . . . Content! So was my husband when he knew / The worst he could by his wife" (V.viii.1-19). Barbara continues, despite Letoy's attempts to silence her, to implicate Letoy's biological daughter since "old whoremasters . . . call their wenches daughters." Letoy's practice seems antipodal to his preoccupations with genus, except for two psychological comforts prevalent in western societies: misery loves company and, perversely, masculine pride can issue from cuckolding others as well as from remaining un-horned. Letoy's understanding plumbs deeper than Joyless's interest in a buff woman who is capable of dominating any old husband (III.iv).

The traditions of his house have left Letoy anguishing over a dilemma. Despite his fear of failing to maintain the purity of his venerated line, his very family heritage has made him acutely aware that pride in the past and the present can stifle continuity. Since the Letoys have led in sponsoring innovation, he is acutely aware of his responsibility to promote the change that is necessary to maintaining generation. He tells Blaze that "My ancestors and I have been beginners / Of all new fashions in the court of England / From before *Primo Ricardi Secundi* / Until this day" (I.v.15-18). Letoy is the antipodal lord of his society. Unlike other lords he dresses like a peddler while he supports a company of actors who dress like lords. Whereas other lords run into debt with shows too often ghost written by impoverished poets, he "write[s] all [his] plays [him]self" (I.v.76). And he underwrites, produces, and directs a magnificent repertoire of pleasurable, healthful stage plays. But if in his post of impresario he exercises control, in living up to his name of Letoy he recognizes the importance of improvisation, of innovation. Thus he creates a liberty in which people can act out vicarious roles; he thereby frees them to experiment with social change without facing horrendously damaging consequences.

When Hughball predicts acclaim for the social physician and the "lord of fancy" who restore the healthful mirth of their participating audience, Letoy claims that his "antiquity" dates from "Ages before the fancies were begot, / And shall beget still new to the world's end" (II.i.7-9). He is declaring his legacy of control; but he is also using sexual metaphors to suggest possibilities beyond that control. While he aims to achieve specific goals and maintains strict directorship in some ways, he also acknowledges the necessity of promoting free play with its unpredictable potential. Estimating that his actors are "all perfect/ But one," Letoy admits that Byplay's "shifts extempore, / (Knowing the purpose what he is to speak to) . . . moves mirth in me 'bove all the rest" (II.i.15-19). And Hughball realizes that Byplay's improvisations will prove invaluable as the spectators become interlocutors. Still, free play incurs risks few will venture. Exhorting his troupe Letoy corrects the absurdly formal speeches and mannered posturings that violate the decorum required by his style of directing. Then he berates Byplay for overgoing directorial attempts to overcontrol:

> But you, sir, are incorrigible, and
> Take license to yourself to add unto
> Your parts your own free fancy, and sometimes
> To alter or diminish what the writer
> With care and skill compos'd; and when you are
> To speak to your coactors in the scene,
> You hold interlocutions with the audients—
> BYPLAY.
> That is a way, my lord, has bin allow'd
> On elder stages to move mirth and laughter.
> LETOY.
> Yes, in the days of Tarlton and Kemp,
> Before the stage was purg'd from barbarism.
> . . . .
> Tonight I'll give thee leave to try thy wit.   [II.ii.39-54]

Three sanctions in this release to curative extemporaneous play assuage Letoy's fear of surrendering some direction to experimentation. First, the circumstances virtually require it; whoever gives up control must recognize dire need. Second, the release is for a specific temporary occasion;

whoever gives up control tries to limit the period of vicarious trial. Third, tradition itself provides a precedent for trying change by improvising and sets rules for opening opportunities to salutary reform. All three imply carnival. All are potentially radical in both senses of maintaining a society's roots and of changing a society at root. Letoy expresses a principle of *The Antipodes* and a principle Brome held to throughout his playwriting career.

The inset play increasingly involves the spectators, who are drawn in by Byplay's dominating, role-shifting performance until, with only general direction by Letoy, it dissolves into *The Antipodes*. "Hoyday! The rest will all be lost," Letoy tells Joyless, turning to instruct Byplay to entice Peregrine to his state marriage with Martha. "We now / Give over the play, and do all by extempore / For your son's good, to sooth him into's wits" (IV.x.116-18). Perhaps recognition of good physic as well as wise counsel (after Brome's fantasy) causes anti-Londoners to richly reward their poets, those antipodal Puritans. Extempore playing proves efficacious in healing and reforming—not as a program, but as a process. The inset play's progress, which encourages vicarious social, political, and finally personal experimentation, takes up the center of *The Antipodes*.

The Antipodes' inset play, though it provokes interaction with everyone, is primarily aimed at relieving Peregrine's mad Mandevillian escape from Joyless's paternal oppressions. In doing so through the commonplace analogy, it extends patriarchy from the absolutism of the family through the arbitrary hierarchy of society to the capricious tyranny of the state. There can be little question of the focus on law in the inset play. Each section of the inset, which begins with Quailpipe's prologue (II.v) and concludes with the marriage masque for Peregrine and Martha, the king of the Antipodes by conquest and its queen by inheritance (IV.xi), opens with a legal concern. The first begins with a gentleman chasing two sergeants who refuse his plea to be arrested and arraigned (II.vi); after a brief intermission the second begins with an unlikely conference between an impoverished lawyer and his rich client, a poet (III.ii); after Peregrine's entry into the play by attacking the performers' tiring house and declaring himself king, the third section begins with an absurd court hearing presided over by Byplay (III.vii); finally, when the Joyless entourage retire still further from the play, Peregrine gathers intelligence so he can judge and correct enormities in his kingdom (IV.i). The opening of each section manifests temporary escape from arbitrary authority. More, the last section indicates the necessity of change in the sociopolitical order, following the popular Renaissance stage tradition of the investigative disguised prince, lynx-eyed Haroun-al-Raschid, Jonson's imitative Justice Overdo, and his descendant, Brome's Cockbrain. Most, the central break is supplied by Peregrine storming the tiring house, taking "strict survey" of the actors' properties, and laying claim to dominion over anti-London, in imitation of the London apprentices' Shrovetide revelry.

Other factors contribute to an atmosphere of carnival exploration of family, social, and political reform through the play set inside *The Antipodes*. In one series of releases the inset's sections progressively focus first on an inverted family and educational system, next on an inverted social hierarchy, then on a perverted judiciary's enforcement of an arbitrary social structure, and climactically on Peregrine's assumption of authority to "reduce" Antipodean mores to English manners. But as Peregrine discovers what are for him abnormalities, he senses how arbitrary manners and mores can be. So he begins his demand for his new subjects' "submission" and "conformity" with mercy. In another pattern of releases, through the insertions Byplay doubles roles, increasing his command of the stage by taking the parts of ever more arbitrary, capricious, and zany authorities. In a final release the inset play's first two sections, which proceed to Peregrine's takeover, lead to the inescapable conclusion that the arbitrary absurdity of anti-London in many ways resembles that of London. And the inset's concluding two sections suggest, by a review of inverted power relationships through the extended family, the society, and the magistracy, that many current inequities need redress.

The opening section of the inset presents a rather straightforward inversion of domestic relations. Habits, manners, even grammar illustrate how servants command mistresses, who rule their husbands; the servants get increasing bonuses, the wives make jointures, the husbands bring dowries. But since in the Antipodes the old normally marry the young, some relations seem to represent London's practices that violate its professions. Gentlemen there are required by their wives to increase family estates by serving as gigolos who satisfy the wives of aged merchants and beget their children; and maids who bear families for aged ladies take precedence over their mistresses. The role of rake there is compelled on unwilling gentry, just as the role of bait is popularly forced on unwilling wives by greedy London merchants. In this odd manner, there patrilineage is reinforced by economics and fiat. What seems askew is not the mores but the moral approval of the Antipodeans. A similar pattern appears in youth ruling age and young women serving as tutors, particularly to senile men. Indeed, Peregrine urges the actors to agree that wisdom comes primarily from the beardless, not the greybeards.

The second section of the inset initially features an "honest lawyer, and though poor, no marvel," who astoundingly counsels mediation rather than litigation to a "spruce young captain" who seeks escape from the feathermaker's duns to not pay his account and needs relief from his coachman's beatings. This section increasingly emphasizes the closeness of apparent oddities in anti-London to abuses in current England. A buff woman, who wins a decree permitting her duel, forces the lawyer to accept a fee rather than a thrashing. "He will take money yet / Rather than blows; and so far he agrees / With our rich lawyers, that sometimes give blows, / And shrewd ones, for their money," Diana observes (III.v.27-30). The entry of a beggar trailed by a gallant who is begging from him suggests a remarkable set of likenesses. Not only do beggars and courtiers prove interchangeable in their insatiable search for funds but "politic young student[s]" prime the pump for larger allowances with gifts to their parents and grandparents. Direct commerce appears through the anti-charity of anti-London lawyers who collect beggars' fees to pay off London lawyers who curse the burden of poverty cases. Direct correspondence is discovered in the universal hypocrisy of usury, particularly among "some that pass for grave and pious churchmen" (III.v.92).

A change of focus from family to state commences with the third section of *The Antipodes'* inset, when the conqueror, Peregrine, admires the adjudication of a "point of justice" by an arbitrary, capricious, and confiscatory judge, Byplay. The greedy male magistrate's domineering enforcement of arbitrary morals parallels London's mores rather than its professed ideals. This "jeering judge" interrupts with sarcastic remarks, refuses to listen to charges or lawyers, and hears the defendant before the plaintiff. Mainly he bullies the citizen into a sycophantic obeisance that recalls Saleware's subservience ("An't please you, sir, my lord, an't like your honor") under the threat of the swordbearer whose place "is to show correction" (III.ix.12). The citizen has brought a breach of promise suit on behalf of his wife against a gentleman who was given clothing to service her. He presents two arguments for his demand that the gentleman "satisfy" his wife: as his commander she makes him a whole tradesman; and gentlemen need to sire children (particularly sons) of citizens who will become the new gentry inheriting the estates their biological fathers lost to citizens. This custom rings familiar tunes satirizing London. But the gentleman antipodally creates discord by accepting imprisonment for violating anti-London's profession and London's practice of the double standard. He chooses to remain faithful, not "stand out with all men's wives / Except mine own" (III.ix.45-46). As a citizen the judge refuses to allow so dangerous a breach of "city custom, / By gentlemen's neglect of tradesmen's wives" and as a gentleman and representative of a rapacious state he abhors letting wealth get away. So he determines to seize the wares and satisfy the wife himself: "I'll do't, and set all straight and right: / Justice is blind, but judges have their sight" (III.ix.75-76). "And feeling, too, in the Antipodes." And in England.

In the final section of the inset, Peregrine, following Hughball's advice, dons a disguise so as to "perceive / What to approve, and what correct" (IV.i.4-5). Resolving to "cherish, or severely punish," he investi-

gates family, social, and state hierarchies, values, and mores. As he
discovers these to be wrongheadedly arbitrary and capriciously greedy,
he decides to use authoritarian compulsion to right them, that is, to
reduce them to London's ideals. But since many reflect London's normative practices or invert them so that suppressors and suppressed merely
exchange roles, what gets revealed is the necessity not of revolution, a 180-
degree spin, but of reformation. It would begin with the recognition of the
irrational basis for many common practices and with the forgiveness of
fallible humans. For arbitrary repression in *The Antipodes* requires the
release of merciful amnesty. Just so, Peregrine gets released from his
father, Joyless's family gets released from a destructive, jealous paternalism, and London gets released from a sociopolitical plague. Thus what
gets prescribed is a process.

The first two scenes recall antipodal family and gender hierarchies
that suggest parallels in London. A drunken old woman plays hooky
from her lessons to enjoy bearbaiting; a gentleman indulging in ostentatious consumption fears to offend his servingman; then a lusty maid
insultingly tries to pick him up. As this scene inverts the anticipated roles
of sexual harassment, it modulates into a set of scenes showing the state's
intervention in family and social habits. When a constable enters, the
aggressor accuses the gentleman and his servingman of being street-
walkers assaulting her virginity. She thereby initiates a paradigm of the
problems produced by the authoritarian enforcement of customs that are
all too often as inequitable as they are arbitrary. For the constable refuses
to hear the gentleman's protests because women by virtue of their antipodal gender role perforce take precedence; he compounds the problem
by accepting her word because of her superior social status. He further
proclaims that one witness is more credible than two (though he is wary of
self-interest) and that the law should always support the weaker side
(despite the contradiction of his previous arguments). When he orders
the two men off to prison, Peregrine is dismayed: "Here's much to be
reformed" (IV.iii.25). Thus the scene's first point, the arbitrary and unjust
nature of customs and their authoritarian enforcement, comes by way
of the shock of recognition during role inversions. The scene's second
point follows when Peregrine orders the gentleman freed and the maid
jailed. At Hughball's prompting the new, just monarch grants clemency
and release because "They are an ignorant nation, / And have my pity
mingled with correction" (IV.iii.32-33) and because this may be her first
offence. Then he advises her to follow his example when her truant
grandmother returns from bearbaiting. Peregrine provides no solution to
the shocking problem, only an understanding, forgiving process for its
resolution: "Go and transgress no more" (IV.iii.38).

The next crucial scene reaffirms both lessons as the Man-scold indicts the law and his punishment of ducking: "The law's a river, is't? Yes, 'tis a river, / Through which great men, and cunning, wade, or swim; / But mean and ignorant must drown in't" (IV.v.7-9). Again, Peregrine is appalled by the reversal of gender roles wherein a man is denied speech or a female brandishes a sword while a male plies a needle: they are "so contrary / In all that we hold proper to each sex," " 'Twill ask long time and study to reduce / Their manners to our government" (IV.v.31-32, 34-35). The scene implies recognition, again through gender role inversion, of the unfairness of the sentence and the arbitrariness of what is proper. It also implies recognition that "reducing" the mores of others, through the claim of leading them back to proper mores, involves compulsion. And it implies that vicarious topsyturvy role playing can create an understanding that offers the potential for valuable reform, though making changes in an enforcing social hierarchy will be much harder to effect than making changes in these "low" domestic concerns, which are "easy to be qualified" (IV.v.36).

The next scenes, which present a parodic inversion of courtiers who talk and roughhouse like lowlifes with carriers who compliment like sophisticates, provide transit through questions of social mobility to concerns of state. The courtiers prove "rude silken clowns" who wrangle over petty gambling, sleazy clothing, and cheap food in sexual bawdry punctuated by small oaths; their flytings lead to slapstick buffetings; their interests are told by broadside ballads. But the transporters emit high-flown compliments, offers of mutual aid, and proposals for a fine lunch graced by conversation about correspondence from the Continent, new ideas at the universities, and politics at court. Since carriers are intellectual but courtiers illiterate in anti-London, Peregrine decrees that "Before I reign / A month among them, they shall change their notes, / Or I'll ordain a course to change their coats. / I shall have much to do in reformation" (IV.ix.35-39). He recognizes the need for meritorious achievement; holders of high status should at least be educated. Such reforms of the social hierarchy have great implications for the state.

As Peregrine improves at identifying madness, Hughball signals that the inset is proceeding "Beyond the line." He introduces Byplay ironically, as "A statesman, studious for the commonwealth, / Solicited by projectors of the country" (IV.ix.56-58). Byplay's entry, amid clamoring projectors grasping bundles of proposals, initiates the inset's presentation of correspondences. It also introduces Brome's customary concern over the waste that results from arbitrary tyranny and its concomitant sycophantic scrambling for status, wealth, and power. Having approved a number of foolish projects, the "statesman" particularly commends increasing wool "By flaying of live horses and new covering them / With sheepskins" (IV.x.16-17). Descending from absurdity to vice, this favorite supports aid for a broke young gambler, a collection for a broken old bawd, and relief for thieves, burglars, conmen, and pimps; meanwhile he advocates the punishment of their victims for permitting damage to the "weal public"—all these apparently caricatures of current state abuses. At each discovery Peregrine becomes more indignant, until he breaks in on plans to take up a collection for a palsied "captain of the cutpurses": "I'll hang ye all." But Byplay leads a chorus who implore mercy, "Let not our ignorance suffer in your wrath / Before we understand your highness' laws; / We went by custom, and the warrant which / We had in your late predecessor's reign," and pledge obedience (IV.x.86-95). Again Peregrine responds with forgiveness: "My mercy / Meets your submission. See you merit it / In your conformity" (IV.x.96-98).

Peregrine is virtually cured, wanting an easy return to London via the marriage masque. So Letoy explains to Joyless how Hughball has directed Peregrine's progress from madness to folly to sanity. Yet all is not done. The last act of the play produces a different cure through still more role playing. Diana, who has associated curing with role playing all along, wonders if Hughball's prescription for Joyless's son might help Joyless:

> But 'tis the real knowledge of the woman
> (Carnal, I think you mean) that carries it.
> . . . .
>
> Nay, right or wrong, I could even wish
> If he were not my husband's son, the doctor
> Had made myself his recipe, to be the means
> Of such a cure.
> . . . .
>
> Perhaps that course might cure your [Joyless's] madness, too,
> Of jealousy, and set all right on all sides.   [IV.xiii.22-29]

Diana turns the play back to the issue that haunts Blaze, Joyless, and Letoy, the issue that haunts Brome's plays, the issue of issue and patriarchal ego, the issue of cuckoldry.

Throughout the insets Diana and Joyless, as well as Peregrine (and occasionally Martha) have been responding to Hughball, the troupe, and Letoy, to the playing, role playing, and free play which can lead to vicarious experiment and cure. Diana and Letoy have also concentrated on curing Joyless's insanely patriarchal jealousy. Ever after Diana accepted Letoy's ring, their repeated show and talk of it have prodded her old husband's dread of having "fallen through the doctor's fingers / Into the lord's hands" (II.iii.58-59). Letoy's psychosocial pressure has barely countered Joyless's attempts to banish his wife from her first play, since Joyless has feared Diana's collaboration with Byplay, both the actor and the action, during Letoy's frequent intermezzos of feasting and courting. "Kissing indeed is prologue to a play, / Compos'd by th' devil, and acted by the Children / Of his Black Revels," he anguishes (II.v.30-32). He is horrified by Diana's empathy for the antipodean custom of contracting with young gentry to impregnate the wives of impotent oldsters. Such experiments in thought, much more Diana's pretense of putting in for a "share amongst" actors who "may want one to act the whore" (III.v.51,54), severely threaten old Joyless. So for his cure Diana risks experimenting with the condition of her own name: "Your jealousy durst not trust me / Behind you in the country, and since I'm here, / I'll see and know and follow th' fashion; if / It be to cuckold you, I cannot help it" (III.vi.54-57). She stresses both the power of custom and the potency of experiment. Here reform and cure are, at the least, analogous. Both threaten Joyless as the antipodal play within the play dissolves into more role playing and scene setting in the final act of *The Antipodes*.

After the inset Joyless finds that he has been locked up for the night and that his host and his wife are missing. Possessed by mad folly he puts *The Antipodes'* crucial problem poignantly: "Why, rather, if [Letoy] did intend my shame / And [Diana's] dishonor, did he not betray me / From her out of his house, to travel in / The bare suspicion of their filthiness?" (V.i.10-14). But even if a husband does not face such an incident and even if his disease is in remission, his dread of cuckoldry remains incurable. Joyless will always face the dilemma that Hughball and Letoy cannot do away with but can try to resolve by compelling a husband onto one of its two painful horns. The perfect resolution can be achieved by their typical cure—let a husband, like Blaze, know that the worst has transpired. More psychologically amenable, but less sure, is to get a husband to trust that his wife is in deed a Diana. Impelling a husband onto this horn is much harder. Since suspicions are rife and the proof of innocence is impossible, credence in this case is ever precarious. To be reasonably sound, then, a husband (or a wife) can either forgive or he (she) can trust the spouse. Letoy and Diana propose the latter cure for Joyless.

The treatment commences with letting Joyless believe the worst and concludes with disabusing him. Charivaresque comedy opens the last act of *The Antipodes*, when Joyless, feeling the horns of his dilemma and his cuckoldry, appears in anguish. Barbara regales Joyless with news of the bedding of Peregrine and Martha, unaware that he suffers the news with reference to Letoy and Diana. Then a taunting and comforting Byplay, having allowed Joyless to purge considerable passion, enters to save Barbara or Joyless or both from the hornmad husband's knife and to usher him to another staging: Letoy's theater-proven testing of Diana. Joyless witnesses their parodic debate. In aphorisms phrased as capping couplets the faithful Diana resists the worldly wise Letoy's successive offers of riches instead of comfort, sensual satisfaction for aged impotence, and vengeance for jealous possessiveness. After the witness exalts his wife's "invincible" fidelity, he realizes that Letoy had Byplay bring him to this testing scene. He might have seen only an act:

> Stay, stay, stay, stay;
> Why may not this be then a counterfeit action,
> Or a false mist to blind me with more error?
> The ill I fear'd may have been done before,
> And all this but deceit to daub it o'er.   [V.vi.18-22]

His observation is exact. Letoy's confessional revelation to keep Joyless from "falling back again" (that he is testing his own daughter out of toying with his own madness) does not in itself assure. Joyless's ultimate tolerance and belief must come from internal reform. For his own health he must accept play, improvisation beyond his control.

In the end Letoy tries to reassert his directorship and paternalism by confessing his part in the role playing and scene setting. He has tested his daughter Diana. He has arranged for her adoption by Truelock. He calls in the Antimasque of Discord and the Masque of Harmony. But, if he wants to succeed, Letoy too has to surrender some control to extemporaneous play. Verification of whether his and Hughball's "cure be perfect yet or no" is granted only by society's applause for whatever reforms issue from improvisation. Such vicarious social experiment may resemble satire's correction in order to restore norms, and it can function to allow temporary release in order to effectively reinstitute received mores. But it can also lead through traditional ways to salutary changes in the family, the society, and the state. The faith and forgiveness that underlie improvisation, carnival, and May-December charivari, all of which promote thinking about the unthinkable and trying the untryable, can encourage reforming the recalcitrant, realizing the unrealizable.

Epilogue

At the end of *The Antipodes* the masque of Harmony with her train supplants the brief show of defiance by Discord and her antimasquers: Wit displaces Folly, Love Jealousy, Wine Melancholy, Health Madness. So Brome, or Letoy, might seem to try to contain any radical potential for reform in the vicarious social experiment of byplay and carnival. But both the lord Letoy and the doctor Hughball subvert containment. Letoy promises to offer whatever "may please, / Though we dive for it to th'Antipodes." He is willing to try inversions and free play again, not on any warrant of success but on the potential for pleasure and cure in release. His uncertainty about the outcome and his faith in the process are doubled by Hughball's plea for approving applause, since "Whether my cure be perfect yet or no, / It lies not in my doctorship to know. / Your approbation may more raise the man, / Than all the College of Physicians can." He is willing to risk radical vicarious experiment, and he allows that his success depends on society's acknowledgment.

Despite the fact that *The Antipodes* also closes with a masque, Brome's proffer of radical questions and consequences through play opposes the play of his fellow junior Caroline professional, Shirley. For the willow garland ceremony at the conclusion of *Hyde Park* does more than contain temporarily released inhibition; it reinforces and consolidates, structures and restricts a social standard that permits little variation from the norms authorized by absolute monarchy through ascribed hierarchy, family patriarchy, and masculine dominion. All the losing venturers for the ladies join in a brotherhood and "obey the Ceremony" because they see "a providence" uniting them with the victors and the trophies in one elite social system, one rule-bound game.

Brome is opposed in mode and in outcome to Ford, whom Shirley most resembles. The conclusion of *The Broken Heart* presents a social conformity that allows no deviation from ideal absolutes and the ceremonies that simultaneously embody, define, and mold them. The requirements established, promulgated, and engendered by the ceremonies of his determinist hierarchical society command characters' obedience to the utmost sacrifice for their essential selves or roles. The ceremonies of marriage and alliance arranged by Calantha are contained by her final testament and jointure, a funeral for her and her bridegroom. Just so, all the characters are virtually foreordained to shatter like flawed crystals.

The interacting demands of the characters and their society, if admirably transcendental, are also self-destructive.

Brome is closest in outcome to Massinger. The conclusion of *The Picture* offers social regeneration in the renewal of two reformed marriages. These mutual rebirths issue from a continually reforming accommodation of charitable, repenting and forgiving reflection and reciprocity among characters and their society. For the characters seem finally to recognize and affirm mutual, perpetual creation and cultivation of selves and society, through mutually arrived upon colors that reflect each other.

Thus the Caroline professional playwrights can be distributed along a sociopolitical spectrum. At one end are the self-encrusting and self-destroying ceremonies that command social control; Ford's tragic characters can be imaged as flawed crystals. Toward the middle is the more moderate social containment of a restricted repertoire of variations of set personal roles; Shirley's comic characters can be imaged as players in an enclosed game. On the other side of the middle is a reforming social accommodation (perhaps appropriation); Massinger's tragicomic characters can be imaged as reflexive and reciprocal portraits of psychosocial and moral colors. At the other end is the social incorporation of potentially radical reform in vicarious social experiment; Brome's comic characters can be imaged as participants in extemporaneous byplay. But the Caroline professional playwrights can be so distributed individually because they can be considered collectively through their common concern with dominant social issues of their time; and these, I believe, open up to ideas used by social scientists of ours. The perspective these colleagues seem to have self-consciously shared, presumably with the privileged audiences who offered them patronage and approving applause, focused on the mutual, interacting creation and maintenance, enforcement and transformation of personality and society.

Notes

For bibliographical information on works cited, see pages 215-25.

1. The Caroline Professionals

1. Muriel C. Bradbrook, *Themes and Conventions of Elizabethan Tragedy;* John F. Danby, *Poets on Fortune's Hill;* T.S. Eliot, *Elizabethan Dramatists.*

2. Bentley, *The Profession of Dramatist in Shakespeare's Time, 1590-1642,* 37.

3. Ibid., 27.

4. For wages see ibid., 106-8.

5. Ibid., 286-87.

6. See Mary Edmond's *Rare Sir William Davenant,* 51-55.

7. More usable accounts of these companies and playhouses than Bentley's *The Jacobean and Caroline Stage* are his rendition for *The* Revels *History of Drama in English,* vol. 4, *1613-1660,* by Lois Potter et al., and Alexander Gurr's *The Shakespearean Stage, 1574-1642.*

8. Besides Edmonds, see the apparatus by A.M. Gibbs, editor of *Sir William Davenant: The Shorter Poems, and Songs from the Plays and Masques.*

9. Martin Butler identifies several acquaintances Ford and Davenant had in common. Undoubtedly the literary coterie of the inns of court provided support for Massinger and Shirley as well as for Ford and Davenant, but Butler glosses over the rivalry. See the opening (201-5) of *"Love's Sacrifice:* Ford's Metatheatrical Tragedy," in *John Ford: Critical Re-Visions,* ed. Michael Neill, 201-31.

10. Davenant's known association with Newcastle did not come until after the closing of the theaters.

11. For the latest account see Andrew Gurr's "Singing through the Chatter: Ford and Contemporary Theatrical Fashion," in Neill, *John Ford: Critical Re-Visions,* 81-96. Also see Michel Grivelet, "Th' Untun'd Kennell: Note sur Thomas Heywood et le théâtre sous Charles Ier"; Gorges Bas, "James Shirley et 'Th' Untun'd Kennell': Une petite guerre des théâtres vers 1630"; and especially Peter Beal, "Massinger at Bay: Unpublished Verses in a War of the Theatres." Despite later additions and revisions, Alfred Harbage's *Cavalier Drama* still proves indispensable.

12. Kevin Sharpe, *Criticism and Compliment.* I disagree with Sharpe inasmuch as he means that during the mid- and later 1630s Davenant looked more to the theater than to preferment for his livelihood (57).

13. Waith, *The Pattern of Tragicomedy in Beaumont and Fletcher;* Anderson's essays and introductions begin with "The Heart and the Banquet: Imagery in Ford's *'Tis Pity* and *The Broken Heart,"* and culminate in *John Ford.*

14. Kaufmann, *Richard Brome, Caroline Playwright.*

15. Butler, *Theater and Crisis, 1632-1642.*

16. Ibid., 7-11.

17. See, for example, the lead essay of Crane's *Critical and Historical Principles of Literary History.*

18. The two most valuable constructive critiques of this heterogeneous grouping are Jean E. Howard's "The New Historicism in Renaissance Studies," and Howard Felperin's *The Uses of the Canon.* Howard offers a selective sampling of representatives and a broad context of analogous motifs and techniques, framing concepts, and stimulation supplied by European theorists from Bakhtin through Foucault to Derrida. Felperin offers the more thoughtful categories and incisive critiques.

19. The breadth of the approach ranges from Burns's *Theatricality: A Study of Convention in the Theatre and in Social Life* to Leach's attention to how people in specific societies act out endlessly repeated dramas of "more or less fixed" social roles and relationships that are variously adaptable to time and place, in *Social Anthropology,* 130.

20. Mead's seminal work is *Mind, Self, and Society;* he is best known through *George Herbert Mead on Social Psychology.* In theorizing, social psychologists are not prone to acknowledge this metaphor. But their language describing experiments—their "theater," "scenario," "scenery," "setting," "staging," "casting," "acting," when a "dramatist" or "showman" "produces" "re-creations" or "scripts"—is revealing. For a sampling see Arthur Aron and Elaine N. Aron's *The Heart of Social Psychology,* 84-85.

21. Of particular interest are Berger and Luckmann's introduction and third section of *The Social Construction of Reality.*

22. Milgram, *Obedience to Authority,* and Zimbardo, with Craig Haney and W. Curtis Banks, "A Pirandellan Prison."

23. See the survey of current interests in Anthony Giddens's *The Constitution of Society,* especially xvi.

24. One compelling reason why I do not examine Davenant here is that he does not seem to stage scenes in the ways that social psychologists do or, conversely, that his plays do not seem to yield dividends when viewed from this perspective.

25. Cook, *The Privileged Playgoers of Shakespeare's London, 1576-1642,* 9. I perceive Massinger's, Ford's, Shirley's, and Brome's audiences through Cook and through Andrew Gurr's *Playgoing in Shakespeare's London.*

26. Cook, *Privileged Playgoers,* 9. Despite differences, Butler agrees with Cook on two essential points: the patrons of the elite companies and houses to which the Caroline professional playwrights were linked consisted of both gentry/prosperous citizenry and courtiers; and the audience held divergent political views.

27. For an excellent entry into how evocations of Elizabeth in politics and drama could be used in opposing ways, see Butler, *Theatre and Crisis,* 198-210. For folk custom revivals see Marcus, *The Politics of Mirth.*

28. See Judson's *The Crisis of the Constitution,* 1-106, and Russell's *Parliaments and English Politics, 1621-29,* 1-84, especially early on, pp. 5, 39-40, 54-55.

29. Cope, *Politics without Parliaments, 1629-1640.*

30. See David Underdown, *Revel, Riot, and Rebellion;* a summation appears on 40-41.

31. Butler also stresses divided allegiances and gives examples: *Theatre and Crisis,* 19-24.

32. Besides Stone's *The Crisis of the Aristocracy, 1558-1664* and *The Causes of the English Revolution, 1529-1642* and Hexter's *Reappraisals in History,* see Sharpe's *Faction and Parliament* and Russell's *Parliaments and English Politics,* 1-84.

33. For Zagorin see *The Court and the Country,* especially 33-118. For Stone's summary see *Causes of the English Revolution,* 105-8. Despite its difficulties, the

persuasive force of this antithesis is indicated by the fact that both recent books on literary and aesthetic culture during the era open with admonitions about it but then, with provisos, rely on it. See Kevin Sharpe's *Criticism and Compliment* and R. Malcolm Smuts's *Court Culture and the Origins of a Royalist Tradition in Early Stuart England*.

34. For seminal analyses see Louis Montrose's "'Eliza, Queene of shepheardes' and the Pastoral of Power," and Stephen Orgel's *The Illusion of Power*.

35. *The Political Works of James I*, 307.

36. Samuel R. Gardiner, *History of England, 1603-42*, 6:83, and J.P. Kenyon, ed., *The Stuart Constitution, 1603-1688*, 71.

37. For a useful survey of the many varieties of argument, both for royal absolutism and for limitations on the monarch, see J.P. Sommerville's *Politics and Ideology in England, 1603-1640*.

38. For the document see Kenyon, *Stuart Constitution*, 29-35. For a statement of its importance see Hexter's "Power, Parliament and Liberty in Early Stuart England," reprinted in *Reappraisals in History*, 163-218; note especially 197-215.

39. See J.G.A. Pocock, *The Ancient Constitution and the Feudal Law*, especially 30-55.

40. I quote *The Dramatic Works in the Beaumont and Fletcher Canon*, ed. Bowers.

41. Danby, *Poets on Fortune's Hill*, 163-66.

42. Sedge, "Social and Ethical Concerns in Caroline Drama," 13-19.

43. Tricomi, *Anticourt Drama in England, 1603-1642*.

44. Because of its availability, the edition I cite for the act.scene/page is James Maidment and W.H. Logan's *The Dramatic Works of Sir William D'Avenant*. I correct the text from the original editions.

45. For an acute account of political subtleties in Caroline drama see Butler's *Theatre and Crisis*, 25-83. Both Butler's and Sharpe's interpretations are usefully read in the dramatic tradition laid out by Tricomi.

46. See Wrightson, "Degrees of People" in *English Society, 1580-1680*.

47. See Stone, *Causes of the English Revolution*, especially 48, 50-51.

48. Cook's table (*Privileged Playgoers*, 51) sums up estimates by Peter Laslett's Cambridge group.

49. Quoted by Stone in *Crisis of the Aristocracy*, 32.

50. See Frances Elizabeth Baldwin, *Sumptuary Legislation and Personal Regulation in England*. For later recurrences see Stone, *Crisis of the Aristocracy*, 27-30.

51. Wilson, "The State of England (1600)," respectively 18-19, 23, 22.

52. Harrison, *Description of England*, 115.

53. Besides Stone, *Crisis of the Aristocracy*, especially 21-198, data and examples are available in Peter Laslett's *The World We Have Lost*, especially 30-50 and 195-205, and in Wrightson, *English Society*, 22-38; Cook sums up: *Privileged Playgoers*, 11-51.

54. See especially *Crisis of the Aristocracy*, 65-128.

55. See Sedge, "Social and Ethical Concerns," 231-32ff.

56. For the sake of reference I cite the act.scene/page of *The Dramatic Works and Poems of James Shirley*, ed. William Gifford and Alexander Dyce, 3:201. But I quote the original editions.

57. See Stone's *Crisis of the Aristocracy*, 335-36, 375-84.

58. On this ambivalence see Theodore B. Leinwand's *The City Staged: Jacobean Comedy, 1603-1613*, 27-37.

59. Quoted by Butler (*Theatre and Crisis*, 166) from p. 279 of Dorothy Gardiner's edition of *The Oxinden and Peyton Letters* (London: Sheldon Press, 1937).

60. I cite and quote *Ben Jonson,* ed. Charles H. Herford et al.

61. I cite and quote *The Complete Works of John Webster,* ed. F.L. Lucas.

62. I cite and quote act.scene/page of a reprint of the 1875 edition of *The Dramatic Works of Shackerley Marmion,* ed. James Maidment and W.H. Logan.

63. I am deeply indebted to Schochet's *Patriarchalism in Political Thought.*

64. An excellent entry is Jonathan Goldberg's "Fatherly Authority: The Politics of Stuart Family Images," 3-32.

65. A telling example is considered by D.E. Underdown, "The Taming of the Scold: The Enforcement of Patriarchal Authority in Early Modern England."

66. Despite compelling attacks on portions of Stone's thesis, I only temper the claims of *The Family, Sex and Marriage in England, 1500-1800* because I focus on the elite circles he knows best. Stone is vulnerable in his extrapolation to all society from the family practices of the aristocracy, in his theory of callous family relationships, and in his greater reliance on ideological tracts than on personal accounts. For a critique of the first, see Trumbach's *The Rise of the Egalitarian Family;* for criticism of the second and third see Pollock's *Forgotten Children: Parent-Child Relations from 1500 to 1900.* For a trenchant attack see MacFarlane's review essay in *History and Theory.* Two considerations allowing my reliance on Stone despite MacFarlane's persuasive *The Origins of English Individualism* are (1) MacFarlane's avowed redress of a previous imbalance because of more information about the privileged (with whom I am concerned) than the rest, and (2) the general perception, expressed in didactic and moral tracts, the drama, and other works from the period, that radical changes were under way.

67. I follow *Certain Sermons or Homilies appointed to Be Read in Churches in the Time of Queen Elizabeth of Famous Memory* (London, 1673). Wing C4091E.

68. See Filmer, *Patriarcha and Other Political Works of Sir Robert Filmer,* ed. Laslett, 96; see also Laslett's helpful outline, 11-20. Filmer's use here of "sons" for all children (or the only children who counted) is not insignificant.

69. For Schochet see *Patriarchalism in Political Thought,* especially 1-17 and 54-158; for Hinton, "Husbands, Fathers, and Conquerors," particularly 291-94.

70. For Gouge, *Of Domesticall Duties,* I cite and quote the first edition.

71. See Aries, *Centuries of Childhood,* 25, 261-62, 268, 329.

72. See Smith, "The London Apprentices As Seventeenth-Century Adolescents," and idem, "Religion and the Conception of Youth in 17th-Century England."

73. See Stone's *Family, Sex and Marriage,* 151-206, and Jean-Louis Flandrin's *Families in Former Times,* 130ff.

74. Ralph A. Houlbrooke provides a judicious evaluation of histories of such matters in *The English Family, 1450-1700,* 68-78.

75. Stone, *Crisis of the Aristocracy,* 651, and Hill, *The Intellectual Origins of the English Revolution,* 273.

76. Sedge, "Social and Ethical Concerns," 94ff.

77. See Thirsk, "The European Debate on Customs of Inheritance, 1500-1700," 177-91, especially 183-86. Also see Houlbrooke, *English Family,* 234-38.

78. Wilson, "State of England," 24.

79. Gouge, *Of Domesticall Duties,* 577.

80. I quote *The Works of Francis Beaumont and John Fletcher,* ed. Arnold Glover and A.R. Waller, 6:12.

81. See Rose, *The Expense of Spirit.* Rose marshals useful evidence from Puritan handbooks and some plays of a wakening awareness of gender problems and a new marital heroism. But she seems to me to rely too readily on

advice that counsels melioration and on striking rather than representative plays.

82. See Part II of Belsey, *The Subject of Tragedy.*

83. Summaries of gender relations appear in Amussen's "Gender, The Family and the Social Order, 1560-1725," and in Wrightson, *English Society,* 118.

84. The dominance of this trinity is emphasized in the fullest annotated bibliography of the topic, Suzanne W. Hull's *Chaste, Silent, and Obedient.*

85. T.E., *The Lawes Resolution,* III.xlii: 204. See as well Doris Mary Stenton, *The English Woman in History,* chapters 3-5.

86. Kelso, *Doctrine for the Lady of the Renaissance,* 1ff., especially 31ff., 78-82; for the centrality of obedience see especially 97ff.; for chastity 24ff., 90, and 97ff.; for silence 100ff. Ann Rosalind Jones updates Kelso in "Nets and Bridles: Early Modern Conduct Books and Sixteenth-century Women's Lyrics."

87. Gouge, *Of Domesticall Duties,* 219.

88. Kahn, *Man's Estate,* 121.

89. For a discussion and list, see Thomas B. Stroup, *Microcosmos,* 179-206.

90. Braithwait, *English Gentlewoman,* 88-89.

91. For satiric stage quips see Linda Woodbridge, *Women and the English Renaissance,* 207-10.

92. See ibid., and Ann Rosalind Jones's "Counterattacks on 'the Bayter of Women': Three Pamphleteers of the Early Seventeenth Century."

93. For Stone see *Crisis of the Aristocracy,* 614-17, and idem, *Family, Sex, and Marriage,* 137-38. For Powell, *English Domestic Relations, 1487-1653,* see especially 104-6, 124-25, 160-63.

94. Gouge, *Of Domesticall Duties,* 219.

95. See Stone, *Crisis of the Aristocracy,* 662-70, idem, *Family, Sex, and Marriage,* 504-5.

96. Jardine, *Still Harping on Daughters.*

97. Kelso, *Doctrine for the Lady,* 38-39 and 58-69. It is worth noting that education and conduct books for women were often appendages to those for gentlemen.

98. I provide brief characterizations of these perspectives, with preliminary bibliographies, in my survey of Shirley's characteristic techniques and in my consideration of the exemplary play for each of the others.

2. Massinger's Tragicomedy of Reformation

1. The most famous portrayal of Massinger as not quite reactionary enough is by T.S. Eliot in *Elizabethan Dramatists,* 134-51. See also Robert A. Fothergill, "The Dramatic Experience of Massinger's *The City Madam* and *A New Way To Pay Old Debts,*" and Michael Neill, "Massinger's Patriarchy: The Social Vision of *A New Way To Pay Old Debts.*"

2. S.R. Gardiner noted this in "The Political Element in Massinger." See Alan G. Gross's modifications sustaining Gardiner with less Whiggishness and without portraying Massinger as a political propagandist aware of the inner politics of the highest circles, "Contemporary Politics in Massinger."

3. For Massinger's associates and patrons I rely on T.A. Dunn, *Philip Massinger,* and Donald S. Lawless, *Philip Massinger and His Associates.* See the corroborations and condensations by Philip Edwards and Colin Gibson in the general introduction and notes to *The Plays and Poems of Philip Massinger.* In *Philip Massinger,*

Doris Adler has questioned some conclusions. Throughout I quote and cite Edwards and Gibson's invaluable edition.

4. For consideration of the mixed motives evident in ingratiating epideictic, see Robert C. Evans's *Ben Jonson and the Poetics of Patronage*, 12-13 and 23-30.

5. After scholarly neglect of this literary institution, John Danby revived interest in it by the late forties; others followed, including Margot Heinemann, *Puritanism and Theatre;* Philip J. Finkelpearl, "The Role of the Court in the Development of Jacobean Drama," and Butler, *Theatre and Crisis*, 100-135, and idem "Massinger's *The City Madam* and the Caroline Audience," especially 159-60 and 185-87. See specifically Michael Brennan, *Literary Patronage in the English Renaissance: The Pembroke Family.*

6. The support is confirmed by John Aubrey in *The Natural History of Wiltshire.* See Edwards and Gibson's introduction: xxxv.

7. See Heinemann, *Puritanism and Theatre*, 102, 116, 213, and the surrounding readings; also see Russell, *Parliaments and English Politics*, especially 12-14, 105-6, 176-80, 255, 287-90. And see Brennan, *Literary Patronage*, 103-98. In calling the Herberts and other families Puritan I am emphasizing the first of three types of Puritan Joseph Mede distinguished in 1623: the "Puritan in Politicks or the Politicall Puritan" is described by J.T. Cliffe as concerned "with such matters as the liberties of the people and the prerogatives of sovereigns." For quotations from and analysis of this letter see Cliffe, *The Puritan Gentry*, 5-6 and note 6, 241.

8. See Lawless, *Philip Massinger,* 44 and 50.

9. See Finkelpearl, "Role of the Court," 153-57.

10. Dunn, *The Concept of Ingratitude in Renaissance English Moral Philosophy.*

11. Throughout this discussion I rely on Stanley Frederick Bonner, *Roman Declamation in the Late Republic and Early Empire;* see especially 46 and 83.

12. See Waith, "John Fletcher and the Art of Declamation," and idem, *Pattern,* 86-98 and 203-7. Waith's study has been extended by Bertha Hensman, *The Shares of Fletcher, Field, and Massinger in Twelve Plays of the Beaumont and Fletcher Canon.*

13. The last several paragraphs digest my argument in *The Moral Art of Philip Massinger.* See the sections on his political inclinations before the discussion of his political plays and on his social preferences before that of his tragedies and satires.

14. Adler presents the latest version of a conservative Massinger. Her nostalgic Elizabethan is more credible than the portraits of a reactionary, but my accommodating reformer challenges her thesis, which appeals to "eternal verities."

15. For an extended argument for my conclusions about the social inclinations and political preferences in Massinger's plays, see my *Moral Art.*

16. See my "The Power of Integrity in Massinger's Women."

17. For a summation see Sedge, "Social and Ethical Concerns," 69-74.

18. The most cogent readings of Massinger as a reactionary are Fothergill's and Neill's. For an analysis of positions and bibliography see my *Moral Art.*

19. See Edwards's overly corrective introduction and notes to *The Bondman,* and Jerzy Limon's *Dangerous Matter,* 62-88.

20. For an epitome of Adler's consistent interpretation, see her *Philip Massinger,* 29-32.

21. See the accounts by Dunn, *Philip Massinger,* 15-30, and Lawless, *Philip Massinger,* 16-25.

22. In the 1650s Cokayne tried to redress the still prevalent neglect; see Edwards and Gibson's introduction to *Plays and Poems,* 1: xix-xxi. For discussion of Massinger's acknowledgments of his artistic debts and of his technical achievements see my "Models for Massinger the Apprentice" in *Moral Art.*

23. Besides Waith, *The Pattern of Tragicomedy*, 36-41, see Dunn, *Philip Massinger*, 55-75.

24. For Massinger's customary moral testing see Philip Edwards, "Massinger the Censor."

25. See her discussion of backgrounds in *sacra rappresentazione*, *Endeavors of Art*, 189-90, 198-20.

26. I extend into Morris Croll's description of a "loose," "trailing," "linked," or reintegrated baroque prose style the generally acknowledged characteristics of Massinger's rhetorical poetry (Hensman, *Shares of Fletcher*, 374-77, Dunn, *Philip Massinger*, 202-66, Waith, *The Pattern of Tragicomedy*, 184-92). But instead of agreeing with their evaluations, I propose that his style represents a deeper sociopolitical probe and a higher aesthetic quality as it mediates between opposed ideals of reaction and revolution. For Croll's 1929 essay with a commentary see *Essays by Morris Croll: "Attic" and Baroque Prose Style*, 207-33, especially sections IIIc-e. Here I merely characterize Massinger's high style and low style. In reading *The Picture* (below) I provide detailed commentary.

27. In "Verbal Formulae in the Plays of Philip Massinger," Cyrus Hoy supplies a suggestive descriptive catalog but an unappreciative appraisal.

28. See Alan C. Dessen, *Jonson's Moral Comedy*.

29. See L.C. Knights's *Drama and Society in the Age of Jonson*, and Leinwand, *The City Staged*.

30. For a compilation of the central contributions masques make to Stuart drama see Marie Cornelia, *The Function of the Masque in Jacobean Tragedy and Tragicomedy;* her study mainly evolves from Stephen Orgel's *The Jonsonian Masque*.

31. In "Philip Massinger: The Spurious Legatee," David L. Frost shows that Massinger used Shakespeare for allusive repertory company reverberations and that both playwrights employed current commonplaces, but that Massinger differs from Shakespeare in mode.

32. These metaphors recur. Notice, for examples, the language at Mathias's departure at the opening and then Sophia's recollection of his venture as a voyage (II.i.71-79) or his comments at the beginning of Act IV when he first notices the change in the picture. See also the lessons Sophia's clown Hilario learns as he is dismissed to be a strolling player and the comments by her would-be seducers, Ubaldo and Ricardo.

33. For the former, shallow reactionary decadence, see Dunn, *Philip Massinger*, 157-58; for the latter, nostalgic reactionary idealism, see Adler, *Philip Massinger*, 71-73.

34. Giddens, *Constitution of Society*, 3ff.

35. See Mead, *Mind, Self, and Society*.

36. See Zimbardo et al., *Influencing Attitudes and Changing Behavior*.

37. Tesser, "Self-generated Attitude Changes."

38. For Mead, see *Philosophy of the Act;* for the best known of many Goffman studies, see *The Presentation of Self in Everyday Life;* for Stebbins see *Teachers and Meaning*. Besides his summary (from 16-20) and his operational definition (from 12) which follow, Stebbins places this perspective among approaches, particularly social perception, ethnomethodology, motivation, and formalization (27-39). For a survey of ideas leading to and following from Mead see Sheldon Stryker's *Symbolic Interactionism*.

39. See Stone's *Crisis*, 609-17, 662-67, and *Family*, 317; Powell, *English Domestic Relations*, 101-91; Rose, *Expense of Spirit*, passim; and chapter two of Florence T. Winston's "The Significance of Women in the Plays of Philip Massinger."

40. Dunn provides an excellent account of Massinger's plotting: each act

builds to its climax while each play fits into one of two categories, building to greater climaxes either in the first, third, and fifth acts, or in the first, third, and fourth acts. He criticizes the structure of *The Picture* (and other plays in the second category) for having an anticlimactic, moralizing last act. But he draws a pre-emptive moral that contradicts the values emphasized by the structure. See *Philip Massinger,* 55-75, especially his abstract and graph, 57-58; on *The Picture* see 69 and 75.

41. My final assertion extends implications in Richard Levin's analysis (*The Multiple Plot in English Renaissance Drama,* 5-20) of insights in William Empson's "Double Plots: Heroic and Pastoral in the Main Plot and Sub-Plot."

42. See Gibson, "Massinger's Hungarian History." Gibson quotes the passage in his introduction to *The Picture,* 284.

43. I select, rearrange, and augment Hoy's classifications (in "Verbal Formulae"), but reinterpret his evidence and oppose Dunn, *Philip Massinger,* 210-14. Colin Gibson in "Massinger's 'Composite Mistresses,'" describes Massinger re-creating commonplaces to restore old significances and invent new ones.

44. See especially 293v of Painter, *The Second Tome of the Palace of Pleasure.* For an estimate of the frequent recurrence of this pattern in Massinger see Francis D. Evenhuis, *Massinger's Imagery,* 106-7.

45. For a compilation of Massinger's pervasive use of lustful and luxurious eating images see Evenhuis, *Massinger's Imagery,* 82-93 and 125-27; for clothing, 131-33.

46. See Dunn, *Philip Massinger,* 97-100.

47. For this tradition see Woodbridge, *Women and the English Renaissance,* 275-99.

3. Ford's Tragedy of Ritual Suffering

1. I take virtually all my biographical and most of my bibliographical data from M. Joan Sargeaunt's *John Ford.* I rely, more than is evident in my notes, on the comprehensive study of sources and characteristics by Robert Davril, *Le Drame de John Ford,* and on the judicious summations and suggestive readings by Donald K. Anderson, Jr. in *John Ford.*

2. Unless I state otherwise, for all Ford's plays I quote *John Fordes Dramatische Werke,* from *Materialien zur Kunde des älteren Englischen Dramas.* For a modern edition of the prose I have to use *The Works of John Ford,* reedited from William Gifford by Alexander Dyce. I cite this edition as well for act.scene/page. My dates specify when Ford's plays were printed. I have no more valid conjecture than anyone else as to when he wrote them. I follow Bang, Sargeaunt, Davril, Anderson, and others in attributing to Ford the anonymous *The Queen,* published by Alexander Goughe in 1653.

3. I owe this information about the connection to Jeremy Maule, who kindly gave me a draft of his essay "'To the memory of the late excellent poet John Fletcher': A New Ford Poem?" which is forthcoming in *Viator.*

4. For more on Newcastle see my account of Shirley's audience in chapter 4, below.

5. Anderson's point that Ford at times portrays the middle classes (*Ford,* 14, 137) disregards Ford's focus on the gentry, nobility, and on occasion royalty, his frequent use of crestless imitators as foils for nobles, and his presentation to the privileged.

6. See Greenfield's "John Ford's Tragedy: The Challenge of Re-Engage-

ment," in *"Concord in Discord": The Plays of John Ford, 1586-1986*, ed. Donald K. Anderson, Jr., 1-26. Critical reliance on moral relativity increased with Irving Ribner's conclusion that these plays exhibit the era's loss of moral certainty. See *Jacobean Tragedy*, 153-75.

7. These carry on an argument waged since Lamb and Hazlitt. See the comprehensive bibliographical essay on Ford criticism through the early seventies by Donald K. Anderson, Jr., "John Ford," in Logan and Smith's *The Later Jacobean and Caroline Dramatists*, 120-51. For Sensabaugh see *The Tragic Muse of John Ford*, 186-90; for Stavig, *John Ford and the Moral Order*, 95-121.

8. See Sensabaugh, *Tragic Muse*, 181-86, and Stavig, *John Ford*, 122-43.

9. Probably the seminal argument for this pattern, now a commonplace, is Ralph J. Kaufmann's "Ford's Tragic Perspective." For a good exposition see Alan Brissenden's "Impediments to Love: A Theme in John Ford."

10. Greenfield, "John Ford's Tragedy," 3.

11. Kathleen McLuskie pursues this same dissatisfaction with critics who have tried to understand Ford's plays through "psychologically motivated narrative" instead of through characters who "behave according to the structural logic of the scenes in which they appear." She takes it to a structural rather than a social end in " 'Language and Matter with a Fit of Mirth': Dramatic Construction in the Plays of John Ford," *John Ford; Critical Re-Visions*, ed. Michael Neill, 97-127. The quotations appear on 100 and 104.

12. Ornstein, *Moral Vision*, 200-221, particularly 201 and 212.

13. Orbison, *The Tragic Vision of John Ford*. Like many, Orbison hypothesizes a chronology that enhances his thematic progression.

14. Eliot, *Elizabethan Dramatists*, 120-33, and Ellis-Fermor, *The Jacobean Drama*, 227-46.

15. For example, see H.J. Oliver, *The Problem of John Ford*, 84 and 124.

16. Ford's few characters who do accept accommodation, for example Auria and Spinella in the tragicomic *The Lady's Trial*, rarely gain critical approval, or even acknowledgment.

17. Barish, *"Perkin Warbeck* as Anti-History."

18. Neill, " 'Anticke Pageantrie': The Mannerist Art of *Perkin Warbeck*"; idem, "The Moral Artifice of *The Lovers Melancholy*"; and idem, "Ford's Unbroken Art: The Moral Design of *The Broken Heart*."

19. Candido, "The 'Strange Truth' of *Perkin Warbeck*."

20. Leech, *John Ford and the Drama of His Time*, 11-12. For documentation and for descriptions of Anderson's edition and Kaufmann's essay see the beginning of my last section, on *The Broken Heart*. And Hamilton, "*The Broken Heart*: Language Suited to a Divided Mind," in *"Concord in Discord,"* ed. Anderson, 171-93.

21. Stavig criticizes taking these early efforts overseriously (*Ford and the Moral Order*, 3-19). I am, however, skeptical that anyone now can be sure of discerning the satiric irony of slight exaggeration in an era that doted on such elaborate ceremonials as the one commemorated by *Honour Triumphant*.

22. In "The Unity of John Ford: *'Tis Pity She's a Whore* and *Christ's Bloody Sweat*," Gilles D. Monsarrat applies Stavig, *John Ford and the Moral Order*, 23-29. For Leech, see *Ford and the Drama*, 23-24.

23. Donald K. Anderson, Jr.'s "Kingship in Ford's *Perkin Warbeck*" argues convincingly for a pragmatic perspective while it recognizes Henry VII's reliance on divine right. Also see Anderson's Regents Renaissance Drama edition.

24. Sedge, "Social and Ethical Concerns," 268-73 and 254-61.

25. Sutton, "Platonic Love in Ford's *The Fancies, Chaste and Noble*."

26. See Anderson on Ford labeling those who spread malicious gossip ignoble: *Ford*, 121ff.

27. I quote act.lines from the edition by W. Bang, *Materialien zur Kunde des
älteren Englischen Dramas*.

28. Besides previous citations, note especially Anderson's seminal "The
Heart and the Banquet: Imagery in Ford's *'Tis Pity* and *The Broken Heart*." Repre-
sentative dissertation abstracts include Peggy Muñoz Simonds, "Iconography and
Iconology in John Ford's *'Tis Pity She's a Whore*," *DAI* 36 (1975): 1537A, and Chikako
Daishin Kumamoto, "John Ford's Theatre of Ceremony: A Formal Study of His
Five Major Plays," *DAI* 43 (1982): 808A-9A.

29. There seems to be a resurgent interest in considering Ford's variations on
earlier plays by way of what gets called his allusiveness, intertextuality, meta-
theatricality, and so on. Almost half of the essayists in Neill's *John Ford: Critical Re-
Visions* (in the order of their appearance Colin Gibson, Kathleen McLuskie,
Michael Neill, Verna Foster, and Martin Butler) rely on such a notion for their
readings.

30. For his summary and concluding caveat see Anderson, *Ford*, 14 and
138-39. For his demonstration see the formal analyses that demark the traits of
each of Ford's unaided plays.

31. All of Artaud's 1938 publication *Le théâtre et son double* is suggestive. His
discussion of Ford appears toward the end of the first essay, "The Theater and the
Plague," 28-31, in Mary Caroline Richards's translation, *The Theater and Its Double*.

32. Rosen, "The Language of Cruelty in Ford's *'Tis Pity She's a Whore*."

33. The debt has been scrutinized by Richard S. Ide in "Ford's *'Tis Pity She's a
Whore* and the Benefts of Belatedness," Mark Stavig in "Shakespearean and
Jacobean Patterns in *'Tis Pity She's a Whore*," both in Anderson, "*Concord in Dis-
cord*": 61-86, 221-40, Dorothy M. Farr in *John Ford and the Caroline Theatre*, 50-55,
Michael Neill in "Deciphering *'Tis Pity*": 169-72, and Sidney R. Homan, Jr. in
"Shakespeare and Dekker as Keys to Ford's *'Tis Pity She's a Whore*."

34. For a transcription and useful analysis see Maule's forthcoming essay in
Viator.

35. Since I am tracing the contribution of dramatic forebears to Ford's ritualistic style I do not cover such obvious sources as Robert Burton's *Anatomy of
Melancholy* for *The Lover's Melancholy*, or Sir Francis Bacon's and Thomas Gains-
ford's histories for *Perkin Warbeck*, or even dramatic analogs. Instead I concentrate
on conspicuous allusions to stage traditions that contribute to the effects Ford
achieves through repetitive parallels. For the others see S. Blaine Ewing, *Burtonian
Melancholy in the Plays of John Ford*, the chapter on sources in Davril, *Le Drame de
John Ford*, and the introductions to the Regents and New Mermaid editions.

36. For a discussion of some of this theme's sources and social implications,
see Lois E. Bueler, "Role-Splitting and Reintegration: The Tested Woman Plot in
Ford."

37. See Levin, *Multiple Plot*, 85-86, and A.P. Hogan's representative "*'Tis Pity
She's a Whore*: The Overall Design."

38. McMaster, "Love, Lust, and Sham: Structural Pattern in the Plays of John
Ford," elaborates on and extends Levin's analysis.

39. Bradbrook, *Themes and Conventions*, 253-55.

40. "The Language of Process" accomplishes far more than Greenfield's
modest claim of describing the affective style of *The Broken Heart* and *The Lover's
Melancholy*. As I do in my general characterization of the styles of Massinger and
the others, I defer detailed commentary until the exemplary play, *The Broken Heart*.

41. Huebert, *John Ford, Baroque English Dramatist*, 142-61.

42. For *The Broken Heart* I quote and cite the Regents Renaissance Drama edition by Donald K. Anderson, Jr.

43. Ribner, *Jacobean Tragedy,* 156 ff. and Burbridge, "The Moral Vision of Ford's *The Broken Heart.*"

44. See Eliot, *Elizabethan Dramatists,* 127; Ornstein, *Moral Vision,* 213ff; Sensabaugh, Burton section of *Tragic Muse;* Stavig, *Ford and the Moral Order,* 146ff; Charles O. McDonald's "The Design of John Ford's *The Broken Heart:* A Study in the Development of Caroline Sensibility"; and Arthur L. Kistner and M.K. Kistner's "The Dramatic Functions of Love in the Tragedies of John Ford." Sharon Hamilton's reading in *"The Broken Heart:* Language Suited to a Divided Mind," in *"Concord in Discord,"* ed. Anderson, is often close to my own, but she persists in moral condemnation.

45. Ure, "Marriage and the Domestic Drama in Heywood and Ford," and Blayney, "Convention, Plot, and Structure in *The Broken Heart.*"

46. See Sargeaunt, *John Ford,* 144-46; Kaufmann's "Ford's 'Waste Land': *The Broken Heart*"; Anderson's *Ford,* 68ff; Orbison, *Tragic Vision,* 120ff; and Neill, "Unbroken Art."

47. Leech, *John Ford,* 10.

48. For the most comprehensive and persuasive case for the play's disasters as foreordained by fate see Neill's "Unbroken Art," 253-56; for the most prominent case for the play's embodiment of the "unknowability of fate" see Anne Barton's "Oxymoron and the Structure of Ford's 'The Broken Heart'."

49. I focus on the social "tragedy of manners" influentially mapped in Anderson's introduction and Kaufmann's "Ford's 'Waste Land'" (especially 177-85). As Neill does in his presentation of Ford's aestheticized stoicism in "Unbroken Art," I modify Kaufmann in one crucial respect. I oppose all three of these critics by regarding role playing as personality-forming rather than personality-thwarting.

50. I quote the translation of Durkheim by Joseph Ward Swain, 414, 387.

51. See Mauss, *A General Theory of Magic,* especially 91-140, on analysis, ideology, and collective states and forces.

52. For an argument and testimony in favor of this substitution see Harry Alpert's influential "Durkheim's Functional Theory of Ritual."

53. Probably the most frequently cited of these have been Sydney Anglo's *Spectacle, Pageantry, and Early Tudor Policy,* Roy Strong's *Splendor at Court,* David Bergeron's *English Civic Pageantry, 1558-1642,* and Stephen Orgel's *The Illusion of Power.* The most directly pertinent recent study is Kevin Sharpe's *Criticism and Compliment.* An excellent mapping and forecast of scholarship is Bergeron's introduction to his collection of essays, *Pageantry in the Shakespearean Theater,* which opens with a reprint of one of Orgel's most provocative critical pieces.

54. For a fine sampler see Marcus, *Politics of Mirth,* 1-20.

55. Greenfield, "Language of Process," 398.

56. See Neill's "Unbroken Art," 250-51, for an illuminating arrangement.

57. See I.i.17ff, II.ii,30ff, II.iii,33ff, III.ii.37-110 passim, IV.ii.140ff, for specific statements; brief reminders abound.

58. See Anderson's edition, xviii-xix. See also Neill's "Unbroken Art," 251-52. In pressing his case for aesthetic stoicism Neill condemns Spartan society for a shallow, arbitrary sanction of surface "*perform*ance" of "outward *forms* of behaviour" and therefore for a violation of internal psyches. Borrowing from the social sciences, I argue that such forms are fundamental to Ford's presentation of the creation and maintenance of society and characters.

59. See the introduction to Morris's New Mermaid edition of *The Broken Heart*, xxvi-xxx.

60. Although I follow Anderson's "The Heart and the Banquet," *Ford*, and his edition, xvii-xviii, Kaufmann's "Ford's 'Waste Land,'" 169-77, Barton's "Oxymoron," and Huebert's *John Ford*, 136-42, I intensify and extend their evidence, place it in a different context, and see it from a different perspective.

61. Eliot, *Elizabethan Dramatists*, 126.

4. *Shirley's Social Comedy of Adaptation to Degree*

1. For Shirley's dedications I quote the original printed edition. Whenever a scholarly edition of a Shirley play is available I cite and quote it. When there is none I quote the original printed edition but cite the textually inadequate act.scene/page of *The Dramatic Works and Poems*, ed. William Gifford and Alexander Dyce. For poems, including prologues and epilogues to the plays, I cite and quote *The Poems*, ed. Ray Livingstone Armstrong. For dates of the plays and most bibliography I rely on Albert Wertheim's essay in Logan and Smith, *Later Jacobean and Caroline Dramatists*, 152-71.

2. See Marvin Morillo, "Shirley's 'Preferment' and the Court of Charles I."

3. Biographical data from Arthur Huntington Nason's doublecheck of Anthony à Wood's *Athenæ Oxoniensis* in *James Shirley, Dramatist: A Biographical and Critical Study*, 3-163, Albert C. Baugh's "Some New Facts about Shirley," Georges Bas's essays, particularly "Two Misrepresented Biographical Documents Concerning James Shirley," and William D. Wolf's "Some New Facts and Conclusions about James Shirley: Residences and Religion" have been comprehensively reviewed and extended in Sandra A. Burner's *James Shirley: A Study of Literary Coteries and Patronage in Seventeenth-Century England*. I am not persuaded by her presupposition of Shirley's Roman Catholic conversion and her hedged construal of what might then have happened. I agree with Bas and Wolf, who find this old hypothesis implausible, particularly since Shirley's children were baptized as Anglicans.

4. See Arthur C. Kirsch's full text of "A Caroline Commentary on the Drama," 257, as well as James G. McManaway's announcement and digest of the text in "Excerpta Quaedam per A.W. Adolescentem," 124.

5. For Wright, see Kirsch, "Caroline Commentary," 258. For Herbert I quote and cite *The Dramatic Records of Sir Henry Herbert, Master of the Revels, 1623-1673*, 19-20, 53.

6. Herbert, *Dramatic Records*, 54-55.

7. I draw information, quotations, and citations involving this masque from Stephen Orgel and Roy Strong's monumental *Inigo Jones: The Theatre of the Stuart Court* 2: 537-65.

8. For assessments in relation to Jonson see Anne Barton's *Ben Jonson, Dramatist*, 300-320 passim and David Rigg's *Ben Jonson: A Life*, 301-37 passim. For a view of Cavendish related to Brome, see my sketch of Brome's audience, below.

9. Wood, *Athenæ Oxoniensis*, 3:739. For an assessment of Shirley's possible contributions to Cavendish's *The Country Captain* see Harbage's *Cavalier Drama*, 74-77.

10. For speculation see Gerald Eades Bentley's "James Shirley and a Group of Unnoted Poems on the Wedding of Thomas Stanley"; for the poems with literary and biographical annotations, see Armstrong's edition.

11. For the text see Armstrong, 13; for R.G. Howarth's as well as Armstrong's full commentary see Armstrong, 66-67.

12. For all citations and quotations of the 1647 folio, where the text is available I use the ongoing *The Dramatic Works in the Beaumont and Fletcher Canon*, ed. Fredson Bowers. Where it is not I use *The Works of Francis Beaumont and John Fletcher*, ed. Arnold Glover and A.R. Waller. For this preface I quote the latter, 1:xi.

13. The political theme of Ben Lucow's *James Shirley* is Shirley's presentation of monarchical absolutism and a hierarchy by ascription. Note especially Lucow's argument, 18-20, and his impressive collection of Shirley's habitual political diction, 148-50.

14. For an interesting but implausible and unverifiable political placement of this play in Charles's court see Butler, *Theatre and Crisis*, 42-44.

15. See Orgel, *Illusion of Power*, 77-83 (the quotation is from 79) and Sharpe, *Criticism and Compliment*, 211-22 (the quotation is from 222). Sharpe here as elsewhere counters an undiscriminating broadside characteristic of Graham Parry's otherwise useful study of the era's noble patronage, *The Golden Age Restor'd: The Culture of the Stuart Court, 1603-42*.

16. Venuti, "The Politics of Allusion: The Gentry and Shirley's *The Triumph of Peace*."

17. Butler, "Politics and the Masque: *The Triumph of Peace*."

18. See Sedge, for example, on Alinda's speech in the middle of *The Doubtful Heir*, "Social and Ethical Concerns," 61-63.

19. Nason, *James Shirley*, 304-7 provides a typical example of critical moral disgust over the Cornari episodes; while Nason's maneuvers facilitate appreciation of Shirley's formal integration of plots, they deny access to Shirley's thematic parallels.

20. All Butler's work emphasizes this thesis; on Shirley see *Theatre and Crisis*, 158-59. Though he does not cite these earlier critics, he modifies and extends tendencies in Sedge's identification of passages and in Morton's "Deception and Social Dislocation: An Aspect of Shirley's Drama," a consideration of caste structure and conflict.

21. The most credible claimant is Morillo.

22. Herbert, *Dramatic Records*, 19. I follow Harbage in *Cavalier Drama*, 78, and especially Bentley in *Profession of Dramatist*, 190-91, in distributing Herbert's blame to the players as well as the playwright.

23. For *The Lady of Pleasure* I quote the critical edition by Marilyn J. Thorssen. For the circumstances of *The Ball* see Hanson T. Parlin, *A Study in Shirley's Comedies of London Life*, 59.

24. See Stone's *Crisis of the Aristocracy*, chapters six and seven, "Estate Management" and "Business."

25. Lucow, *James Shirley*, 93-94.

26. See Sedge, "Social and Ethical Concerns," 317ff. Besides Morillo's essay, see his introduction to *The Humorous Courtier*, especially 64-79.

27. Butler, *Theatre and Crisis*, 44. Butler's extended argument runs 166-80.

28. See Nason, *James Shirley*, 54-68.

29. For a listing of Shirley's prodigals, see the tabulations of Robert Stanley Forsythe in *The Relations of Shirley's Plays to the Elizabethan Drama*, 100-101. Only two ladies appear: besides Lady Aretina there is Lady Plot, an adulterous philanderer and treacherous go-between in *The Example*.

30. See Herbert, *Dramatic Records*, 54-55.

31. Although in *Criticism and Compliment* (44-47) Sharpe catalogs the rough

satire in *The Gamester,* he elides my main issue: Shirley targets blatant abuses that draw attention away from some problems that were becoming evident in his traditional hierarchy; rather than defending it with Ford, testing it with Brome, or reforming it with Massinger, he assumes its righteousness.

32. See Cogan, "James Shirley's *The Example:* Some Reconsiderations," 317-31.

33. The persuasive center of Butler's discussion appears in *Theatre and Crisis,* 166-70; the concessions my argument builds on appear on 172-75, especially 174-75.

34. The italics are Forsythe's in *Relations,* 50. His general discussion of debts covers 49-53.

35. Lucow's unappreciative discussion of masque elements in Shirley includes the characters' useful remarks on the genre: *James Shirley,* 38-40, 46-49.

36. See ibid., especially 40, 46, and 137-38.

37. I differ on some interpretations and I modify some of McGrath's valuable ideas. My central revisions involve (1) transforming her idea of language as a moral sign to my consideration of language as a sociopolitical instrument and (2) suggesting that some of the gaps she reads as Shirley's distrust of the duplicity or the inadequacy of language are better read as the effects of Shirley's Fletcherian reversing, surprising plots. Both of these substitute a playfulness with language and wit for a distrust of them. As I do in my general characterization of the style of each Caroline professional playwright, I defer detailed commentary until the exemplary play, *Hyde Park.*

38. Javitch, *Poetry and Courtliness in Renaissance England,* and Whigham, *Ambition and Privilege.*

39. See Garfinkel, *Studies in Ethnomethodology.* The most understandable and useful description and bibliography I know is John C. Heritage's "Ethnomethodology." I believe that ethnomethodology parallels Whigham's kinds of assumptions and analyses more helpfully than does either Pierre Bourdieu's provocative *Outline of a Theory of Practice,* which is cited by Whigham, or the suggestive Mead, who is cited by Richard A. Lanham in a discussion of Castiglione, *The Motives of Eloquence: Literary Rhetoric in the Renaissance,* 152-53.

40. I quote the first edition of Garfinkel, *Studies in Ethnomethodology,* 1.

41. For Forsythe's detailed list of *Love Tricks* analogs see *Relations,* 117-36.

42. Wertheim, "Games and Courtship in James Shirley's *Hyde Park,*" expands on Levin, *Multiple Plot,* 96-101, summed up from his "The Triple Plot of *Hyde Park.*"

43. For representative examples see McLuskie in *The* Revels *History of Drama in English,* ed. Potter, 253-56, and especially Lucow, *James Shirley,* 69-76. The fullest account of the play's sociopolitical implications is Butler's *Theatre and Crisis,* 175-79.

44. Butler's entire discussion extends through 175-79 of *Theatre and Crisis;* this section primarily appears on 175-78; the section on role-playing overlaps, 177-79.

45. See Levin, *Multiple Plot,* 98, for example.

5. Brome's Comedy of Types and Inversions

1. Kaufmann's valuable *Richard Brome, Caroline Playwright,* despite placing Brome in what now seems an obsolescent view of his times, incisively interprets his works; particularly observe 1-16. McLuskie, in *The* Revels *History of Drama in English,* ed. Potter, 237-48.

2. Sedge, "Social and Ethical Concerns," 330. I rely on Catherine Shaw's review of relevant data about Brome's life (*Richard Brome,* 17-33) and use her

comprehensive treatment of his works. Brome plays a major part in Butler's *Theatre and Crisis*.

3. Shaw, *Richard Brome*, 18, 149 n.5.

4. For both lords see Butler, *Theatre and Crisis*, 193-98. For more about Newcastle see my account of Shirley's audience, above.

5. See Richard H. Perkinson, "Topographical Comedy in the Seventeenth Century," Theodore Miles, "Place-Realism in a Group of Caroline Plays," and Shaw, *Richard Brome*, 87.

6. See Shaw, *Richard Brome*, 77-78 and 70, Kaufmann, *Richard Brome*, 151-68, and John Freehafer, "Brome, Suckling, and Davenant's Theater Project of 1639."

7. Burke, "Popular Culture in Seventeenth-Century London," in Barry Reay, ed., *Popular Culture in Seventeenth-Century England*, 48.

8. Kaufmann, *Richard Brome*, 168-74.

9. For *A Jovial Crew* I cite and quote the edition by Ann Haaker.

10. Butler, *Theatre and Crisis*, 274.

11. Hill, *World Turned Upside Down*, 32-45, especially 39.

12. Because of its fullness and availability, the edition I cite for the act.scene/page of all Brome's works apart from *The Antipodes* and *A Jovial Crew* is John Pearson's inadequate *The Dramatic Works of Richard Brome*. I correct the text from original editions.

13. For examples see Barry Reay's "Introduction" and Bernard Capp's "Popular Literature" in Reay, *Popular Culture in Seventeenth-Century England*, 21, 209-11.

14. Besides Kaufmann, *Richard Brome*, 151-68, and Freehafer, "Brome, Suckling," see Sedge, "Social and Ethical Concerns," 252-54, Shaw, *Richard Brome*, 68-74, and Tricomi's caveats in *Anticourt Drama*, 182-84.

15. See Bentley's *The Jacobean and Caroline Stage* 1: 332-34, along with the biographical accounts already cited. For Butler, see *Theatre and Crisis*, 220-29.

16. Kaufmann, *Richard Brome*, 109-30. For a catalog of the attributes that were commonly ridiculed see the gleanings of George F. Sensabaugh in "Love Ethics in Platonic Court Drama 1625-1642."

17. Kaufmann's useful discussion of Brome's stage usurers (*Richard Brome*, 131-50) omits the tradition of Renaissance stage usurers and fails to acknowledge that Brome sometimes offers reform as well as condemnation to loan sharks.

18. See ibid., 67-87, Shaw, *Richard Brome*, especially 79, and Butler, *Theatre and Crisis*, 155-57.

19. See Kaufmann, *Richard Brome*, 68-74.

20. For the tone of these see Haaker's bibliographical essay in Logan and Smith, *The Later Jacobean and Caroline Dramatists*, 185, and Shaw's summation in *Richard Brome*, 136-37. For responses see Shaw's individual readings.

21. See Shaw, *Richard Brome*, 58-59 and 81.

22. See Shaw (ibid., 85), who quotes with approval Sedge, "Social and Ethical Concerns," 171.

23. The quotation (Shaw, *Richard Brome*, 174) caps a discussion beginning at 171; Kaufmann's agreement is suggested on 56; Shaw sums up uneasily, 87-92; she also provides a helpful survey of previous critics.

24. Ibid., 88.

25. My view of Brome's appropriative parody focuses more on its employment to attack social problems and it deals less with literary questions than do Robert N. Watson's helpful ideas about Jonson's appropriative imitation. See his *Ben Jonson's Parodic Strategy: Literary Imperialism in the Comedies*.

26. Kaufmann's discussion, which has dominated criticism, provides an important example of the problem (*Richard Brome*, 36-46). His moral assumptions about Brome, 37-38, seem to lead to foregone conclusions about artistic demerits when Brome's presentation does not seem as conservative as Kaufmann postulated.

27. For suggestive criticism on his debts see ibid., 36; for specific parallels see Joe Lee Davis's *The Sons of Ben: Jonsonian Comedy in Caroline England*, 148-50, 152-56, 188-90.

28. See particularly Shaw's discussions on 35-37, 57-58, and 68-69 of *Richard Brome*.

29. See the accounts in Kaufmann, *Richard Brome*, 151-68, and Freehafer, "Brome, Suckling."

30. Kaufmann, *Richard Brome*, 109-30. Although Kaufmann's interpretation seems obvious now, the fact that for three centuries the play was apparently accepted as a cheap imitation of the voguish pattern of courtly tragicomedy indicates how hyperbolic this subgenre became.

31. On Brome's use of songs generally see R.W. Ingram's "The Musical Art of Richard Brome's Comedies."

32. See Cope's argument in *The Theater and the Dream*, note 4, 297-98.

33. The quotation appears on 135 of ibid.; the discussion extends to 169.

34. Butler, *Theatre and Crisis*, 224-27, sums up his analysis of this play's implications when seen through the masque.

35. Shaw, *Richard Brome*, 139-43. As I do in my general characterization of the style of each Caroline professional playwright, I defer detailed commentary until the exemplary play, *The Antipodes*.

36. See Charles Read Baskervill's *The Elizabethan Jig and Related Song Drama*, 198, 319.

37. For *The Antipodes* I cite and quote the edition by Ann Haaker.

38. See Donaldson on *The Antipodes* and its tropes in *The World Upside Down*, 78-98, and Butler on estates, *Theatre and Crisis*, 210-14.

39. Davis, "Richard Brome's Neglected Contribution," expanded in *The Sons of Ben*, 65-80; the quotation appears on 75.

40. For Donaldson on *The Antipodes* and on Gluckman, see *World Upside Down*, particularly 96-97, 14-16. For Barber's seminal formulation see *Shakespeare's Festive Comedy*.

41. Cope, *Theater and the Dream*, 147-59.

42. Davis, *Sons of Ben*, 71-74; Kaufmann, *Richard Brome*, 61; and Haaker, "Introduction," *The Antipodes*, xiii.

43. The quotations, from *Theatre and Crisis*, 214 and 220, virtually frame Butler's discussion.

44. For the first, see ibid., 194, 207, 219; for the second, 228-33ff.

45. In *The Reversible World: Symbolic Inversion in Art and Society*, ed. Barbara A. Babcock, 39-94, particularly 41-52. The tradition of *adynata* issuing from Virgilian tradition, popular sources, or both, may overlap. See Ernst Robert Curtius's *European Literature and the Latin Middle Ages*, 94-98.

46. Davis, *Society and Culture in Early Modern France*, 97-123, 124-51; my subsequent quotation appears on 143.

47. See Reay and Burke in Reay's *Popular Culture*, 21 and 34-39.

48. Turner, *The Forest of Symbols*, 93-111, and van Gennep, *The Rites of Passage*. For a helpful account and bibliography of this revision by Turner and others see Babcock's "Introduction" to *Reversible World*, 13-36.

Works Cited

Adler, Doris. *Philip Massinger.* Boston: Twayne, 1987.

Alpert, Harry. "Durkheim's Functional Theory of Ritual." *Sociology and Social Research* 23 (1938): 103-8.

Amussen, Susan D. "Gender, The Family and the Social Order 1560-1725." *Order and Disorder in Early Modern England.* Ed. Anthony Fletcher and John Stephenson. Cambridge: Cambridge Univ. Press, 1985. 196-217.

Anderson, Donald K., Jr., ed. *"Concord in Discord": The Plays of John Ford, 1586-1986.* New York: AMS Press, 1986.

———. "The Heart and the Banquet: Imagery in Ford's *'Tis Pity* and *The Broken Heart.*" *Studies in English Literature, 1500-1900* 2 (1962): 209-17.

———. *John Ford.* Boston: Twayne, 1972.

———. "Kingship in Ford's *Perkin Warbeck.*" *English Literary History* 27 (1960): 177-93.

Anglo, Sydney. *Spectacle, Pageantry, and Early Tudor Policy.* Oxford: Clarendon Press, 1969.

Aries, Philippe. *Centuries of Childhood.* Trans. Robert Baldick. London: Jonathan Cape, 1962.

Aron, Arthur, and Elaine N. Aron. *The Heart of Social Psychology.* Lexington, Mass.: Lexington Books, D.C. Heath, 1986.

Artaud, Antonin. *The Theater and Its Double.* Trans. Mary Caroline Richards. New York: Grove Press, 1958.

Babcock, Barbara A., *The Reversible World: Symbolic Inversion in Art and Society.* Ithaca: Cornell Univ. Press, 1978.

Bakhtin, Mikhail. *Rabelais and His World.* Trans. Helene Iswolsky. Cambridge, Mass.: MIT Press, 1968.

Baldwin, Frances Elizabeth. *Sumptuary Legislation and Personal Regulation in England.* Baltimore: Johns Hopkins Univ. Press, 1926.

Barber, C.L. *Shakespeare's Festive Comedy.* Princeton: Princeton Univ. Press, 1959.

Barish, Jonas A. "*Perkin Warbeck* as Anti-History." *Essays in Criticism* 20 (1970): 151-71.

Barry, Lording. *Ram Alley or Merrie Tricks: Materials for the Study of Old English Drama,* n.s. 23. Louvain: Librairie Universitaire, 1952.

Barton, Anne. *Ben Jonson, Dramatist.* Cambridge: Cambridge Univ. Press, 1984.

———. "Oxymoron and the Structure of Ford's 'The Broken Heart,'" *Essays and Studies 1980* n.s. 33:70-94.

Bas, Georges. "James Shirley et 'Th' Untun'd Kennel': Une petite guerre des théâtres vers 1630." *Etudes Anglaises* 16 (1963): 11-22.

———. "Two Misrepresented Biographical Documents Concerning James Shirley." *Review of English Studies* n.s. 27 (1976): 303-10.

Baskervill, Charles Read. *The Elizabethan Jig and Related Song Drama.* Chicago: Univ. of Chicago Press, 1929.

Baugh, Albert C. "Some New Facts about Shirley." *Modern Language Review* 17 (1922): 228-35.

Beal, Peter. "Massinger at Bay: Unpublished Verses in a War of the Theatres." *Yearbook of English Studies* 10 (1980): 190-203.

Beaumont, Francis, and John Fletcher. *The Dramatic Works in the Beaumont and Fletcher Canon*. Ed. Fredson Bowers. 6 vols. to date. Cambridge: Cambridge Univ. Press, 1966-.

―――. *The Works of Francis Beaumont and John Fletcher*. Ed. Arnold Glover and A.R. Waller. 10 vols. Cambridge: Cambridge Univ. Press, 1905-12.

Belsey, Catherine. *The Subject of Tragedy: Identity and Difference in Renaissance Drama*. London: Methuen, 1985.

Bentley, Gerald Eades. *The Jacobean and Caroline Stage*. 7 vols. Oxford: Oxford Univ. Press, 1941-68.

―――. "James Shirley and a Group of Unnoted Poems on the Wedding of Thomas Stanley." *Huntington Library Quarterly* 2 (1939): 219-31.

―――. *The Profession of Dramatist in Shakespeare's Time, 1590-1642*. Princeton: Princeton Univ. Press, 1971.

Berger, Peter L., and Thomas Luckmann. *The Social Construction of Reality*. Garden City, N.Y.: Doubleday, 1966.

Bergeron, David. *English Civic Pageantry, 1558-1642*. Columbia: Univ. of South Carolina Press, 1971.

―――, ed. *Pageantry in the Shakespearean Theater*. Athens: Univ. of Georgia Press, 1985.

Blayney, Glenn H. "Convention, Plot, and Structure in *The Broken Heart*." *Modern Philology* 56 (1958): 1-9.

Bonner, Stanley Frederick. *Roman Declamation in the Late Republic and Early Empire*. Liverpool: Univ. Press of Liverpool, 1949.

Bourdieu, Pierre. *Outline of a Theory of Practice*. Trans. Richard Nice. Cambridge: Cambridge Univ. Press, 1977.

Bradbrook, Muriel C. *Themes and Conventions of Elizabethan Tragedy*. Cambridge: Cambridge Univ. Press, 1935.

Brathwait, Richard. *The English Gentlewoman*. London, 1631. STC 3565.

Brennan, Michael. *Literary Patronage in the English Renaissance: The Pembroke Family*. London: Routledge, 1988.

Brissenden, Alan. "Impediments to Love: A Theme in John Ford." *Renaissance Drama* 7 (1964): 95-102.

Bristol, Michael D. *Carnival and Theater: Plebeian Culture and the Structure of Authority in Renaissance England*. London: Methuen, 1985.

Brome, Richard. *The Antipodes*. Ed. Ann Haaker. Lincoln: Univ. of Nebraska Press, 1966.

―――. *The Dramatic Works of Richard Brome*. Ed. John Pearson. 3 vols. London: 1873. New York: AMS Press, 1966.

―――. *A Jovial Crew*. Ed. Ann Haaker. Lincoln: Univ. of Nebraska Press: 1968.

Bueler, Lois E. "Role-Splitting and Reintegration: The Tested Woman Plot in Ford." *Studies in English Literature, 1500-1900* 20 (1980): 325-40.

Burbridge, Roger T. "The Moral Vision of Ford's *The Broken Heart*." *Studies in English Literature, 1500-1900* 10 (1970): 397-407.

Burner, Sandra A. *James Shirley: A Study of Literary Coteries and Patronage in Seventeenth-Century England*. Lanham, Md.: Univ. Press of America, 1988.

Burns, Elizabeth. *Theatricality: A Study of Convention in the Theatre and in Social Life*. London: Longman, 1972.

Butler, Martin. "Massinger's *The City Madam* and the Caroline Audience." *Renaissance Drama* 13 (1982): 157-87.

————. "Politics and the Masque: *The Triumph of Peace.*" *Seventeenth Century* 2 (1987): 117-41.

————. *Theatre and Crisis, 1632-1642.* Cambridge: Cambridge Univ. Press, 1984.

Candido, Joseph. "The 'Strange Truth' of *Perkin Warbeck.*" *Philological Quarterly* 59 (1980): 300-316.

Certain Sermons or Homilies appointed to Be Read in Churches in the Time of Queen Elizabeth of Famous Memory. London, 1673. Wing C4091E.

Clark, Ira. *The Moral Art of Philip Massinger.* Lewisburg: Bucknell Univ. Press, 1992.

————. "The Power of Integrity in Massinger's Women." *The Renaissance Englishwoman in Print: Counterbalancing the Canon.* Ed. Anne M. Haselkorn and Betty S. Travitsky. Amherst: Univ. of Massachusetts Press, 1990. 63-79.

Cleaver, Robert. *A Godly Form of Household Government.* London, 1598. STC 5382-5388.

Cliffe, J.T. *The Puritan Gentry: The Great Puritan Families of Early Stuart England.* London: Routledge & Kegan Paul, 1984.

Cogan, Nathan. "James Shirley's *The Example:* Some Reconsiderations." *Studies in English Literature, 1500-1900* 17 (1977): 317-31.

Cook, Ann Jennalie. *The Privileged Playgoers of Shakespeare's London, 1576-1642.* Princeton: Princeton Univ. Press, 1981.

Cope, Esther S. *Politics without Parliaments, 1629-1640.* London: Allen & Unwin, 1987.

Cope, Jackson I. *The Theater and the Dream: From Metaphor to Form in Renaissance Drama.* Baltimore: Johns Hopkins Univ. Press, 1973.

Cornelia, Marie. *The Function of the Masque in Jacobean Tragedy and Tragicomedy.* Jacobean Dramatic Studies no. 77. Salzburg: Universität Salzburg, 1978.

Crane, R.S. *Critical and Historical Principles of Literary History.* Chicago: Univ. of Chicago Press, 1971.

Croll, Morris. *Essays by Morris Croll: "Attic" and Baroque Prose Style; The Anti-Ciceronian Movement.* Ed. J. Max Patrick, Robert O. Evans, and John M. Wallace. Princeton: Princeton Univ. Press, 1966.

Curtius, Ernst Robert. *European Literature and the Latin Middle Ages.* Trans. Willard R. Trask. New York: Pantheon, 1953.

Danby, John F. *Poets on Fortune's Hill.* London: Faber & Faber, 1952. Reprinted by the same publisher in 1964 as *Elizabethan and Jacobean Poets.*

Danson, Lawrence. "Jonsonian Comedy and the Discovery of the Social Self." *Publications of the Modern Language Association* 99 (1984): 179-93.

Davenant, Sir William. *The Dramatic Works of Sir William D'Avenant.* Ed. James Maidment and W.H. Logan. 5 vols. London: 1872-74. New York: Russell & Russell, 1964.

————. *The Shorter Poems, and Songs from the Plays and Masques.* Ed. A.M. Gibbs. Oxford: Clarendon Press, 1972.

Davis, Joe Lee. "Richard Brome's Neglected Contribution to Comic Theory." *Studies in Philology* 40 (1943): 520-28.

————. *The Sons of Ben: Jonsonian Comedy in Caroline England.* Detroit: Wayne State Univ. Press, 1967.

Davis, Natalie Zemon. *Society and Culture in Early Modern France.* Stanford: Stanford Univ. Press, 1975.

Davril, Robert. *Le Drame de John Ford.* Paris: Marcel Didier, 1954.

Dessen, Alan C. *Jonson's Moral Comedy.* Evanston: Northwestern Univ. Press, 1971.

Dod, John, and Robert Cleaver. *A Plaine and Familiar Exposition of the Ten Commandments.* London, 1604. STC 6968-6979.

Donaldson, Ian. *The World Upside Down.* Oxford: Oxford Univ. Press, 1970.

Doran, Madeline. *Endeavors of Art.* Madison: Univ. of Wisconsin Press, 1964.

Du Bosc, Jacques. *The Compleat Woman.* Trans. N.N. London, 1639. STC 7266.

Dunn, Catherine E. *The Concept of Ingratitude in Renaissance English Moral Philosophy.* Washington, D.C.: Catholic Univ. of America Press, 1946.

Dunn, T.A. *Philip Massinger: The Man and the Playwright.* London: Thomas Nelson and Sons for University College of Ghana, 1957.

Durkheim, Émile. *The Elementary Forms of the Religious Life: A Study in Religious Sociology.* Trans. Joseph Ward Swain. London: Allen & Unwin, 1915.

E., T. *The Lawes Resolution of Womens Rights.* London: J. More, 1632. STC 7437.

Edmond, Mary. *Rare Sir William Davenant.* New York: St. Martin's, 1987.

Edwards, Philip. "Massinger the Censor." *Essays on Shakespeare and Elizabethan Drama in Honor of Hardin Craig.* Ed. Richard Hosley. Columbia: Univ. of Missouri Press, 1962. 341-50.

Eliot, T.S. *Elizabethan Dramatists.* London: Faber & Faber, 1963.

Ellis-Fermor, Una. *The Jacobean Drama.* London: Methuen, 1936.

Empson, William. "Double Plots: Heroic and Pastoral in the Main and Sub-Plot." *Some Versions of Pastoral.* London: Chatto & Windus, 1935. 27-86.

Evans, Robert C. *Ben Jonson and the Poetics of Patronage.* Lewisburg: Bucknell Univ. Press, 1989.

Evenhuis, Francis D. *Massinger's Imagery.* Jacobean Drama Studies no. 24. Salzburg: Universität Salzburg, 1973.

Ewing, S. Blaine. *Burtonian Melancholy in the Plays of John Ford.* Princeton: Princeton Univ. Press, 1940.

Farr, Dorothy M. *John Ford and the Caroline Theatre.* London: Macmillan, 1979.

Felperin, Howard. *The Uses of the Canon: Elizabethan Literature and Contemporary Theory.* Oxford: Clarendon Press, 1990.

Filmer, Sir Robert. *Patriarcha and Other Political Works of Sir Robert Filmer.* Ed. Peter Laslett. Oxford: Basil Blackwell, 1949.

Finkelpearl, Philip J. "The Role of the Court in the Development of Jacobean Drama." *Criticism* 24 (1982): 138-58.

Flandrin, Jean-Louis. *Families in Former Times.* Trans. Richard Southern. Cambridge: Cambridge Univ. Press, 1979.

Ford, John. *The Broken Heart.* Ed. Donald K. Anderson, Jr. Lincoln: Univ. of Nebraska Press, 1968.

———. *The Broken Heart.* Ed. Brian Morris. London: Ernest Benn, 1965.

———. *John Fordes Dramatische Werke.* Materialien zur Kunde des älteren Englischen Dramas. Ed. W. Bang. Louvain: A. Uystrpuyst, 1908; Ed. Henry De Vocht. Librairie Universitaire, 1927.

———. *Perkin Warbeck.* Ed. Donald K. Anderson, Jr. Lincoln: Univ. of Nebraska Press, 1965.

———. *The Queen, or the Excellency of her Sex.* Ed. W. Bang. Materialien zur Kunde des älteren Englischen Dramas 13. Louvain: A. Uystrpuyst, 1906.

———. *The Works of John Ford.* Ed. William Gifford and Alexander Dyce. 3 vols. London: James Toovey, 1869.

Forsythe, Robert Stanley. *The Relations of Shirley's Plays to the Elizabethan Drama.* New York: Columbia Univ. Press, 1914.

Fothergill, Robert A. "The Dramatic Experience of Massinger's *The City Madam* and *A New Way To Pay Old Debts.*" *University of Toronto Quarterly* 43 (1973): 68-86.

Freehafer, John. "Brome, Suckling, and Davenant's Theater Project of 1639." *Texas Studies in Language and Literature* 10 (1968): 367-83.

Frost, David L. "Philip Massinger: The Spurious Legatee." *The School of Shake-speare*. Cambridge: Cambridge Univ. Press, 1968. 77-118.

Gardiner, Samuel R. *History of England, 1603-42*. 10 vols. London: Longmans, 1883-84.

———. "The Political Element in Massinger." *Contemporary Review* 28 (1876): 495-507; reprinted in *New Shakespeare Society's Transactions (1875-76)*, 314-31.

Garfinkel, Harold. *Studies in Ethnomethodology*. Englewood Cliffs: Prentice-Hall, 1967. Augmented ed. Cambridge: Polity Press, 1984.

Gibson, Colin. "Massinger's Hungarian History." *Yearbook of English Studies* 2 (1972): 89-92.

———. "Massinger's 'Composite Mistresses.'" *Journal of the Australian Universities Language and Literature Assn.* 29 (1968): 44-51.

Giddens, Anthony. *The Constitution of Society: Outline of the Theory of Structuration*. Berkeley: Univ. of California Press, 1984.

Goffman, Erving. *The Presentation of Self in Everyday Life*. Garden City, N.Y.: Doubleday, 1959.

Goldberg, Jonathan. "Fatherly Authority: The Politics of Stuart Family Images." *Rewriting the Renaissance: The Discourses of Sexual Difference in Early Modern Europe*. Ed. Margaret W. Ferguson et al. Chicago: Univ. of Chicago Press, 1986. 3-32.

Gouge, William. *Of Domesticall Duties*. London: John Haviland for William Bladen, 1622. STC 12119.

Greenfield, Thelma N. "The Language of Process in Ford's *The Broken Heart*." *Publications of the Modern Language Association* 87 (1972): 397-405.

Grivelet, Michel. "Th' Untun'd Kennell: Note sur Thomas Heywood et le théâtre sous Charles Ier." *Etudes Anglaises* 7 (1954): 101-6.

Gross, Alan G. "Contemporary Politics in Massinger." *Studies in English Literature, 1500-1900* 6 (1966): 279-90.

Gurr, Andrew. *Playgoing in Shakespeare's London*. Cambridge: Cambridge Univ. Press, 1987.

———. *The Shakespearean Stage, 1574-1642*. Cambridge: Cambridge Univ. Press, 1972.

Harbage, Alfred. *Cavalier Drama*. New York: Modern Language Association, 1936.

Harrison, William. *Description of England*. Ed. George Edelen. Ithaca: Cornell Univ. Press, 1968.

Heinemann, Margot. *Puritanism and Theatre: Thomas Middleton and Opposition Drama under the Early Stuarts*. Cambridge: Cambridge Univ. Press, 1980.

Hensman, Bertha. *The Shares of Fletcher, Field, and Massinger in Twelve Plays of the Beaumont and Fletcher Canon*. Jacobean Drama Studies, number 6. 2 vols. Salzburg: Universität Salzburg, 1974.

Herbert, Sir Henry. *The Dramatic Records of Sir Henry Herbert, Master of the Revels, 1623-1673*. Ed. Joseph Quincy Adams. New Haven: Yale Univ. Press, 1917.

Heritage, John C. "Ethnomethodology." *Social Theory Today*. Ed. Anthony Giddens and Jonathan H. Turner. Stanford: Stanford Univ. Press, 1987. 224-72.

Hexter, J.H. *Reappraisals in History*. Expanded ed. Chicago: Univ. of Chicago Press, 1979.

Hill, Christopher. *The Intellectual Origins of the Puritan Revolution*. Oxford: Oxford Univ. Press, 1965.

———. *The World Turned Upside Down*. Middlesex: Penguin, 1972.

Hinton, R.W.K. "Husbands, Fathers, and Conquerors." *Political Studies* 15 (1967): 291-300.

Hogan, A.P. "*'Tis Pity She's a Whore:* The Overall Design." *Studies in English Literature, 1500-1900* 17 (1977): 303-16.

Homan, Sidney R., Jr. "Shakespeare and Dekker as Keys to Ford's *'Tis Pity She's a Whore.*" *Studies in English Literature, 1500-1900* 7 (1967): 269-76.

Houlbrooke, Ralph A. *The English Family, 1450-1700.* Themes in British Social History. London: Longman, 1984.

Howard, Douglas, ed. *Philip Massinger: A Critical Reassessment.* Cambridge: Cambridge Univ. Press, 1985.

Howard, Jean. "The New Historicism in Renaissance Studies." *English Literary Renaissance* 16 (1986): 13-43.

Hoy, Cyrus. "Verbal Formulae in the Plays of Philip Massinger." *Studies in Philology* 56 (1959): 600-618.

Huebert, Ronald. *John Ford, Baroque English Dramatist.* Montreal: McGill-Queen's Univ. Press, 1977.

Hull, Suzanne W. *Chaste, Silent, and Obedient: English Books for Women, 1475-1640.* San Marino: Huntington Library Press, 1982.

Ingram, R.W. "The Musical Art of Richard Brome's Comedies." *Renaissance Drama* 7 (1976): 219-52.

James I. *The Political Works of James I.* Ed. and introd. Charles Howard McIlwain. Cambridge, Mass.: Harvard Univ. Press, 1918.

Jardine, Lisa. *Still Harping on Daughters: Women and Drama in the Age of Shakespeare.* Sussex: Harvester Press, 1983.

Javitch, Daniel. *Poetry and Courtliness in Renaissance England.* Princeton: Princeton Univ. Press, 1978.

Jones, Ann Rosalind. "Counterattacks on 'the Bayter of Women': Three Pamphleteers of the Early Seventeenth Century." *The Renaissance Englishwoman in Print: Counterbalancing the Canon.* Ed. Anne M. Haselkorn and Betty S. Travitsky. Amherst: Univ. of Massachusetts Press, 1990. 45-62.

———. "Nets and Bridles: Early Modern Conduct Books and Sixteenth-century Women's Lyrics." *The Ideology of Conduct.* Ed. Nancy Armstrong and Leonard Tennenhouse. London: Methuen, 1987. 39-72.

Jonson, Ben. *Ben Jonson.* Ed. Charles H. Herford and Percy and Evelyn Simpson. 11 vols. Oxford: Clarendon Press, 1925-52.

Judson, Margaret Atwood. *The Crisis of the Constitution: An Essay in Constitutional and Political Thought in England, 1603-1645.* New Brunswick: Rutgers Univ. Press, 1949.

Kahn, Coppélia. *Man's Estate: Masculine Identity in Shakespeare.* Berkeley: Univ. of California Press, 1981.

Kaufmann, R.J. "Ford's Tragic Perspective." *Texas Studies in Language and Literature* 1 (1960): 522-37. Rpt. in *Elizabethan Drama: Modern Essays in Criticism.* Ed. R.J. Kaufmann. New York: Oxford Univ. Press, 1961. 356-72.

———. "Ford's 'Waste Land': *The Broken Heart.*" *Renaissance Drama* 3 (1970): 167-87.

———. *Richard Brome, Caroline Playwright.* New York: Columbia Univ. Press, 1961.

Kelso, Ruth. *Doctrine for the Lady of the Renaissance.* Urbana: Univ. of Illinois Press, 1956.

Kenyon, J.P., ed. *The Stuart Constitution, 1603-1688: Documents and Commentary.* 2nd ed. Cambridge Univ. Press, 1986.

Kirsch, Arthur C. "A Caroline Commentary on the Drama." *Modern Philology* 66 (1969): 256-61.

Kistner, Arthur L., and M.K. Kistner. "The Dramatic Functions of Love in the Tragedies of John Ford." *Studies in Philology* 70 (1973): 62-76.

Knights, L.C. *Drama and Society in the Age of Jonson*. London: Chatto & Windus, 1937.

Kunzle, David. "World Upside Down: The Iconography of a European Broadsheet Type." *The Reversible World: Symbolic Inversion in Art and Society*. Ed. Barbara A. Babcock. Ithaca: Cornell Univ. Press, 1978.

Lanham, Richard A. *The Motives of Eloquence: Literary Rhetoric in the Renaissance*. New Haven: Yale Univ. Press, 1976.

Laslett, Peter. *The World We Have Lost*. 2d ed. New York: Charles Scribner's Sons, 1971.

Lawless, Donald S. *Philip Massinger and His Associates*. Ball State Monograph Number 10. Publications in English, Number 6. Muncie, Indiana: Ball State Univ. Press, 1967.

Leach, Edmund. *Social Anthropology*. New York: Oxford Univ. Press, 1982.

Leech, Clifford. *John Ford and the Drama of His Time*. London: Chatto & Windus, 1957.

Leggatt, Alexander. *Citizen Comedy in the Age of Shakespeare*. Toronto: Univ. of Toronto Press, 1973.

Leinwand, Theodore B. *The City Staged: Jacobean Comedy, 1603-1613*. Madison: Univ. of Wisconsin Press, 1986.

Levin, Richard. *The Multiple Plot in English Renaissance Drama*. Chicago: Univ. of Chicago Press, 1971.

———. "The Triple Plot of *Hyde Park*." *Modern Language Review* 62 (1967): 17-27.

Limon, Jerzy. *Dangerous Matter: English Drama and Politics in 1623/24*. Cambridge: Cambridge Univ. Press, 1986.

Logan, Terence P., and Denzell S. Smith. *The Later Jacobean and Caroline Dramatists*. Lincoln: Univ. of Nebraska Press, 1978.

Lucow, Ben. *James Shirley*. Boston: Twayne, 1981.

McDonald, Charles O. "The Design of John Ford's *The Broken Heart*: A Study in the Development of Caroline Sensibility." *Studies in Philology* 59 (1962): 141-61.

MacFarlane, Alan. *The Origins of English Individualism: The Family, Property, and Social Transition*. Oxford: Basil Blackwell, 1978.

———. Review of Lawrence Stone, *The Family, Sex and Marriage in England, 1500-1800*. *History and Theory* 18 (1979): 103-26.

McGrath, Juliet. "James Shirley's Uses of Language." *Studies in English Literature, 1500-1900* 6 (1966): 323-39.

McManaway, James G. "Excerpta Quaedam per A.W. Adolescentem." *Studies in Honor of DeWitt T. Starnes*. Ed. Thomas P. Harrison et al. Austin: Univ. of Texas, 1967. 117-29.

McMaster, Juliet. "Love, Lust, and Sham: Structural Pattern in the Plays of John Ford." *Renaissance Drama* 2 (1969): 157-66.

Marcus, Leah. *The Politics of Mirth: Jonson, Herrick, Milton, and Marvell, and the Defense of Old Holiday Pastimes*. Chicago: Univ. of Chicago Press, 1986.

Marmion, Shakerly. *The Dramatic Works of Shackerley Marmion*. Ed. James Maidment and W.H. Logan. London: 1875. New York: Benjamin Blom, 1967.

Massinger, Philip. *The Plays and Poems of Philip Massinger*. Ed. Philip Edwards and Colin Gibson. 5 vols. Oxford: Clarendon Press, 1976.

Mauss, Marcel. *A General Theory of Magic*. Trans. Robert Brain. London: Routledge & Kegan Paul, 1972.

Mead, George Herbert. *George Herbert Mead on Social Psychology*. Ed. Anselm Strauss. Chicago: Univ. of Chicago Press, 1964.

———. *Mind, Self, and Society: From the Standpoint of a Social Behaviorist*. Chicago: Univ. of Chicago Press, 1934.

————. *Philosophy of the Act.* Univ. of Chicago Press, 1938.

Miles, Theodore. "Place-Realism in a Group of Caroline Plays." *Review of English Studies* 18 (1942): 428-40.

Milgram, Stanley. *Obedience to Authority.* New York: Harper & Row, 1974.

Monsarrat, Gilles D. "The Unity of John Ford: *'Tis Pity She's a Whore* and *Christ's Bloody Sweat.*" *Studies in Philology* 77 (1980): 247-70.

Montrose, Louis Adrian. "'Eliza, Queene of shepheardes' and the Pastoral of Power." *English Literary Renaissance* 10 (1980): 143-82.

Morillo, Marvin. "Shirley's 'Preferment' and the Court of Charles I." *Studies in English Literature, 1500-1900* 1 (1961): 101-17.

Morton, Richard. "Deception and Social Dislocation: An Aspect of Shirley's Drama." *Renaissance Drama* 9 (1966): 227-45.

Mullaney, Steven. *The Place of the Stage: License, Play, and Power in Renaissance England.* Chicago: Univ. of Chicago Press, 1988.

Nason, Arthur Huntington. *James Shirley, Dramatist: A Biographical and Critical Study.* University Heights, N.Y.: Nason, 1915.

Neill, Michael. "'Anticke Pageantrie': The Mannerist Art of *Perkin Warbeck.*" *Renaissance Drama* 7 (1976): 117-50.

————. "Ford's Unbroken Art: The Moral Design of *The Broken Heart.*" *Modern Language Review* 75 (1980): 249-68.

————. "Massinger's Patriarchy: The Social Vision of *A New Way To Pay Old Debts.*" *Renaissance Drama* 10 (1979): 185-213.

————. "The Moral Artifice of *The Lovers Melancholy.*" *English Literary Renaissance* 8 (1978): 85-106.

————, ed. *John Ford: Critical Re-Visions.* Cambridge: Cambridge Univ. Press, 1988.

Oliver, H.J. *The Problem of John Ford.* Melbourne: Melbourne Univ. Press, 1955.

Orbison, Tucker. *The Tragic Vision of John Ford.* Salzburg: Universität Salzburg, 1974.

Orgel, Stephen. *The Illusion of Power: Political Theatre in the English Renaissance.* Berkeley: Univ. of California Press, 1975.

————. *The Jonsonian Masque.* Cambridge, Mass.: Harvard Univ. Press, 1965.

————, and Roy Strong. *Inigo Jones: The Theatre of the Stuart Court.* 2 vols. London and Berkeley: Sotheby Parke Bernet and Univ. of California Press, 1973.

Ornstein, Robert. *The Moral Vision of Jacobean Tragedy.* Madison: Univ. of Wisconsin Press, 1960.

Painter, William. *The Second Tome of the Palace of Pleasure.* London: Henry Bynneman, 1567. STC 19124.

Parlin, Hanson T. *A Study in Shirley's Comedies of London Life.* Bulletin of the Univ. of Texas No. 371, Studies in English No. 2. Austin, 1914.

Parry, Graham. *The Golden Age Restor'd: The Culture of the Stuart Court, 1603-42.* New York: St. Martin's Press, 1981.

Perkinson, Richard H. "Topographical Comedy in the Seventeenth Century." *English Literary History* 3 (1936): 270-90.

Pocock, J.G.A. *The Ancient Constitution and the Feudal Law.* Cambridge: Cambridge Univ. Press, 1957.

Pollock, Linda. *Forgotten Children: Parent-Child Relations from 1500 to 1900.* Cambridge: Cambridge Univ. Press, 1983. •

Potter, Lois, ed., *The* Revels *History of Drama in English,* vol. 4, *1613-1660.* London: Methuen, 1981.

Powell, Chilton Latham. *English Domestic Relations, 1487-1653.* New York: Columbia Univ. Press, 1917.

Reay, Barry, ed. *Popular Culture in Seventeenth-Century England.* New York: St. Martin's Press, 1985.

Ribner, Irving. *Jacobean Tragedy: The Quest for Moral Order*. London: Methuen, 1962.

Riggs, David. *Ben Jonson: A Life*. Cambridge, Mass.: Harvard Univ. Press, 1989.

Righter, Anne. *Shakespeare and the Idea of the Play*. London: Chatto & Windus, 1962.

Roberts, Jeanne A. "John Ford's Passionate Abstractions." *Southern Humanities Review* 7 (1973): 322-32.

Rose, Mary Beth. *The Expense of Spirit: Love and Sexuality in English Renaissance Drama*. Ithaca: Cornell Univ. Press, 1988.

Rosen, Carol C. "The Language of Cruelty in Ford's *'Tis Pity She's a Whore*." *Comparative Drama* 8 (1974): 356-68.

Russell, Conrad. *Parliaments and English Politics, 1621-29*. Oxford: Clarendon Press, 1979.

Sargeaunt, M. Joan. *John Ford*. Oxford: Basil Blackwell, 1935.

Schochet, Gordon J. *Patriarchalism in Political Thought*. Oxford: Basil Blackwell, 1975.

Sedge, Douglas. "Social and Ethical Concerns in Caroline Drama." Ph.D. diss., Univ. of Birmingham, 1966.

Sensabaugh, George F. "Love Ethics in Platonic Court Drama, 1625-1642." *Huntington Library Quarterly* 1 (1937-38): 277-304.

———. *The Tragic Muse of John Ford*. Stanford: Stanford Univ. Press, 1944.

Sharpe, Kevin. *Criticism and Compliment: The Politics of Literature in the England of Charles I*. Cambridge: Cambridge Univ. Press, 1987.

———, ed. *Faction and Parliament: Essays on Early Stuart History*. Oxford: Clarendon Press, 1978.

Shaw, Catherine. *Richard Brome*. Boston: Twayne, 1980.

Shirley, James. *The Dramatic Works and Poems of James Shirley*. Ed. William Gifford and Alexander Dyce. 6 vols. London: J. Murray, 1833. New York: Russell & Russell, 1966.

———. *The Humourous Courtier*. Ed. Marvin Morillo. New York: Garland, 1979.

———. *The Lady of Pleasure*. Ed. Marilyn J. Thorssen. New York: Garland, 1980.

———. *The Poems*. Ed. Ray Livingstone Armstrong. Morningside Heights, N.Y.: King's Crown Press, 1941.

Smith, Steven R. "The London Apprentices as Seventeenth-Century Adolescents." *Past & Present* 61 (1973): 149-61.

———. "Religion and the Conception of Youth in 17th-Century England." *History of Childhood Quarterly* 2 (1975): 493-516.

Smuts, R. Malcolm. *Court Culture and the Origins of a Royalist Tradition in Early Stuart England*. Philadelphia: Univ. of Pennsylvania Press, 1987.

Sommerville, J.P. *Politics and Ideology in England, 1603-1640*. London: Longmans, 1986.

Stavig, Mark. *John Ford and the Moral Order*. Madison: Univ. of Wisconsin Press, 1968.

Stebbins, Robert A. *Teachers and Meaning: Definitions of Classroom Situations*. Monographs and Theoretical Studies in Sociology and Anthropology in Honour of Nels Anderson, pub. 10. Gen. ed. K. Ishwaran. Leiden: Brill, 1975.

Stenton, Doris Mary. *The English Woman in History*. New York: Macmillan, 1959.

Stone, Lawrence. *The Causes of the English Revolution, 1529-1642*. London: Routledge & Kegan Paul, 1972.

———. *The Crisis of the Aristocracy, 1558-1641*. Oxford: Oxford Univ. Press, 1965.

———. *The Family, Sex and Marriage in England, 1500-1800*. London: Weidenfeld & Nicholson, 1977.

Strong, Roy. *Splendor at Court: Renaissance Spectacle and the Theater of Power*. Boston: Houghton Mifflin, 1973.

Stroup, Thomas B. *Microcosmos: The Shape of the Elizabethan Play.* Lexington: Univ. of Kentucky Press, 1965.

Stryker, Sheldon. *Symbolic Interactionism: A Social Structural Version.* Menlo Park, Calif. Benjamin/Cummings, 1980.

Sutton, Juliet. "Platonic Love in Ford's *The Fancies, Chaste and Noble.*" *Studies in English Literature, 1500-1900* 7 (1967): 299-309.

Swetnam, the Woman-hater, Arraigned by Women. London: 1620. STC 23544.

Tesser, Abraham. "Self-generated Attitude Change." *Advances in Experimental Social Psychology* 11. Ed. Leonard Berkowitz. New York: Academic Press, 1978. 289-338.

Thirsk, Joan. "The European Debate on Customs of Inheritance, 1500-1700." *Family and Inheritance,* ed. Jack Goody. Cambridge: Cambridge Univ. Press, 1976. 177-91.

Tricomi, A.H. *Anticourt Drama in England, 1603-1642.* Charlottesville: Univ. of Virginia Press, 1989.

Trumbach, Ralph. *The Rise of the Egalitarian Family.* New York: Academic Press, 1978.

Turner, Victor. "Betwixt and Between: The Liminal Period of *Rites de Pasage.*" *The Forest of Symbols.* Ithaca: Cornell Univ. Press, 1967. 93-111.

Underdown, David. *Revel, Riot, and Rebellion: Popular Politics and Culture in England, 1603-1660.* Oxford: Clarendon Press, 1985.

―――. "The Taming of the Scold: The Enforcement of Patriarchal Authority in Early Modern England." *Order and Disorder in Early Modern England.* Ed. Anthony Fletcher and John Stevenson. Cambridge: Cambridge Univ. Press, 1985. 116-36.

Ure, Peter. "Marriage and the Domestic Drama in Heywood and Ford." *English Studies* 32 (1951): 200-216.

van Gennep, Arnold. *The Rites of Passage.* Trans. Monika Vizedom and Gabrielle L. Caffee. Chicago: Univ. of Chicago Press, 1960.

Venuti, Lawrence. "The Politics of Allusion: The Gentry and Shirley's *The Triumph of Peace.*" *English Literary Renaissance* 16 (1986): 182-205.

Waith, Eugene M. "John Fletcher and the Art of Declamation." *Publications of the Modern Language Association* 66 (1951): 226-34.

―――. *The Pattern of Tragicomedy in Beaumont and Fletcher.* New Haven: Yale Univ. Press, 1952.

Watson, Robert N. *Ben Jonson's Parodic Strategy: Literary Imperialism in the Comedies.* Cambridge, Mass.: Harvard Univ. Press, 1987.

Webster, John. *The Complete Works of John Webster.* Ed. F.L. Lucas. 4 vols. London: Chatto & Windus, 1927.

Wertheim, Albert. "Games and Courtship in James Shirley's *Hyde Park.*" *Anglia* 90 (1972): 71-91.

Whigham, Frank. *Ambition and Privilege: The Social Tropes of Elizabethan Courtesy Theory.* Berkeley: Univ. of California Press, 1985.

―――. "Sexual and Social Mobility in *The Duchess of Malfi.*" *Publications of the Modern Language Association* 100 (1985): 167-86.

Wilson, Sir Thomas. "The State of England (1600)." Ed. F.J. Fisher. *Camden Miscellany,* 3rd series 52 (1936).

Winston, Florence T. "The Significance of Women in the Plays of Philip Massinger." Ph.D. diss., Univ. of Kansas, 1972.

Wolf, William D. "Some New Facts and Conclusions about James Shirley: Residences and Religion." *Notes and Queries* 29 (1982): 133-34.

Wood, Anthony à. *Athenæ Oxoniensis.* Ed. Philip Bliss. 4 vols. London, 1813-20.

Woodbridge, Linda. *Women and the English Renaissance: Literature and the Nature of Womankind, 1540-1620.* Urbana: Univ. of Illinois Press, 1984.

Wrightson, Keith. *English Society, 1580-1680.* New Brunswick: Rutgers Univ. Press, 1982.

Zagorin, Perez. *The Court and the Country.* London: Routledge & Kegan Paul, 1969.

Zimbardo, Philip G., E.B. Ebbesen, and C. Maslach. *Influencing Attitudes and Changing Behavior.* Reading, Mass.: Addison-Wesley, 1977.

Zimbardo, Philip G., with Craig Haney and W. Curtis Banks. "A Pirandellan Prison." *New York Times Magazine,* 8 April 1973, 38-60.

Index